GUNDAM

THE ORIGIN

GARMA

SECTION III

CREATED BY

HAJIME YATATE
YOSHIYUKI TOMINO

矢立肇・富野由悠季

MECHANICAL DESIGN

KUNIO OKAWARA

大河原邦男

PRESENTED BY

YOSHIKAZU
YASUHIKO

安彦良和

ASSISTANT: MASATO

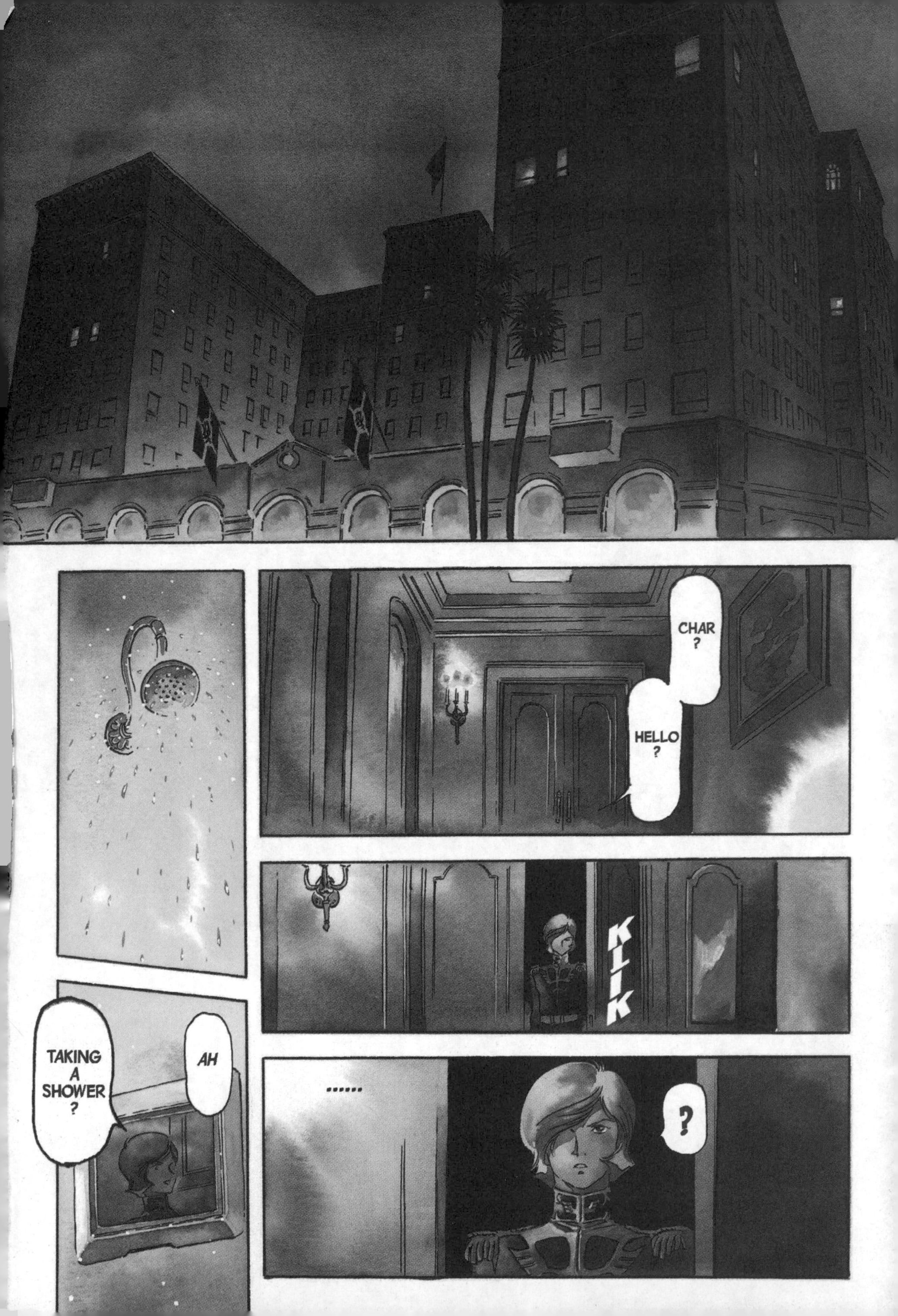
CHAR ?
HELLO ?
KLIK
?
......
AH
TAKING A SHOWER ?

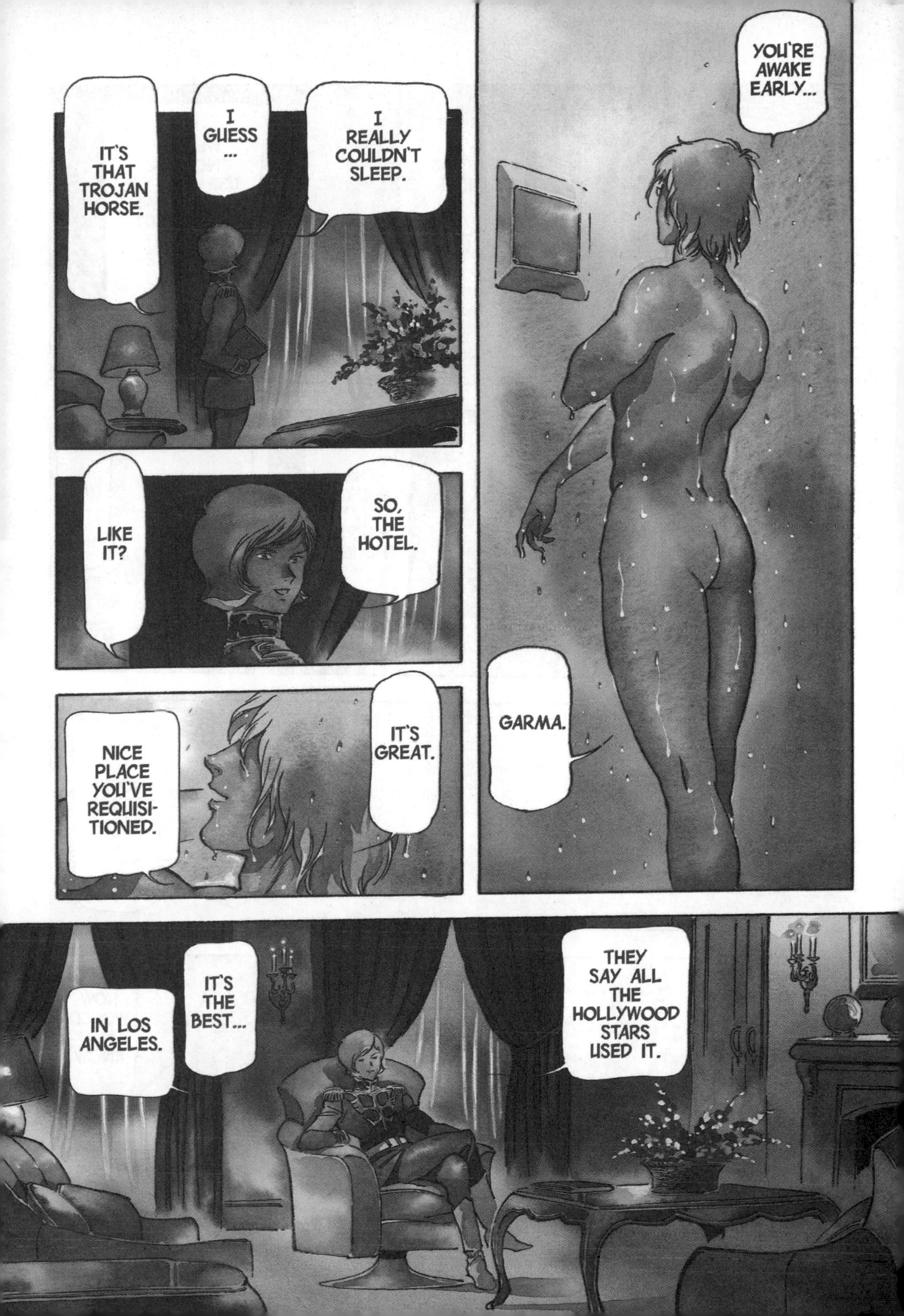
YOU'RE AWAKE EARLY...
GARMA.
I REALLY COULDN'T SLEEP.
I GUESS ...
IT'S THAT TROJAN HORSE.
SO, THE HOTEL.
LIKE IT?
IT'S GREAT.
NICE PLACE YOU'VE REQUISITIONED.
THEY SAY ALL THE HOLLYWOOD STARS USED IT.
IT'S THE BEST...
IN LOS ANGELES.

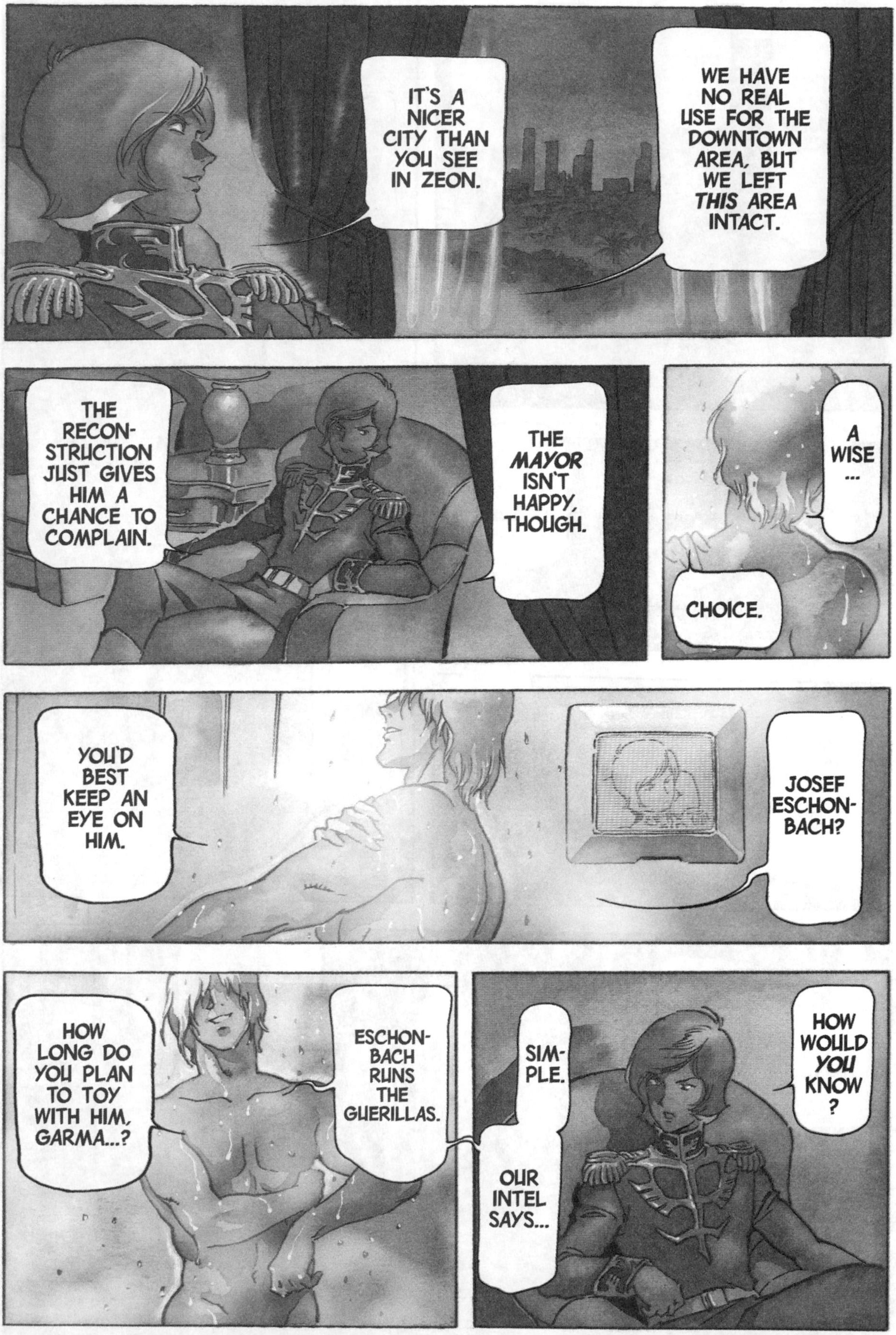
WE HAVE NO REAL USE FOR THE DOWNTOWN AREA, BUT WE LEFT *THIS* AREA INTACT.
IT'S A NICER CITY THAN YOU SEE IN ZEON.
A WISE ...
CHOICE.
THE *MAYOR* ISN'T HAPPY, THOUGH.
THE RECON-STRUCTION JUST GIVES HIM A CHANCE TO COMPLAIN.
JOSEF ESCHON-BACH?
YOU'D BEST KEEP AN EYE ON HIM.
HOW WOULD *YOU* KNOW?
SIM-PLE.
OUR INTEL SAYS...
ESCHON-BACH RUNS THE GUERILLAS.
HOW LONG DO YOU PLAN TO TOY WITH HIM, GARMA...?

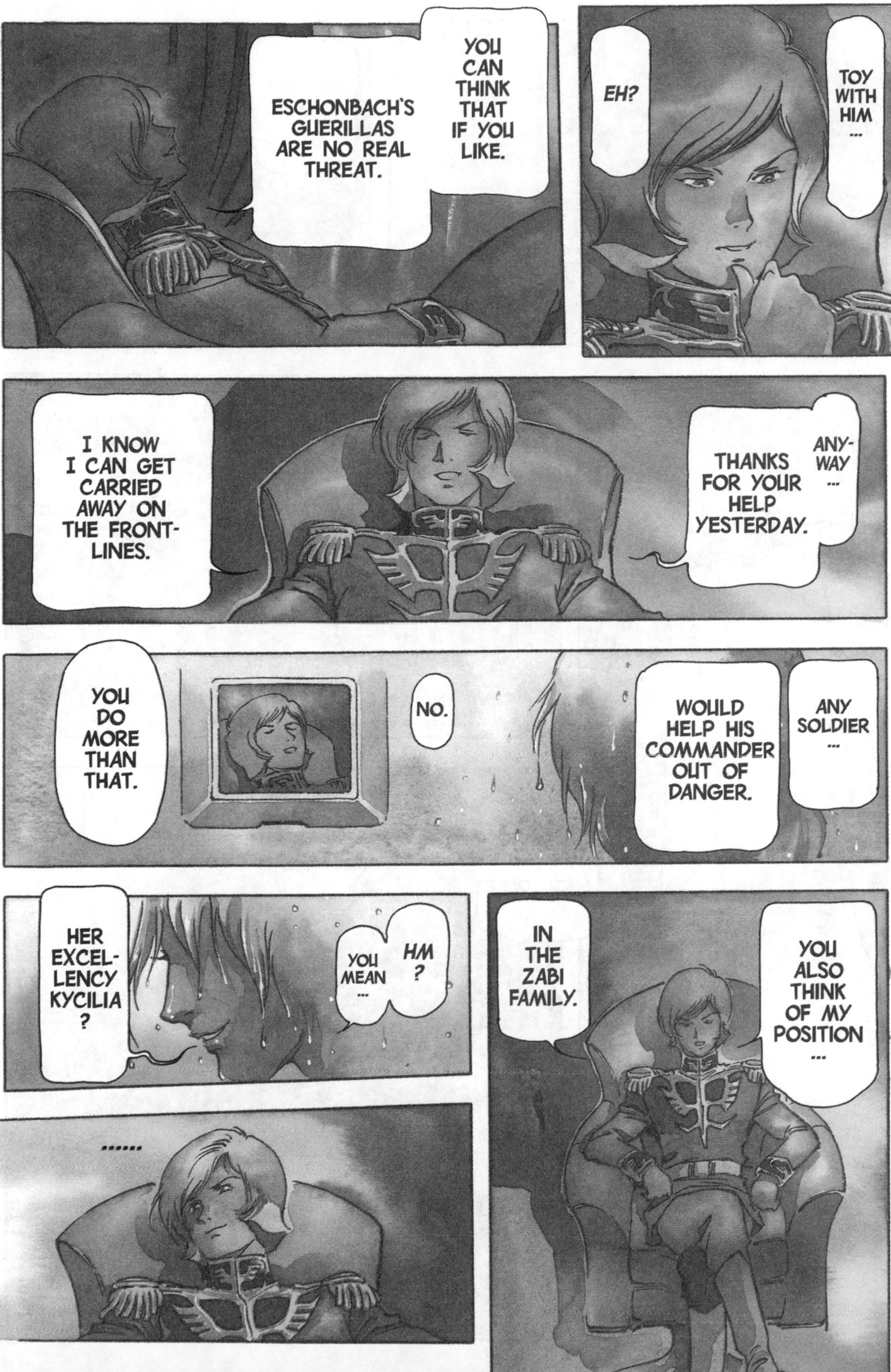
TOY WITH HIM ...
EH?
YOU CAN THINK THAT IF YOU LIKE.
ESCHONBACH'S GUERILLAS ARE NO REAL THREAT.
ANY-WAY ...
THANKS FOR YOUR HELP YESTERDAY.
I KNOW I CAN GET CARRIED AWAY ON THE FRONT-LINES.
ANY SOLDIER ...
WOULD HELP HIS COMMANDER OUT OF DANGER.
NO.
YOU DO MORE THAN THAT.
YOU ALSO THINK OF MY POSITION ...
IN THE ZABI FAMILY.
HM?
YOU MEAN ...
HER EXCEL-LENCY KYCILIA?
......

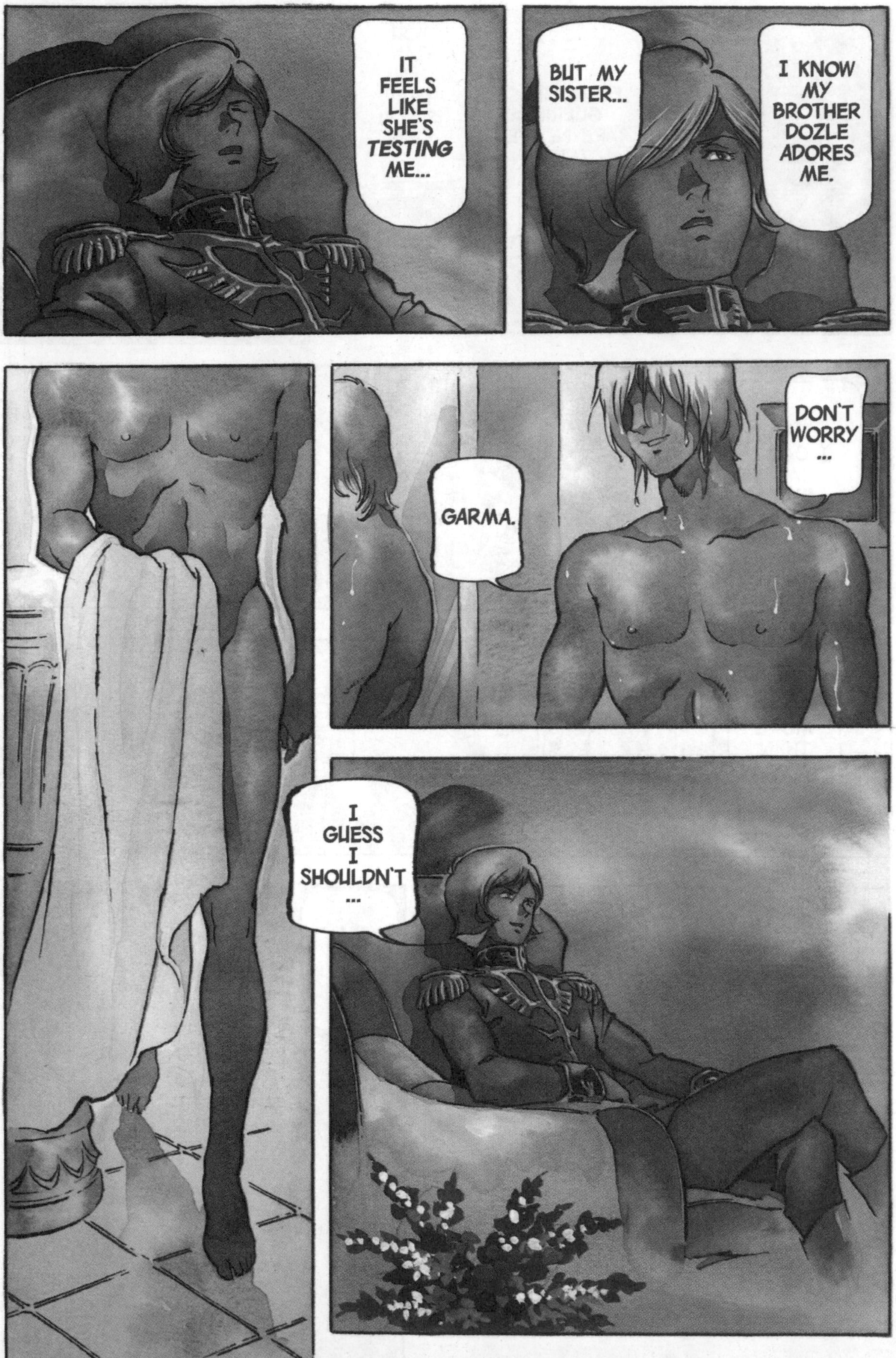
I KNOW MY BROTHER DOZLE ADORES ME.
BUT MY SISTER...
IT FEELS LIKE SHE'S *TESTING* ME...
DON'T WORRY ...
GARMA.
I GUESS I SHOULDN'T ...

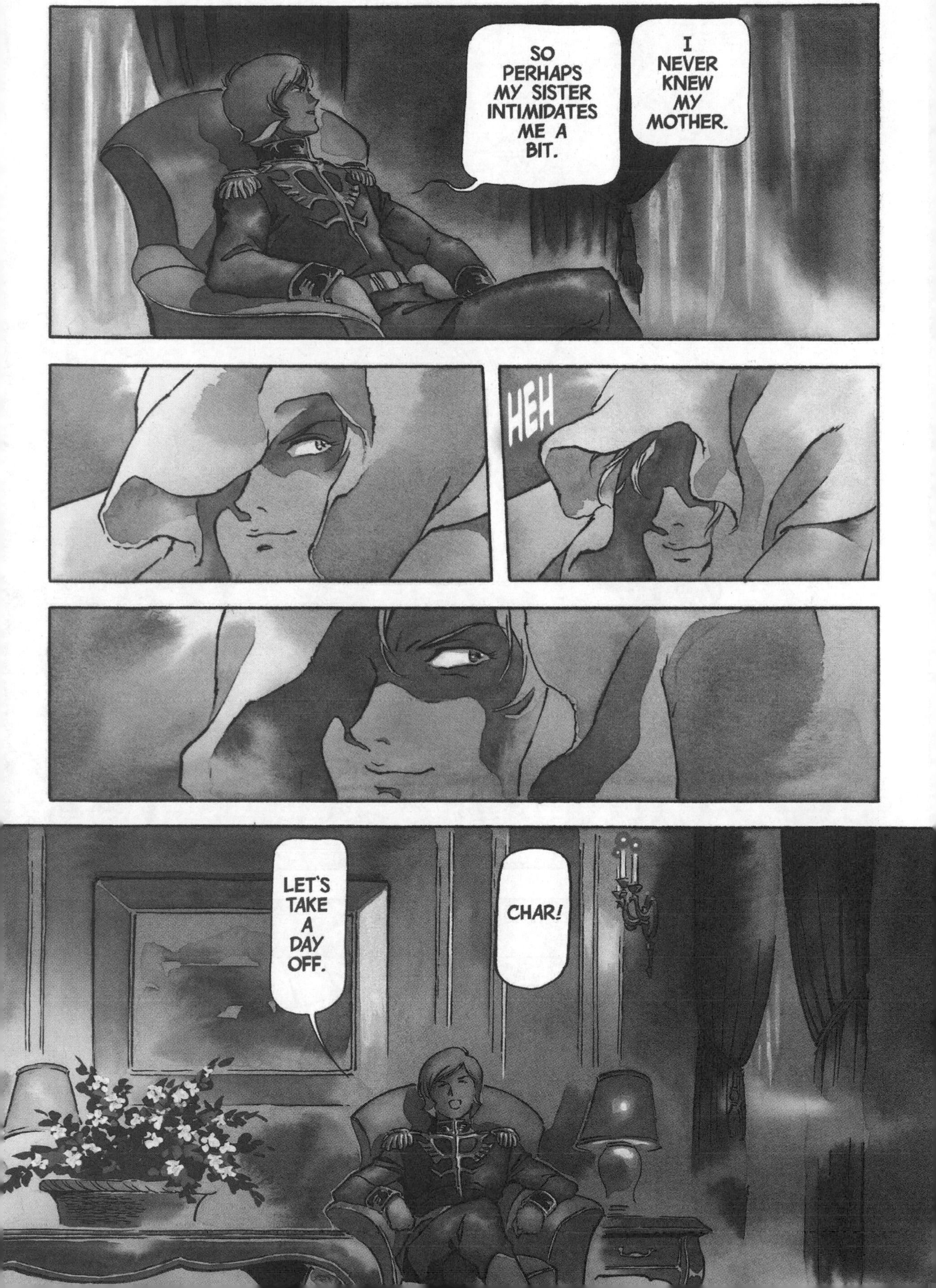
I NEVER KNEW MY MOTHER.
SO PERHAPS MY SISTER INTIMIDATES ME A BIT.
HEH
CHAR!
LET'S TAKE A DAY OFF.

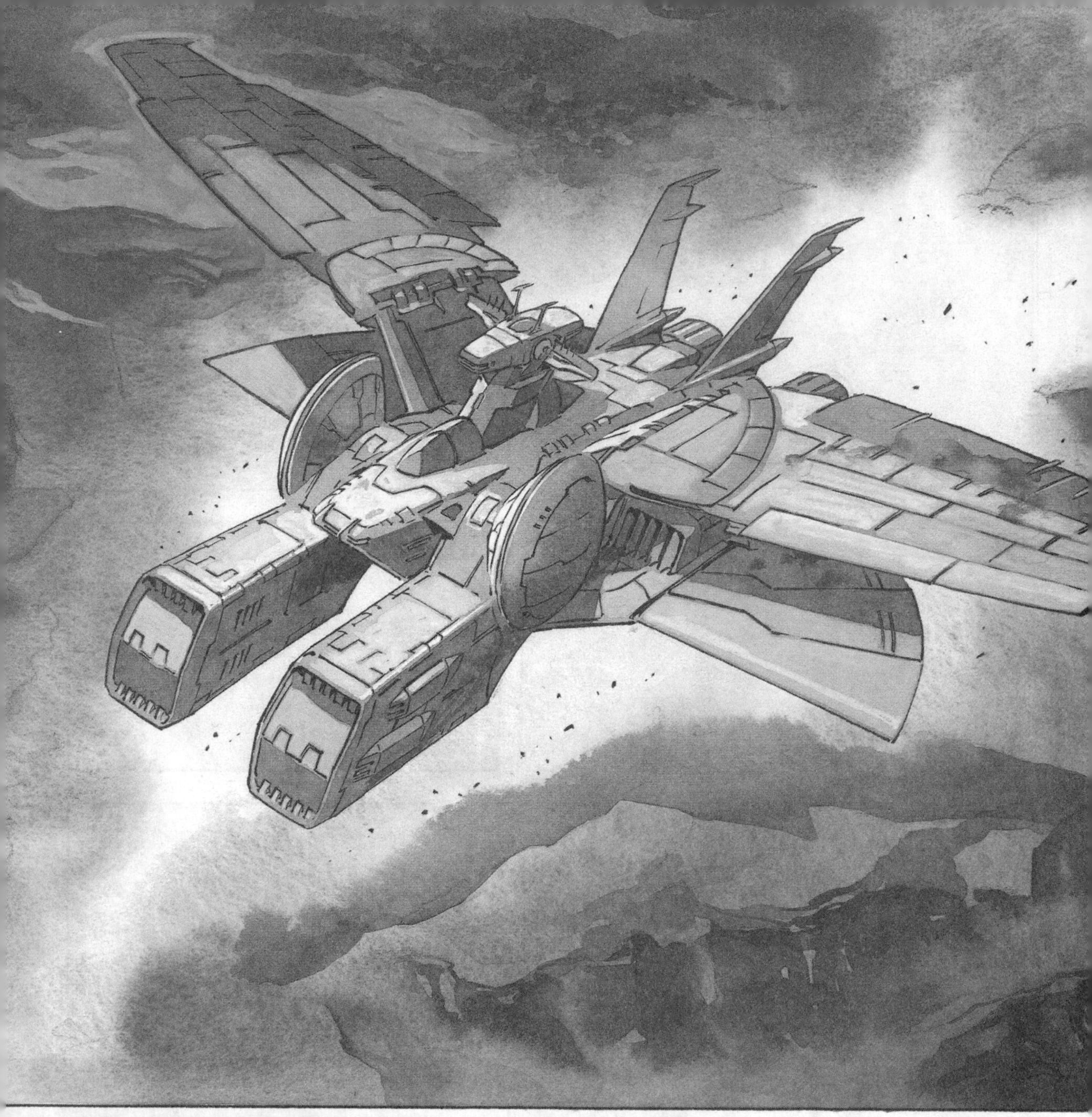

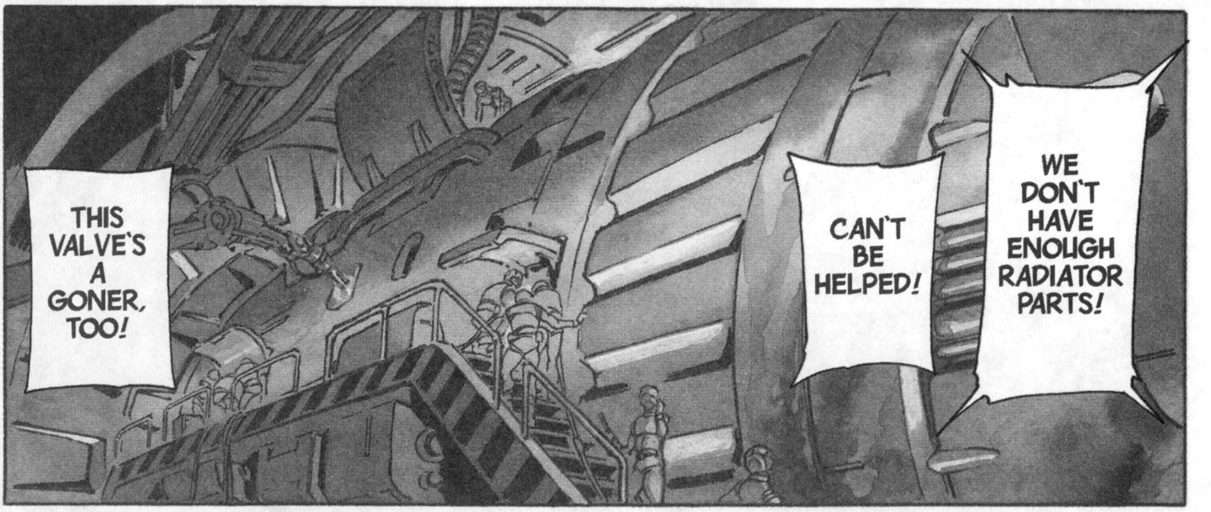
WE DON'T HAVE ENOUGH RADIATOR PARTS!
CAN'T BE HELPED!
THIS VALVE'S A GONER, TOO!

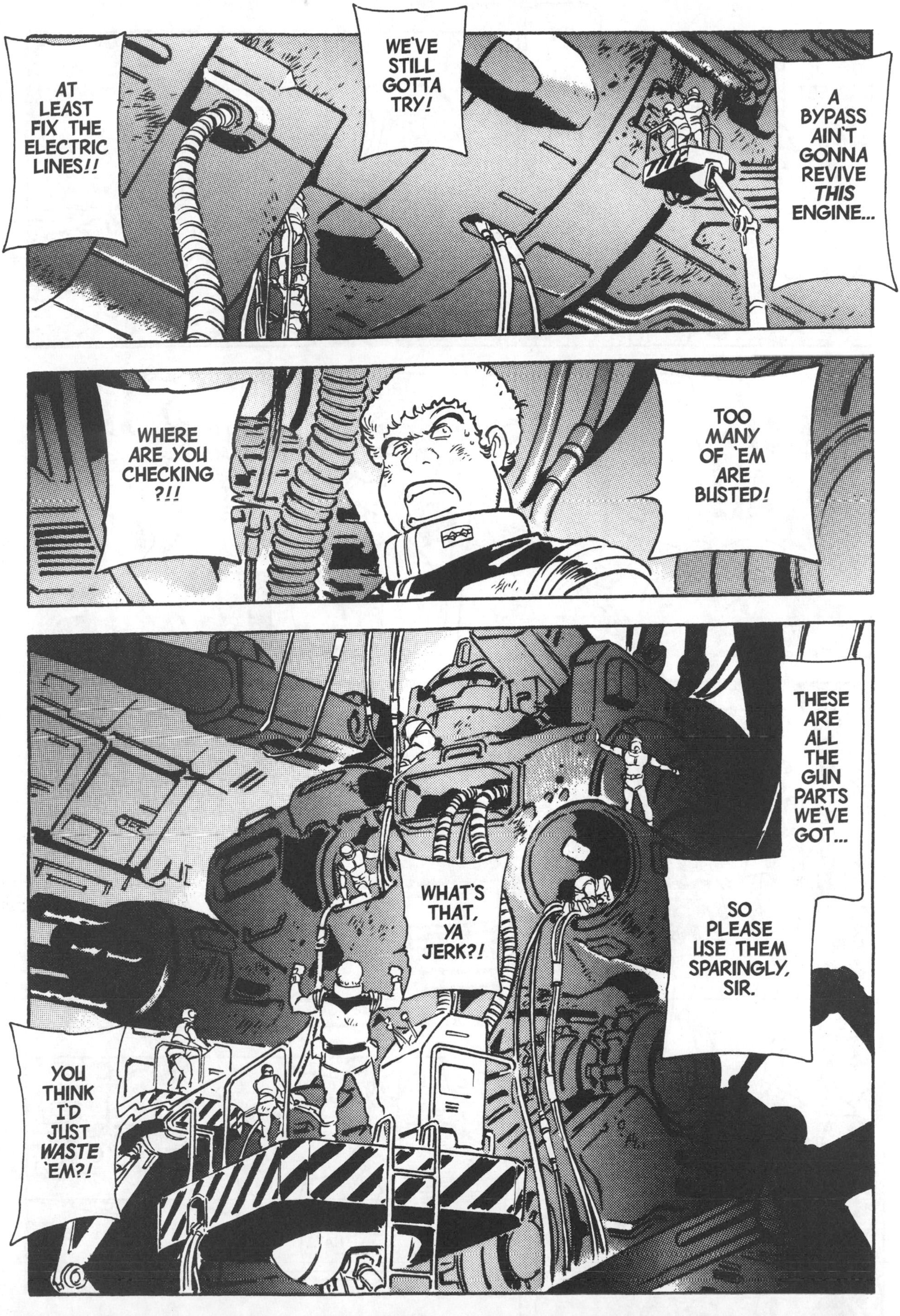
A BYPASS AIN'T GONNA REVIVE *THIS* ENGINE...
WE'VE STILL GOTTA TRY!
AT LEAST FIX THE ELECTRIC LINES!!
TOO MANY OF 'EM ARE BUSTED!
WHERE ARE YOU CHECKING?!!
THESE ARE ALL THE GUN PARTS WE'VE GOT...
SO PLEASE USE THEM SPARINGLY, SIR.
WHAT'S THAT, YA JERK?!
YOU THINK I'D JUST *WASTE* 'EM?!

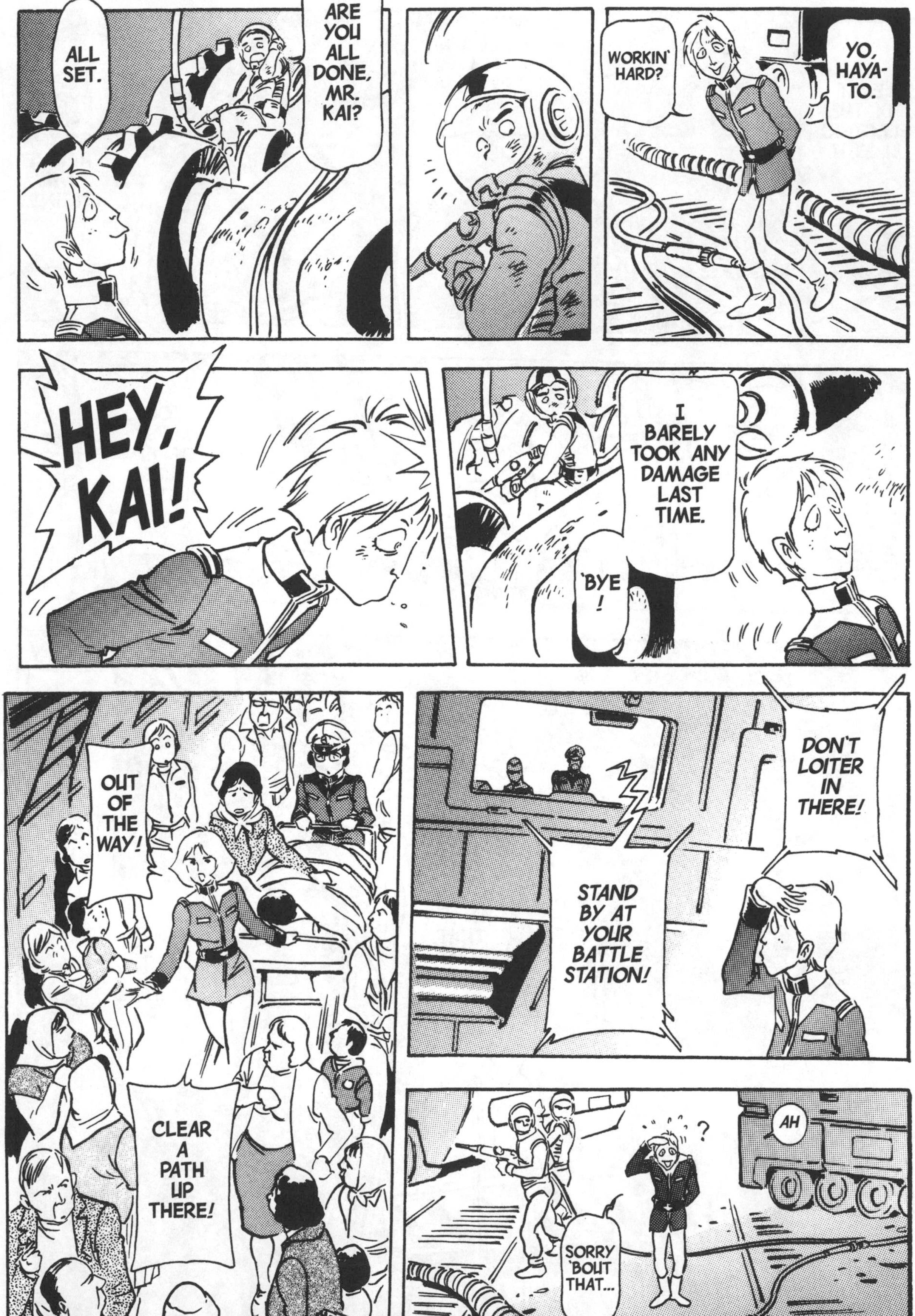
YO, HAYA-TO.
WORKIN' HARD?
ARE YOU ALL DONE, MR. KAI?
ALL SET.
I BARELY TOOK ANY DAMAGE LAST TIME.
'BYE!
HEY, KAI!
DON'T LOITER IN THERE!
STAND BY AT YOUR BATTLE STATION!
AH
SORRY 'BOUT THAT...
OUT OF THE WAY!
CLEAR A PATH UP THERE!

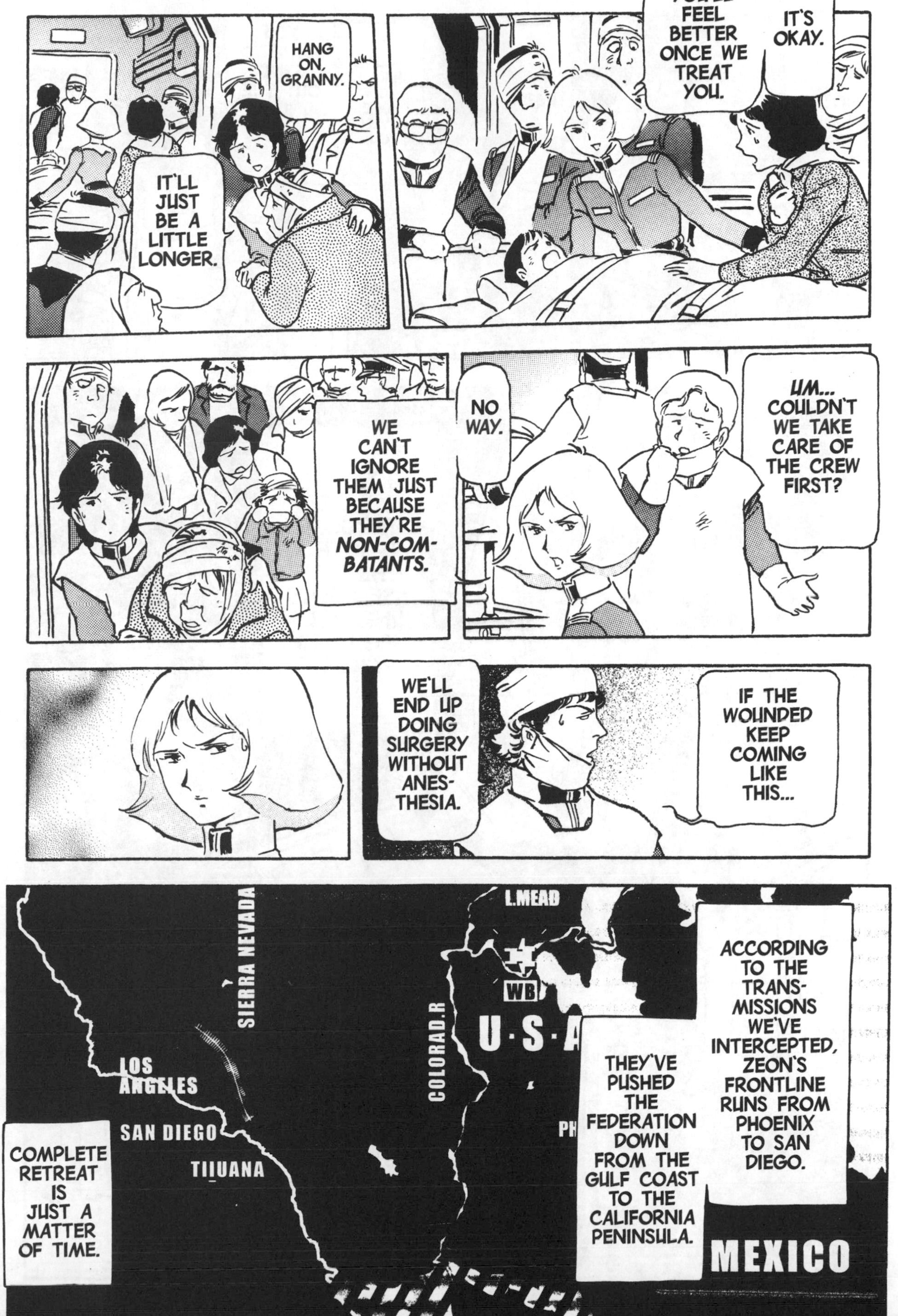
IT'S OKAY.
YOU'LL FEEL BETTER ONCE WE TREAT YOU.
HANG ON, GRANNY.
IT'LL JUST BE A LITTLE LONGER.
UM... COULDN'T WE TAKE CARE OF THE CREW FIRST?
NO WAY.
WE CAN'T IGNORE THEM JUST BECAUSE THEY'RE NON-COMBATANTS.
IF THE WOUNDED KEEP COMING LIKE THIS...
WE'LL END UP DOING SURGERY WITHOUT ANESTHESIA.
ACCORDING TO THE TRANSMISSIONS WE'VE INTERCEPTED, ZEON'S FRONTLINE RUNS FROM PHOENIX TO SAN DIEGO.
L.MEAD
WB
U.S.A
PH
MEXICO
COLORAD.R
SIERRA NEVADA
LOS ANGELES
SAN DIEGO
TIJUANA
THEY'VE PUSHED THE FEDERATION DOWN FROM THE GULF COAST TO THE CALIFORNIA PENINSULA.
COMPLETE RETREAT IS JUST A MATTER OF TIME.

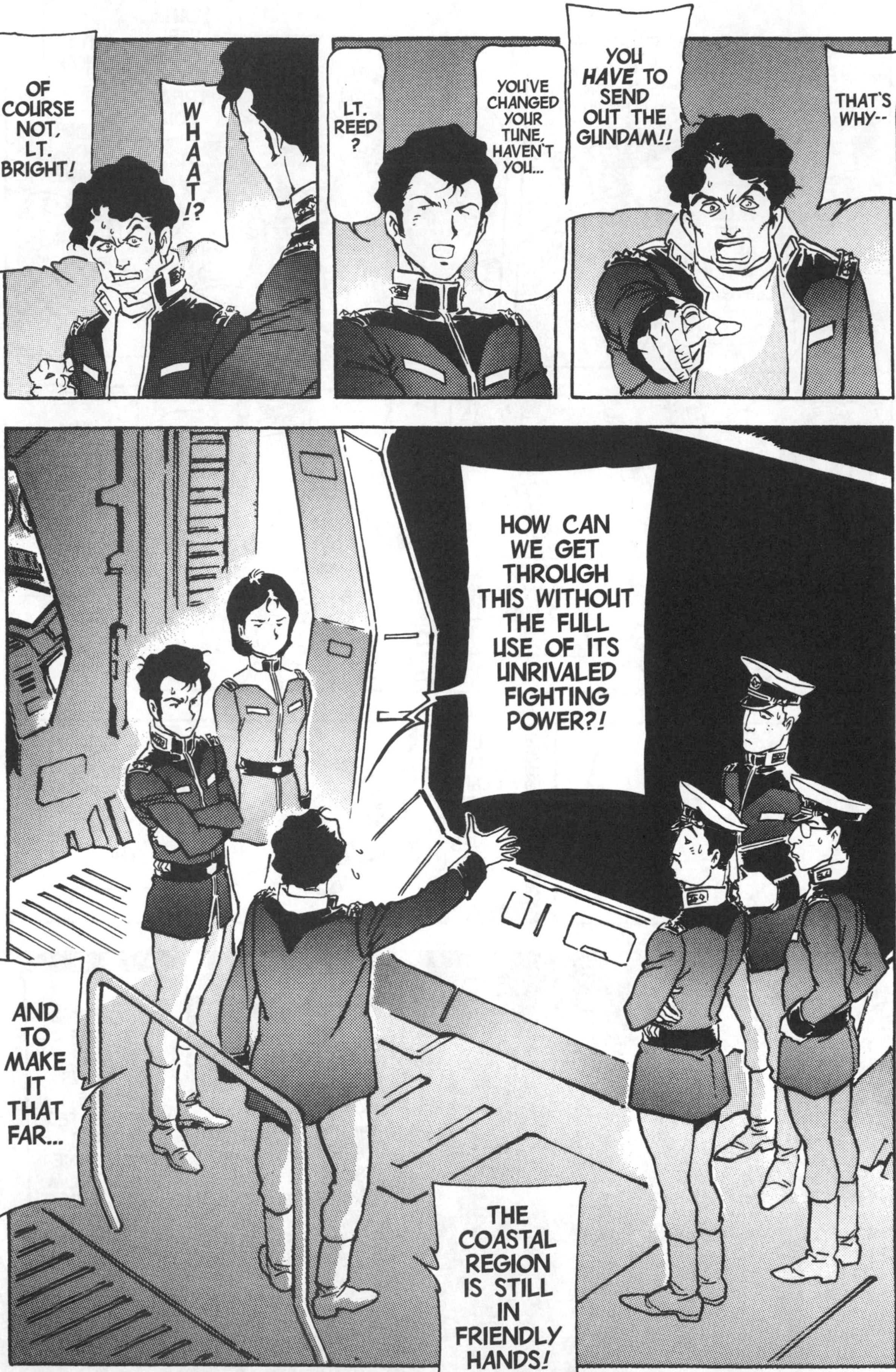
THAT'S WHY--
YOU *HAVE* TO SEND OUT THE GUNDAM!!
YOU'VE CHANGED YOUR TUNE, HAVEN'T YOU...
LT. REED?
WHAAAT!?
OF COURSE NOT, LT. BRIGHT!
HOW CAN WE GET THROUGH THIS WITHOUT THE FULL USE OF ITS UNRIVALED FIGHTING POWER?!
AND TO MAKE IT THAT FAR...
THE COASTAL REGION IS STILL IN FRIENDLY HANDS!

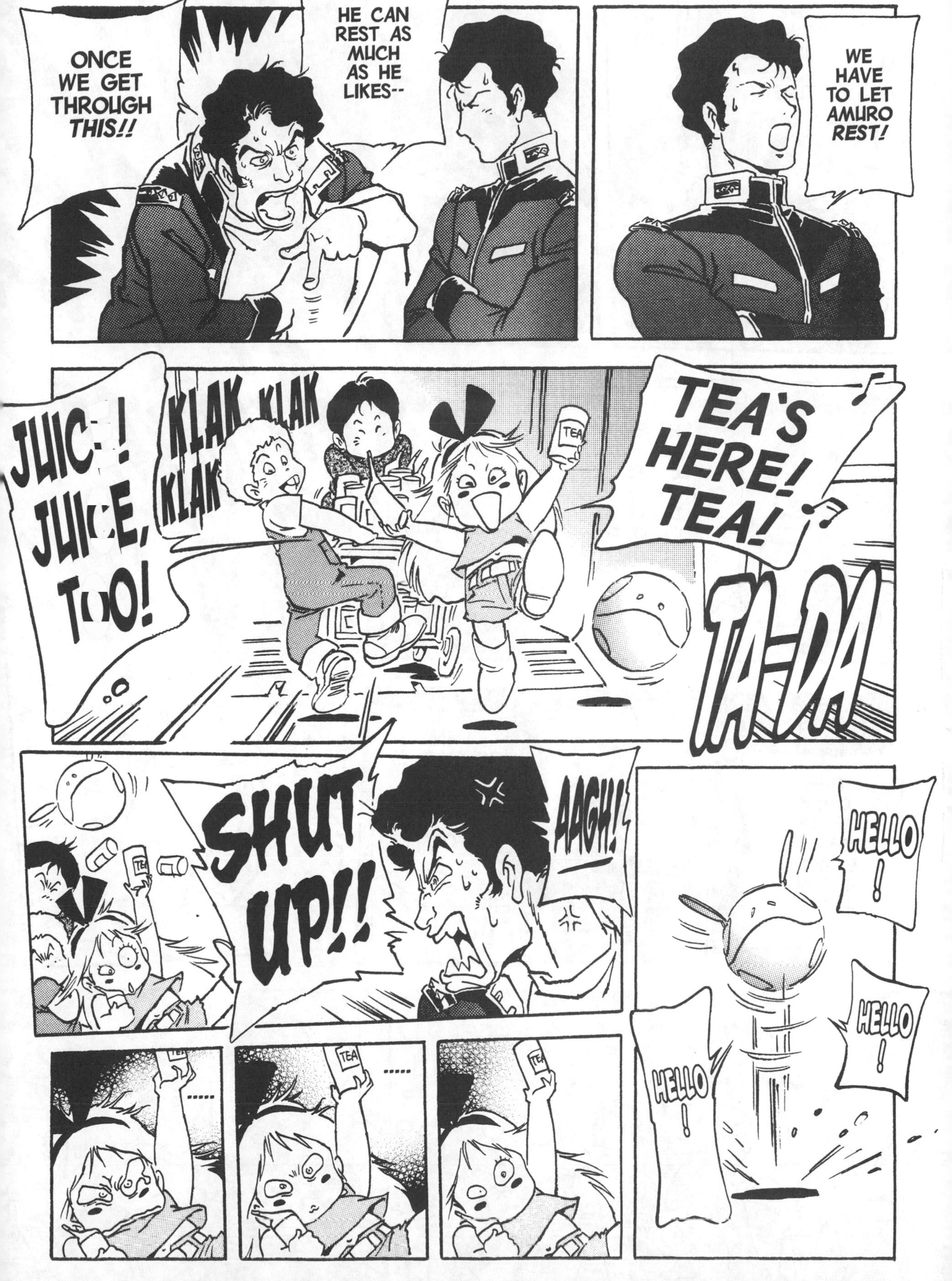
WE HAVE TO LET AMURO REST!
HE CAN REST AS MUCH AS HE LIKES--
ONCE WE GET THROUGH THIS!!
TEA'S HERE! TEA!
TA-DA
KLAK KLAK
KLAK
JUICE! JUICE, TOO!
HELLO!
HELLO!
HELLO!
AAGH!
SHUT UP!!
.....
.....
.....

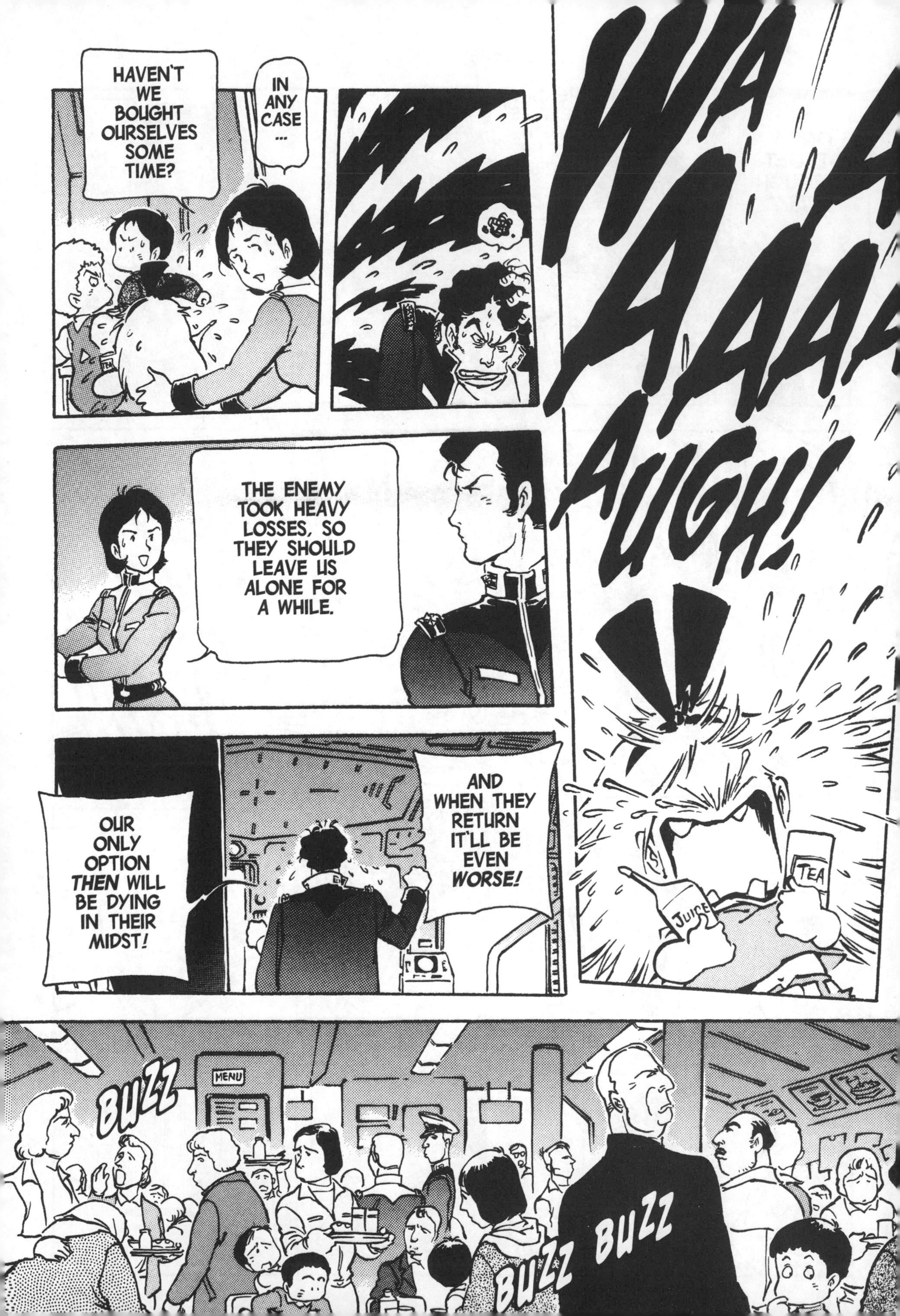
WAAAAAAAUGH!
JUICE
TEA
IN ANY CASE...
HAVEN'T WE BOUGHT OURSELVES SOME TIME?
TEA
THE ENEMY TOOK HEAVY LOSSES, SO THEY SHOULD LEAVE US ALONE FOR A WHILE.
AND WHEN THEY RETURN IT'LL BE EVEN *WORSE!*
OUR ONLY OPTION *THEN* WILL BE DYING IN THEIR MIDST!
BUZZ BUZZ
MENU
BUZZ

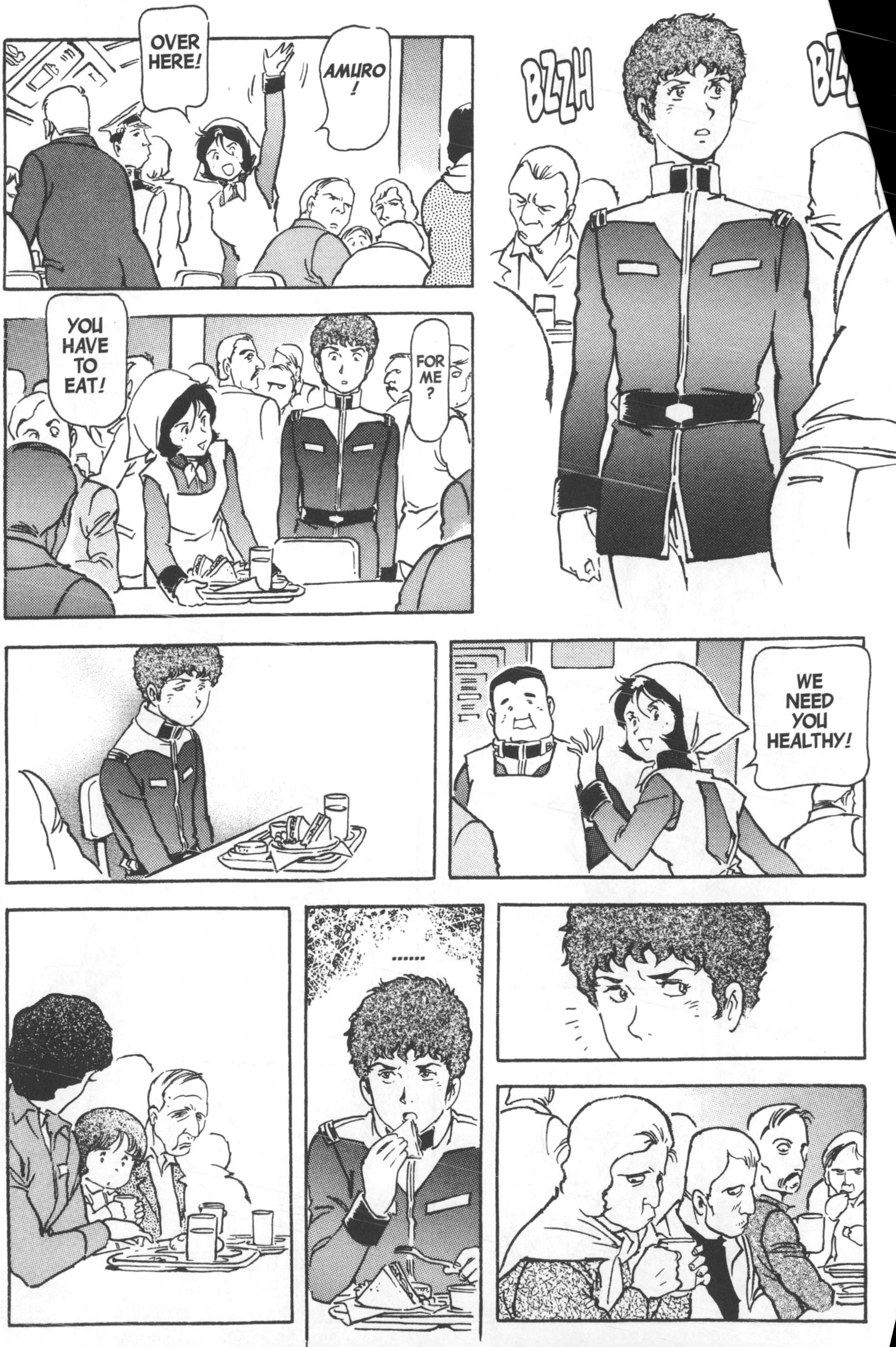
BZZH
BZZ
AMURO!
OVER HERE!
FOR ME?
YOU HAVE TO EAT!
WE NEED YOU HEALTHY!
......

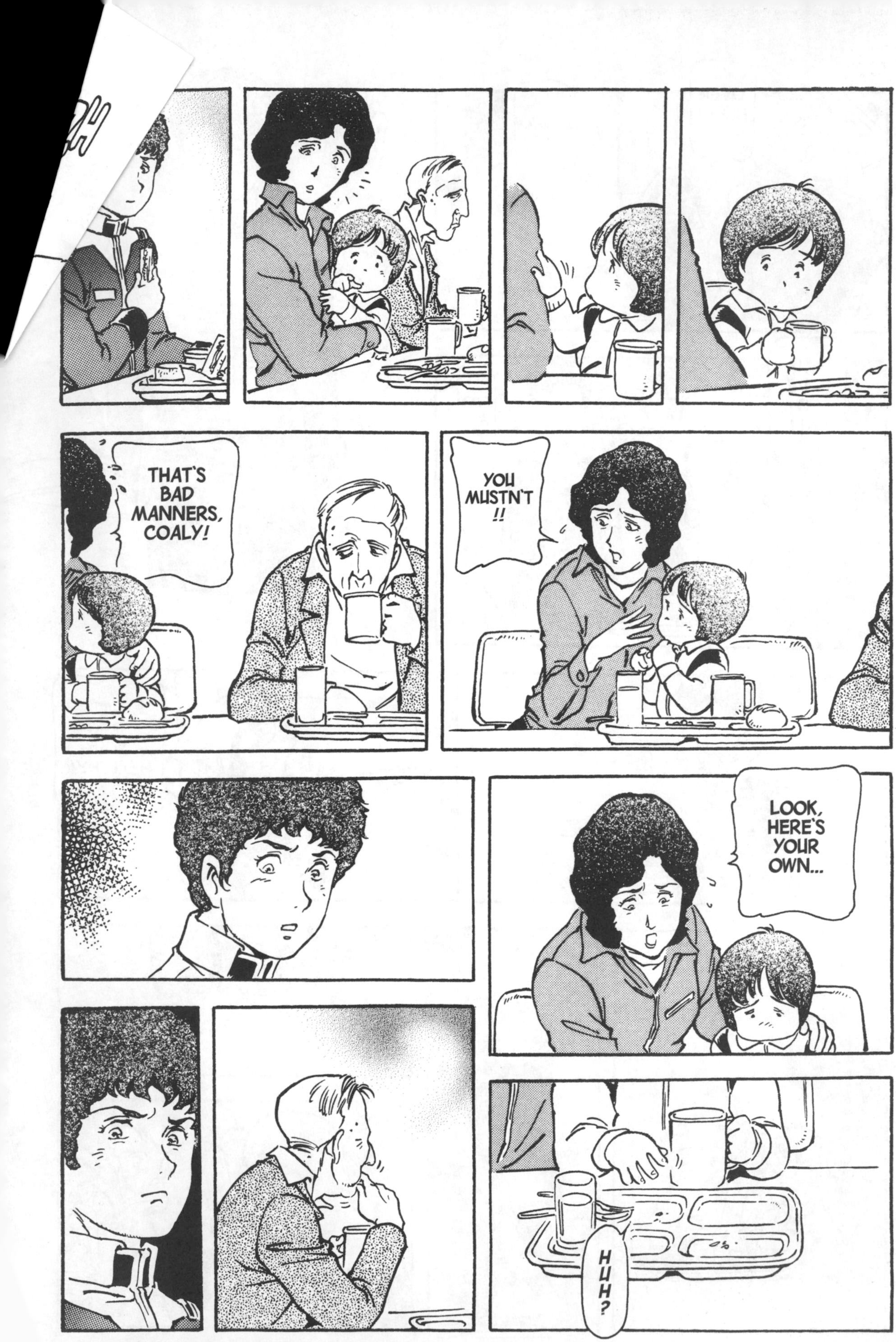
YOU MUSTN'T !!
THAT'S BAD MANNERS, COALY!
LOOK, HERE'S YOUR OWN...
HUH?

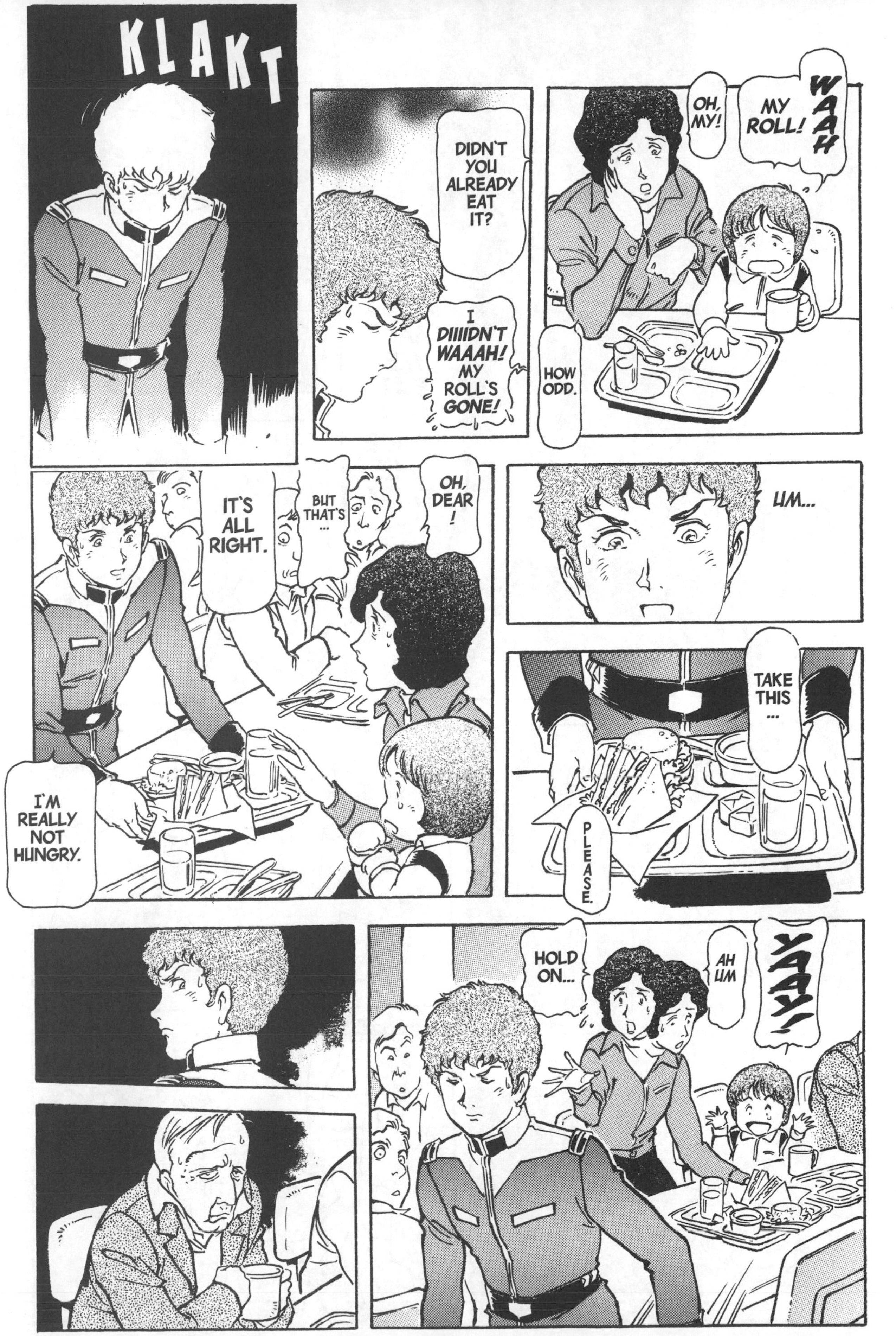
WAAH
MY ROLL!
OH, MY!
HOW ODD.
DIDN'T YOU ALREADY EAT IT?
I DIIIIDN'T WAAAH! MY ROLL'S GONE!
KLAKT
UM...
TAKE THIS...
PLEASE.
OH, DEAR!
BUT THAT'S...
IT'S ALL RIGHT.
I'M REALLY NOT HUNGRY.
YAAY!
AH UM
HOLD ON...

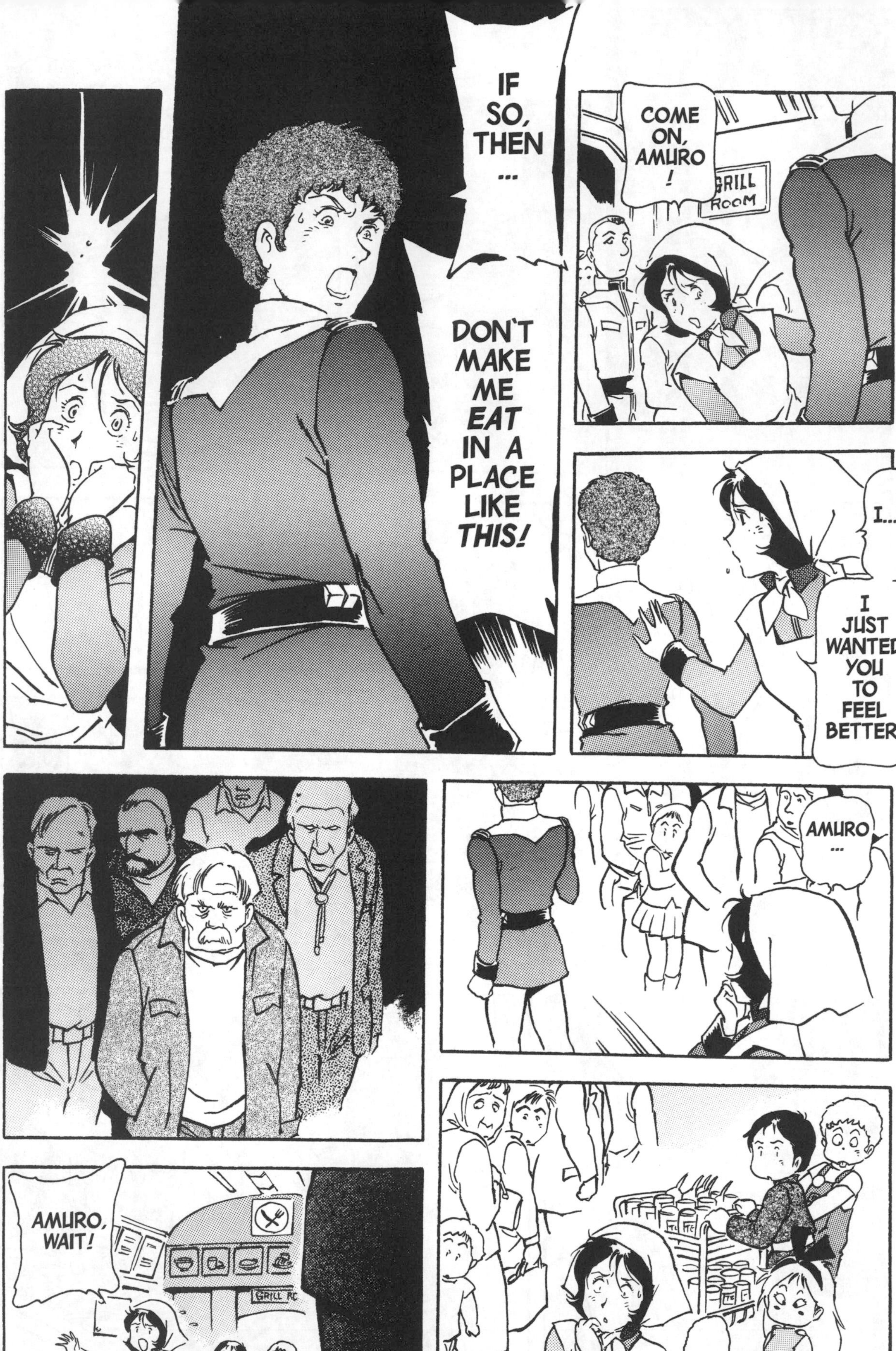
COME ON, AMURO!
GRILL ROOM
I...
I JUST WANTED YOU TO FEEL BETTER.
IF SO, THEN...
DON'T MAKE ME *EAT* IN A PLACE LIKE *THIS!*
AMURO...
......
AMURO, WAIT!

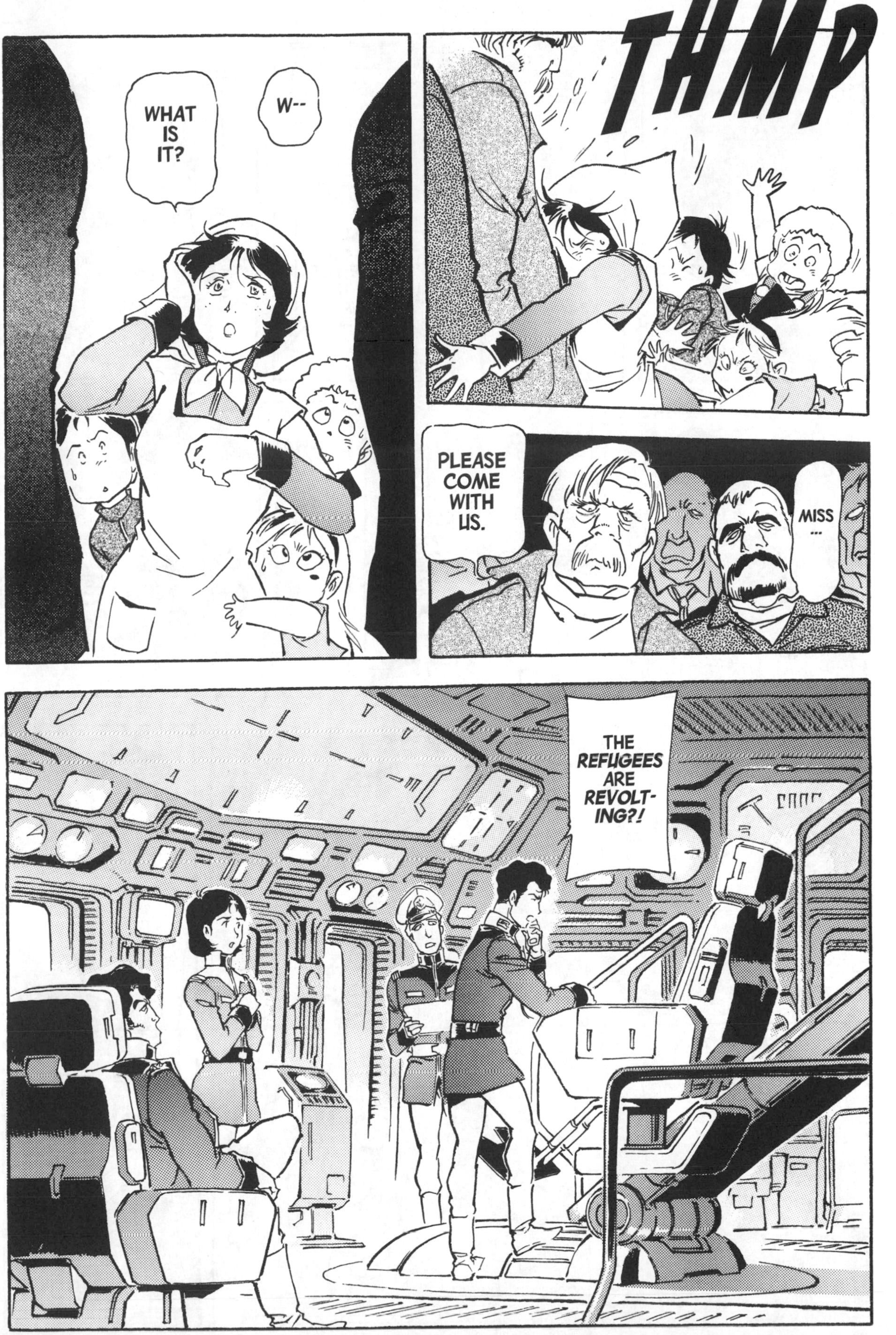
THMP
MISS...
PLEASE COME WITH US.
W--
WHAT IS IT?
THE REFUGEES ARE REVOLTING?!

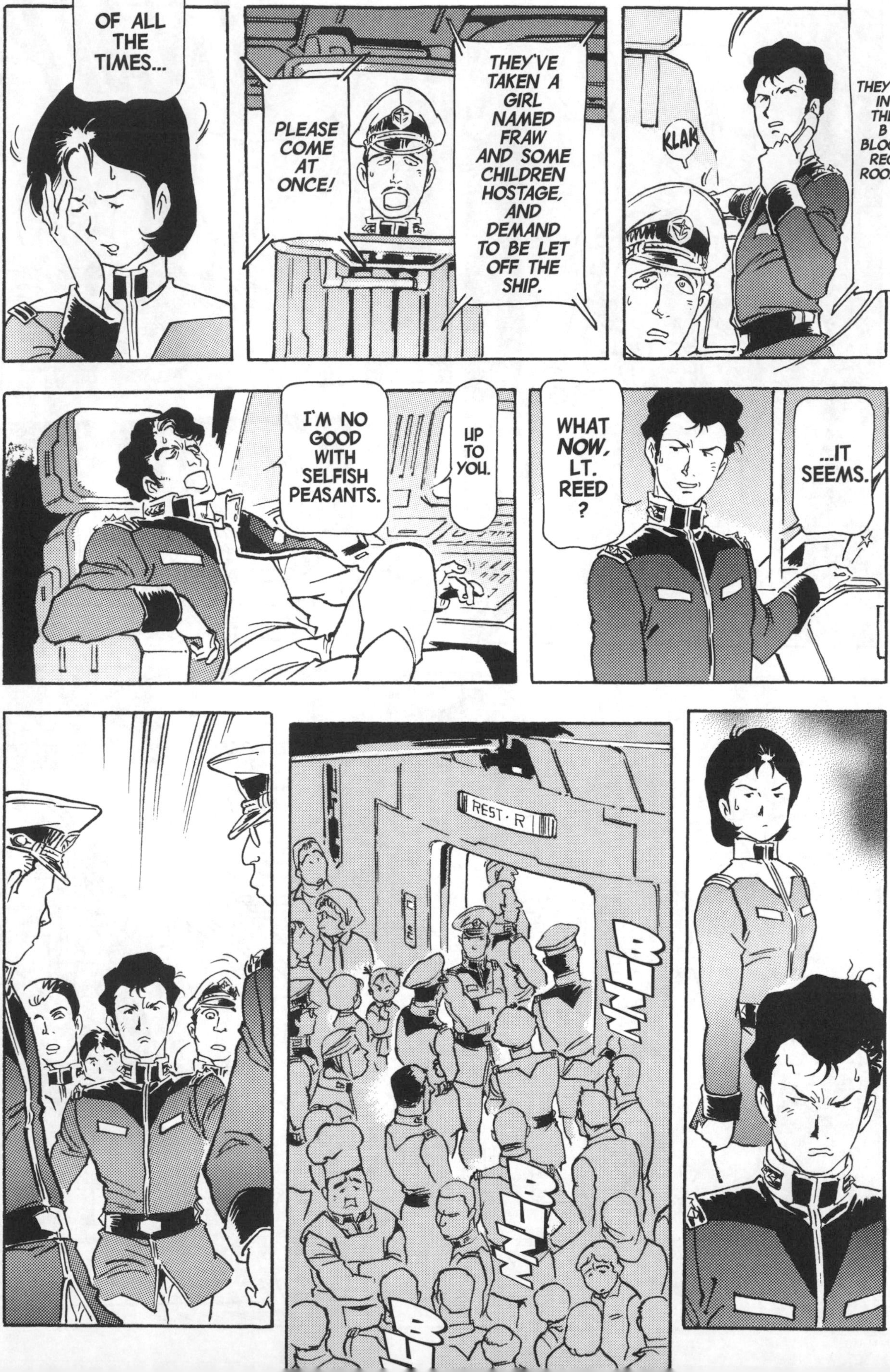
THEY'RE IN THE B BLOCK REC ROOM.
KLAK
THEY'VE TAKEN A GIRL NAMED FRAW AND SOME CHILDREN HOSTAGE, AND DEMAND TO BE LET OFF THE SHIP.
PLEASE COME AT ONCE!
OF ALL THE TIMES...
...IT SEEMS.
WHAT NOW, LT. REED?
UP TO YOU.
I'M NO GOOD WITH SELFISH PEASANTS.
REST · R

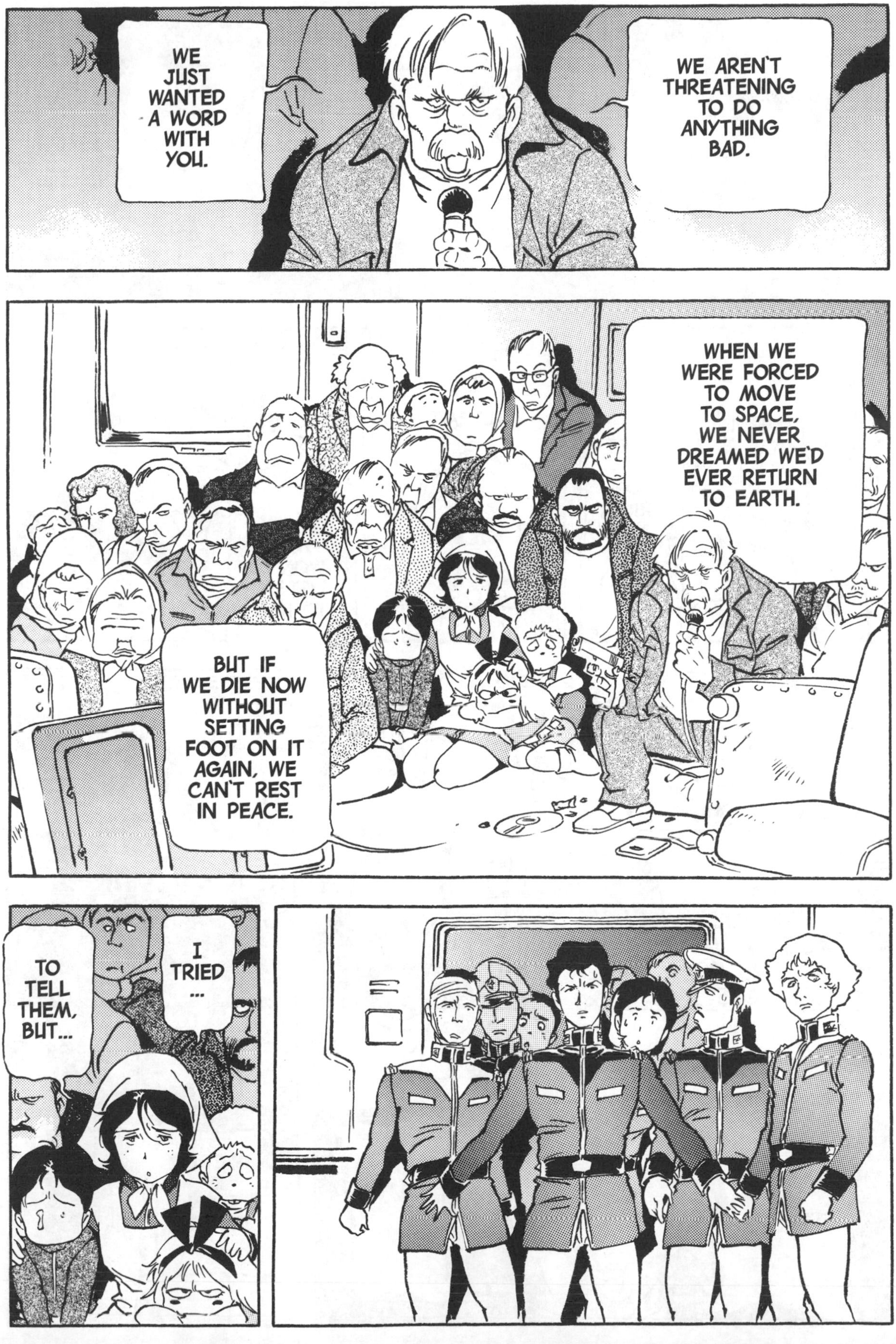
WE AREN'T THREATENING TO DO ANYTHING BAD.
WE JUST WANTED A WORD WITH YOU.
WHEN WE WERE FORCED TO MOVE TO SPACE, WE NEVER DREAMED WE'D EVER RETURN TO EARTH.
BUT IF WE DIE NOW WITHOUT SETTING FOOT ON IT AGAIN, WE CAN'T REST IN PEACE.
I TRIED...
TO TELL THEM, BUT...

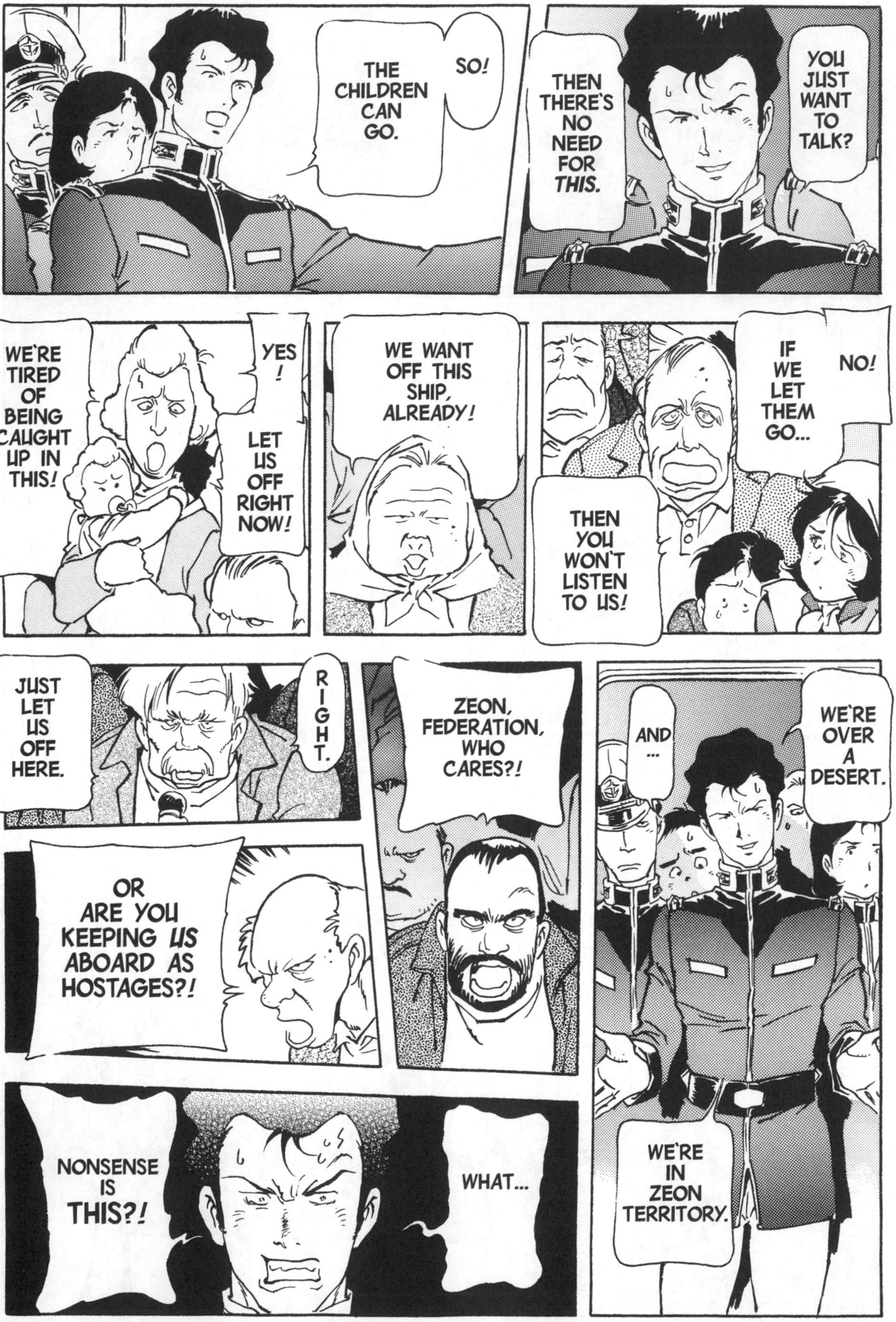
YOU JUST WANT TO TALK?
THEN THERE'S NO NEED FOR *THIS*.
SO!
THE CHILDREN CAN GO.
NO!
IF WE LET THEM GO...
THEN YOU WON'T LISTEN TO US!
WE WANT OFF THIS SHIP, ALREADY!
YES!
LET US OFF RIGHT NOW!
WE'RE TIRED OF BEING CAUGHT UP IN THIS!
WE'RE OVER A DESERT.
AND...
WE'RE IN ZEON TERRITORY.
ZEON, FEDERATION, WHO CARES?!
RIGHT.
JUST LET US OFF HERE.
OR ARE YOU KEEPING *US* ABOARD AS HOSTAGES?!
WHAT...
NONSENSE IS THIS?!

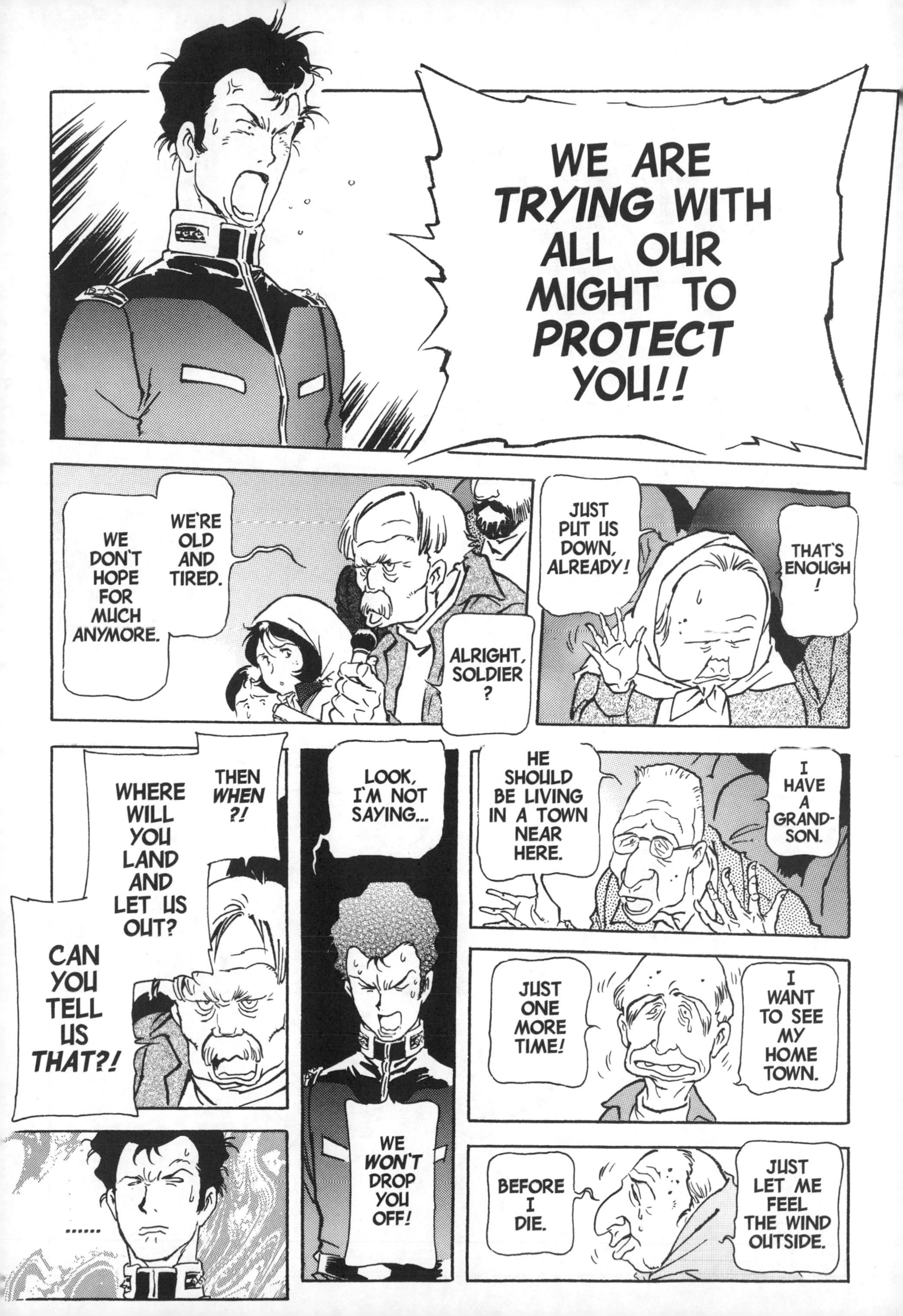
WE ARE *TRYING* WITH ALL OUR MIGHT TO *PROTECT* YOU!!
THAT'S ENOUGH!
JUST PUT US DOWN, ALREADY!
WE'RE OLD AND TIRED.
WE DON'T HOPE FOR MUCH ANYMORE.
ALRIGHT, SOLDIER?
I HAVE A GRAND-SON.
HE SHOULD BE LIVING IN A TOWN NEAR HERE.
I WANT TO SEE *MY* HOME TOWN.
JUST ONE MORE TIME!
JUST LET ME FEEL THE WIND OUTSIDE.
BEFORE I DIE.
LOOK, I'M NOT SAYING...
WE *WON'T* DROP YOU OFF!
THEN *WHEN*?!
WHERE WILL YOU LAND AND LET US OUT?
CAN YOU TELL US *THAT?!*
......

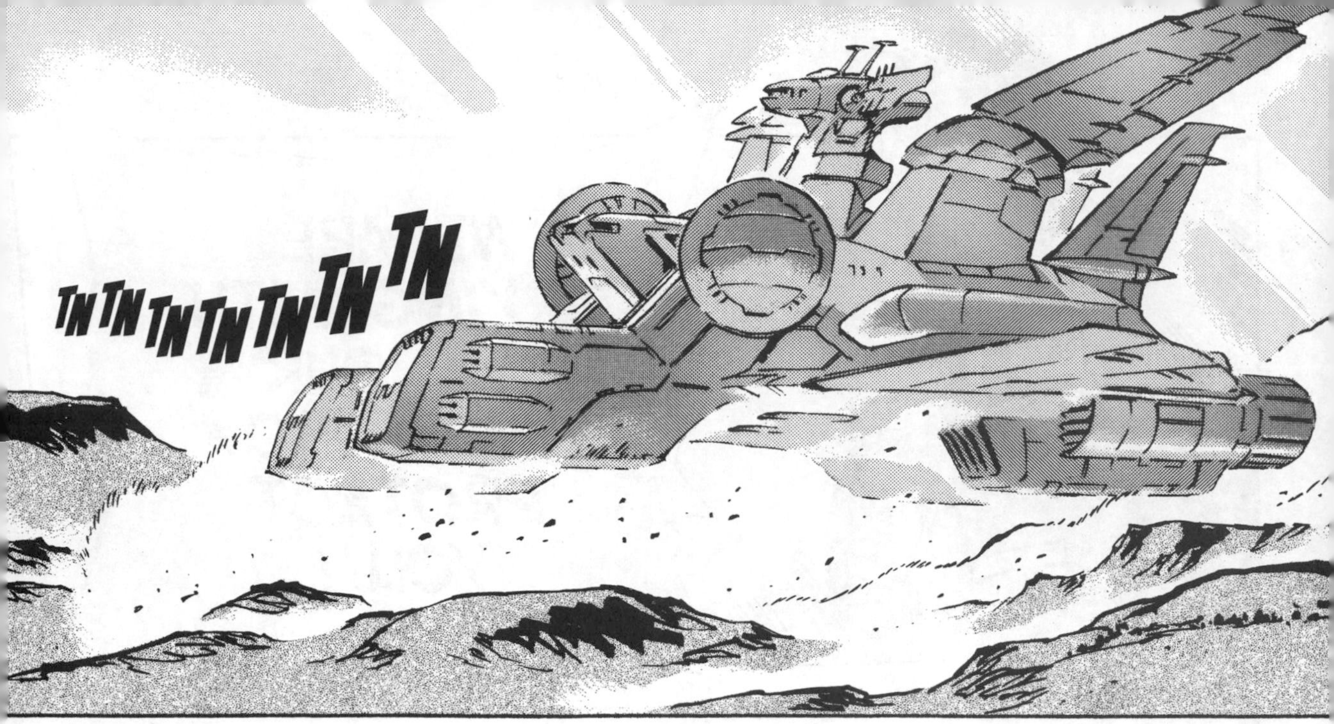
TN TN TN TN TN TN TN

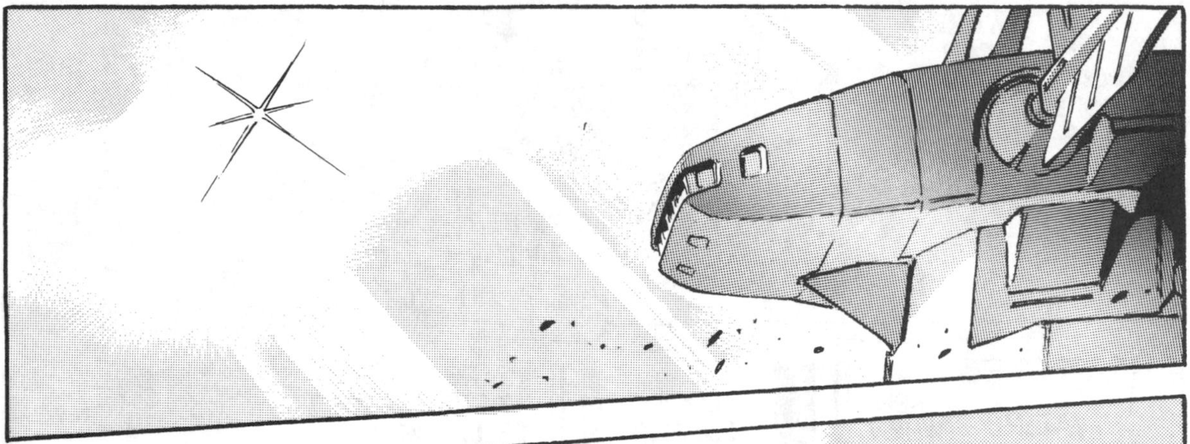

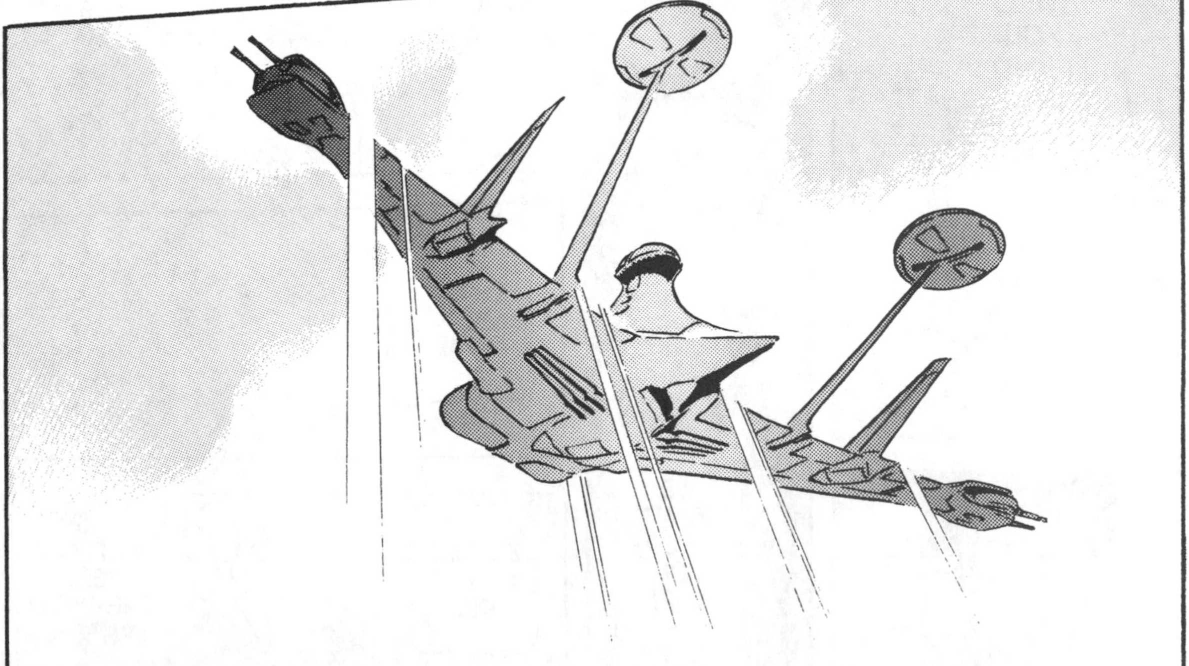

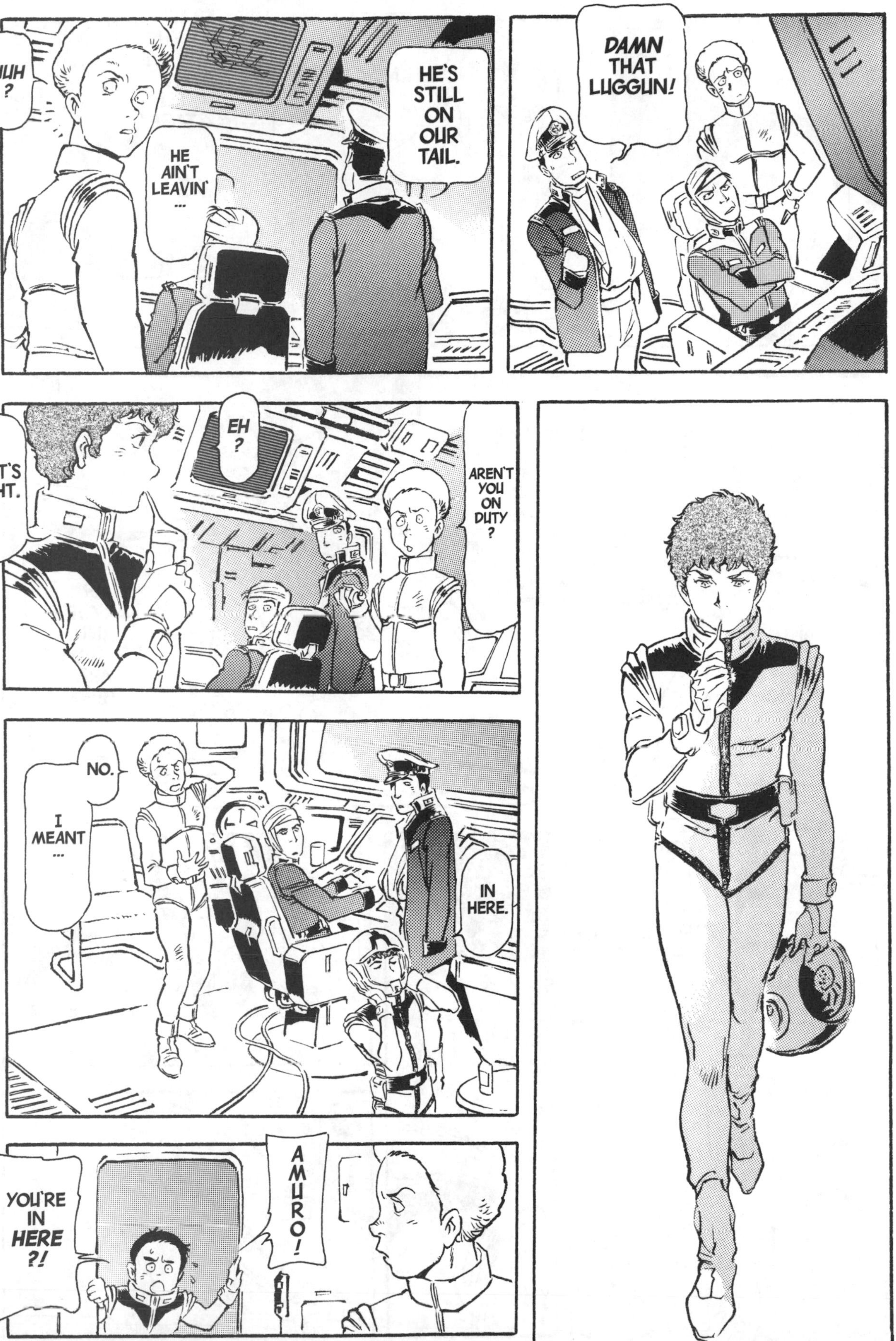
DAMN THAT LUGGUN!
HE'S STILL ON OUR TAIL.
HUH?
HE AIN'T LEAVIN'...
AREN'T YOU ON DUTY?
EH?
THAT'S RIGHT.
NO.
I MEANT...
IN HERE.
AMURO!
YOU'RE IN HERE?!

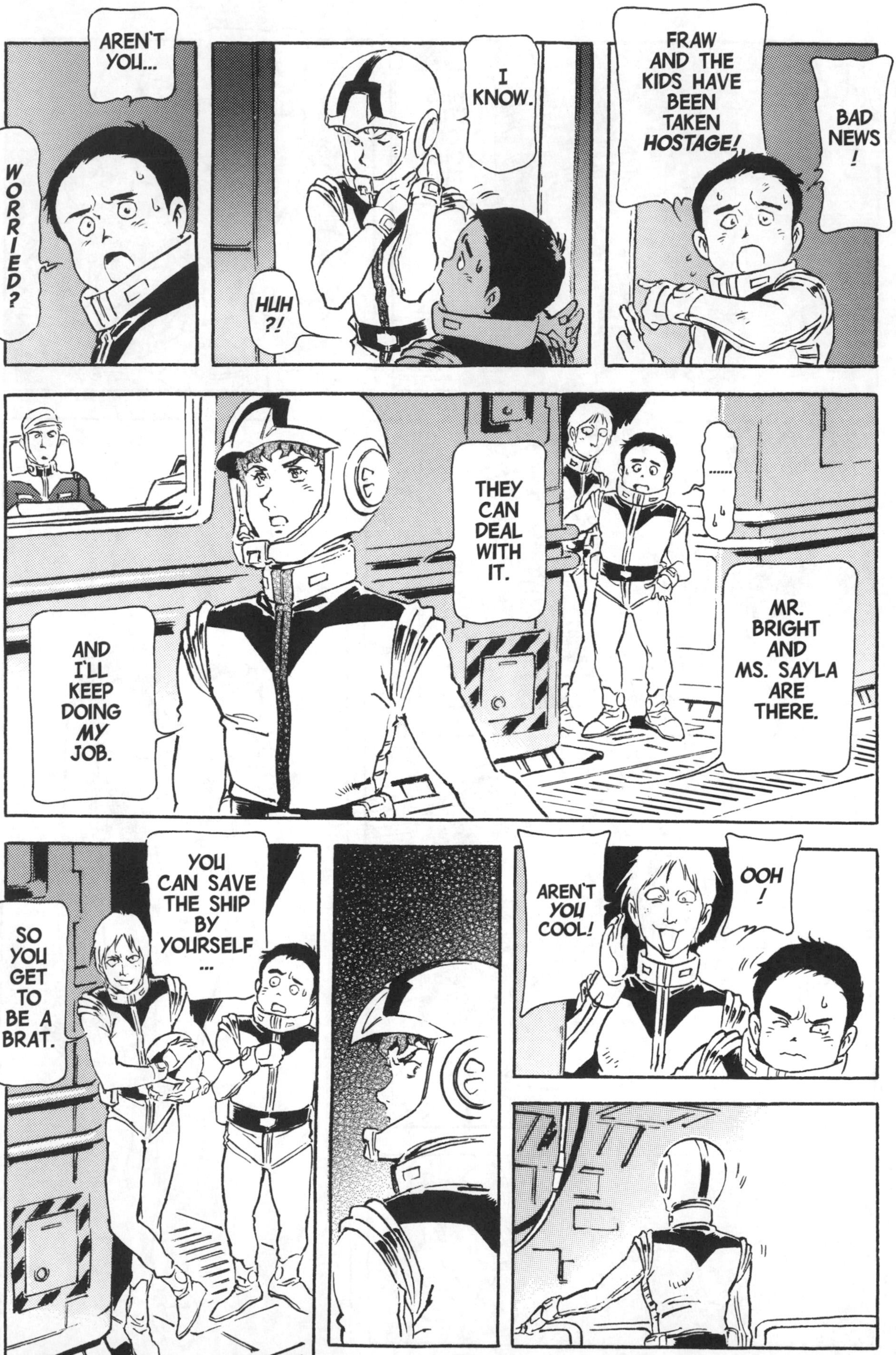
BAD NEWS!
FRAW AND THE KIDS HAVE BEEN TAKEN HOSTAGE!
I KNOW.
HUH?!
AREN'T YOU...
WORRIED?
......
MR. BRIGHT AND MS. SAYLA ARE THERE.
THEY CAN DEAL WITH IT.
AND I'LL KEEP DOING MY JOB.
OOH!
AREN'T YOU COOL!
YOU CAN SAVE THE SHIP BY YOURSELF...
SO YOU GET TO BE A BRAT.

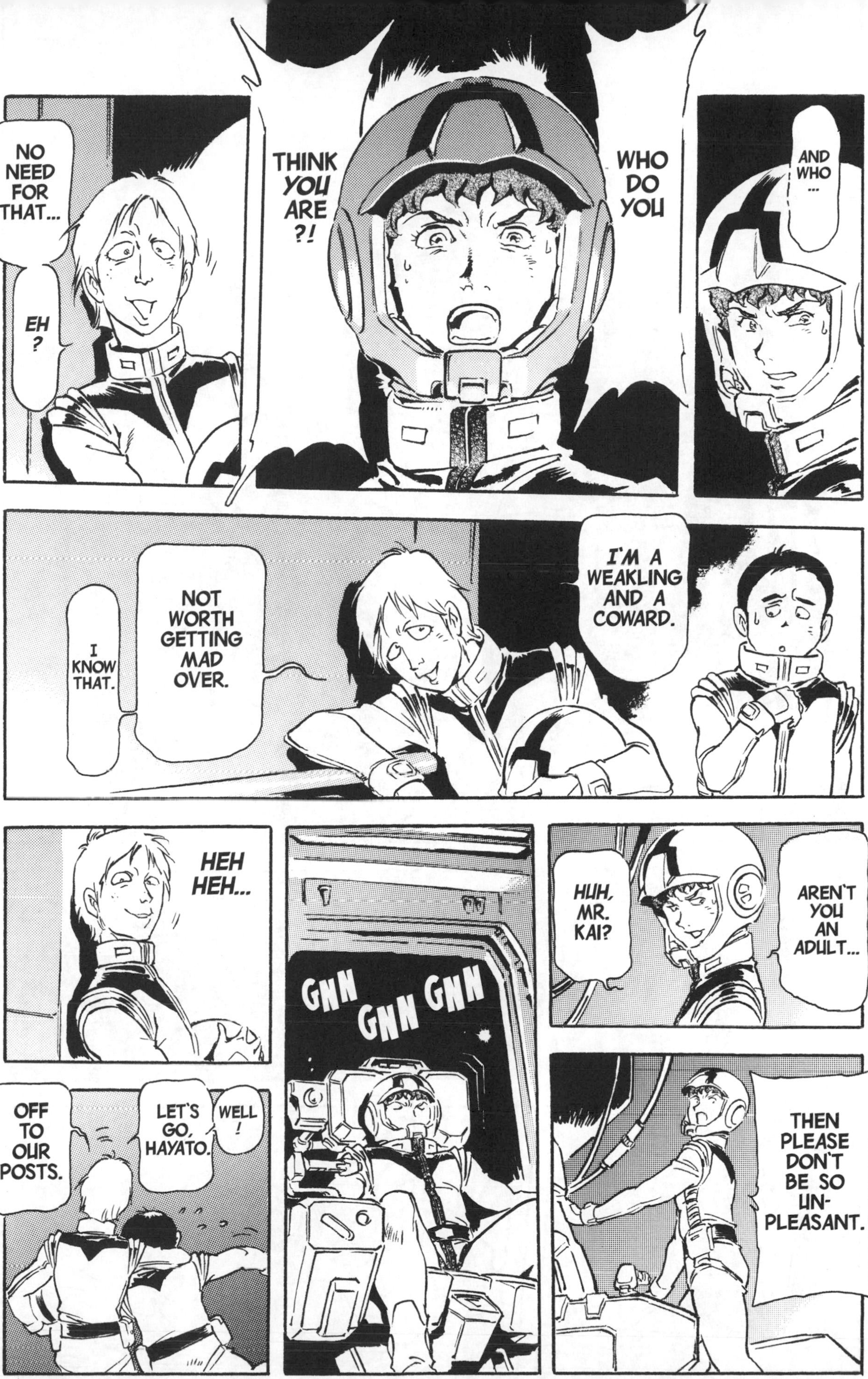
AND WHO ...
WHO DO YOU
THINK YOU ARE ?!
NO NEED FOR THAT...
EH ?
I'M A WEAKLING AND A COWARD.
NOT WORTH GETTING MAD OVER.
I KNOW THAT.
AREN'T YOU AN ADULT...
HUH, MR. KAI?
THEN PLEASE DON'T BE SO UN-PLEASANT.
GNN GNN GNN
HEH HEH...
WELL !
LET'S GO, HAYATO.
OFF TO OUR POSTS.

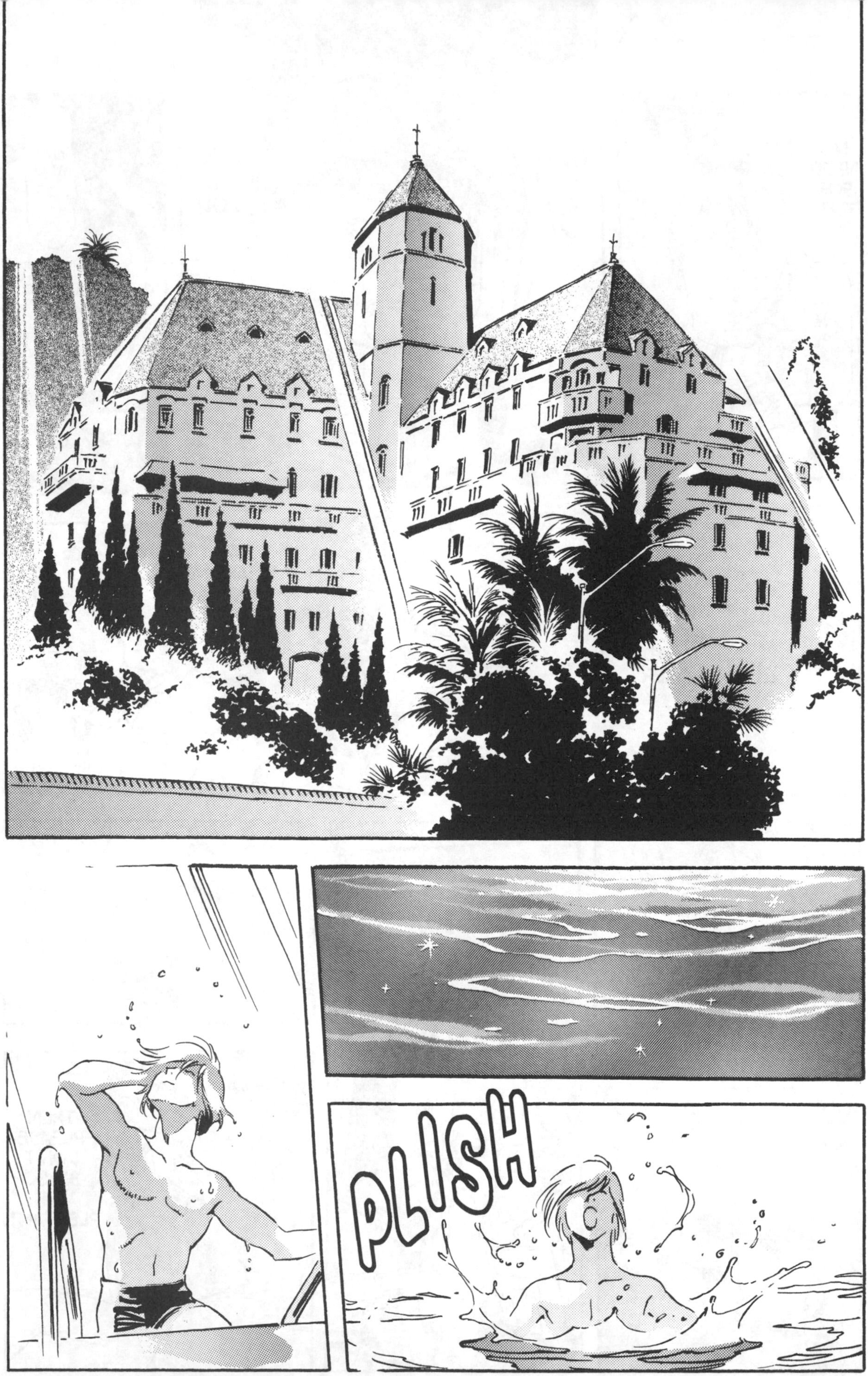
PLISH

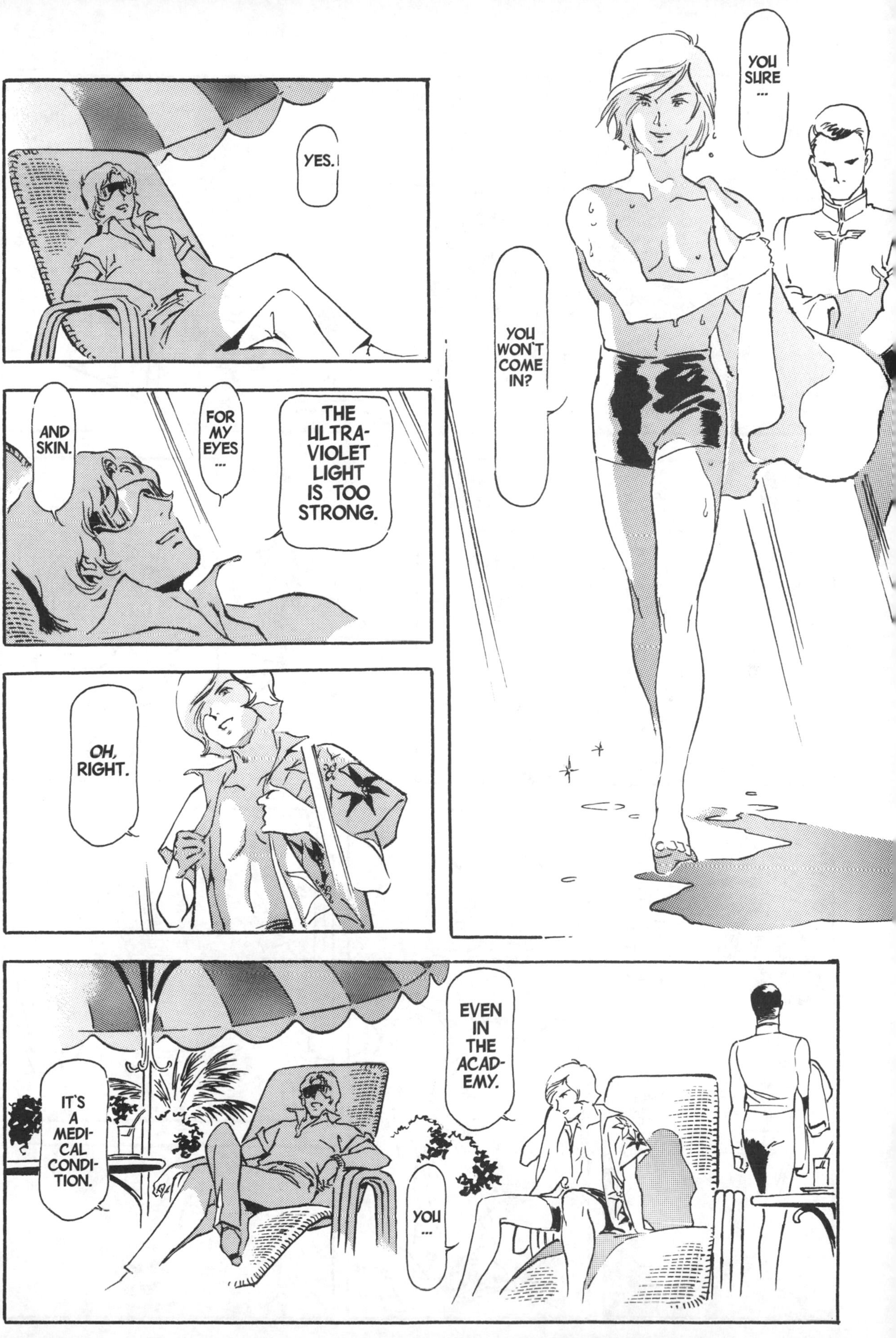
YOU SURE ...
YOU WON'T COME IN?
YES.
THE ULTRA-VIOLET LIGHT IS TOO STRONG.
FOR MY EYES ...
AND SKIN.
OH, RIGHT.
EVEN IN THE ACADEMY.
YOU ...
IT'S A MEDICAL CONDITION.

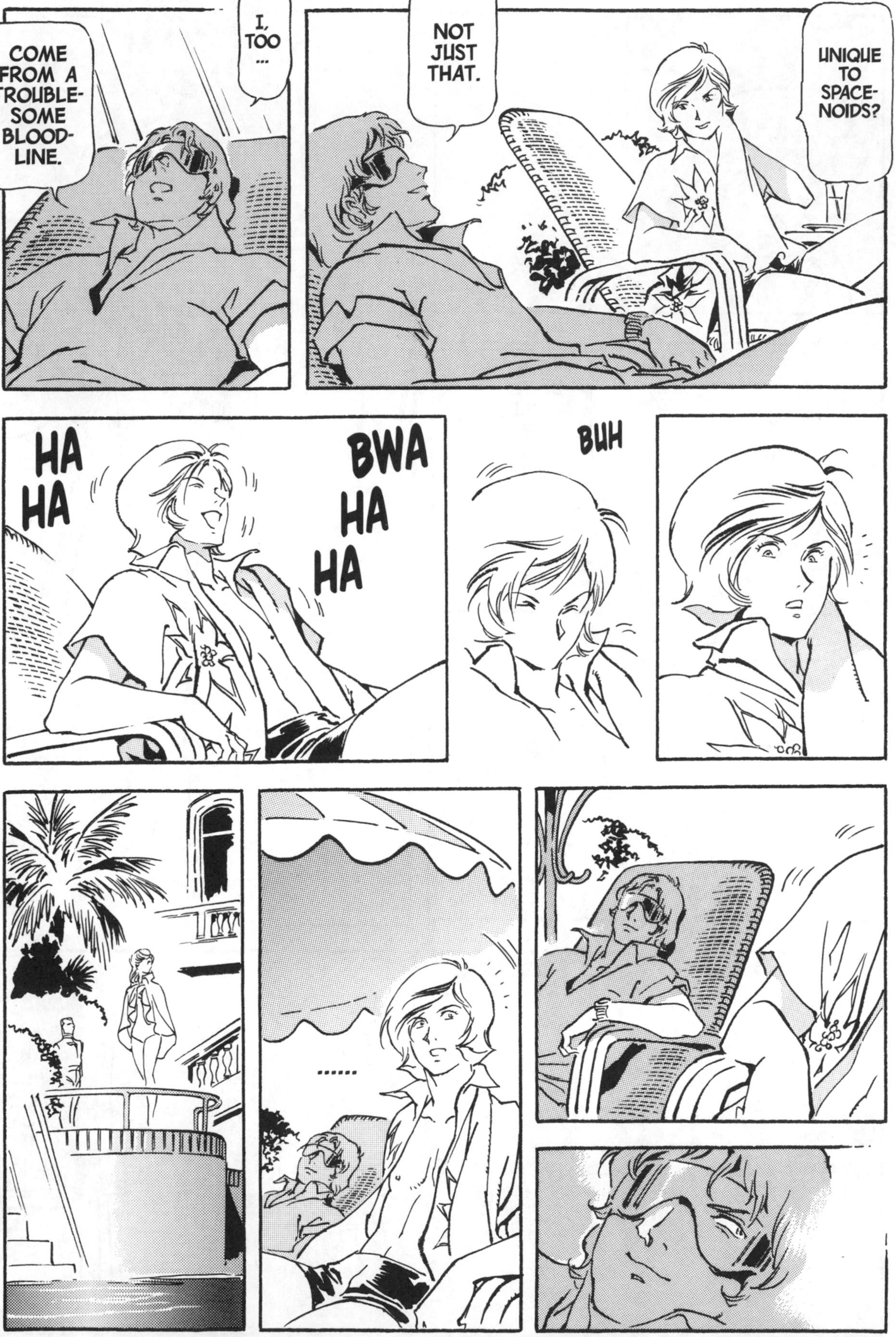
UNIQUE TO SPACE-NOIDS?
NOT JUST THAT.
I, TOO ...
COME FROM A TROUBLE-SOME BLOOD-LINE.
BUH
BWA HA HA
HA HA
......

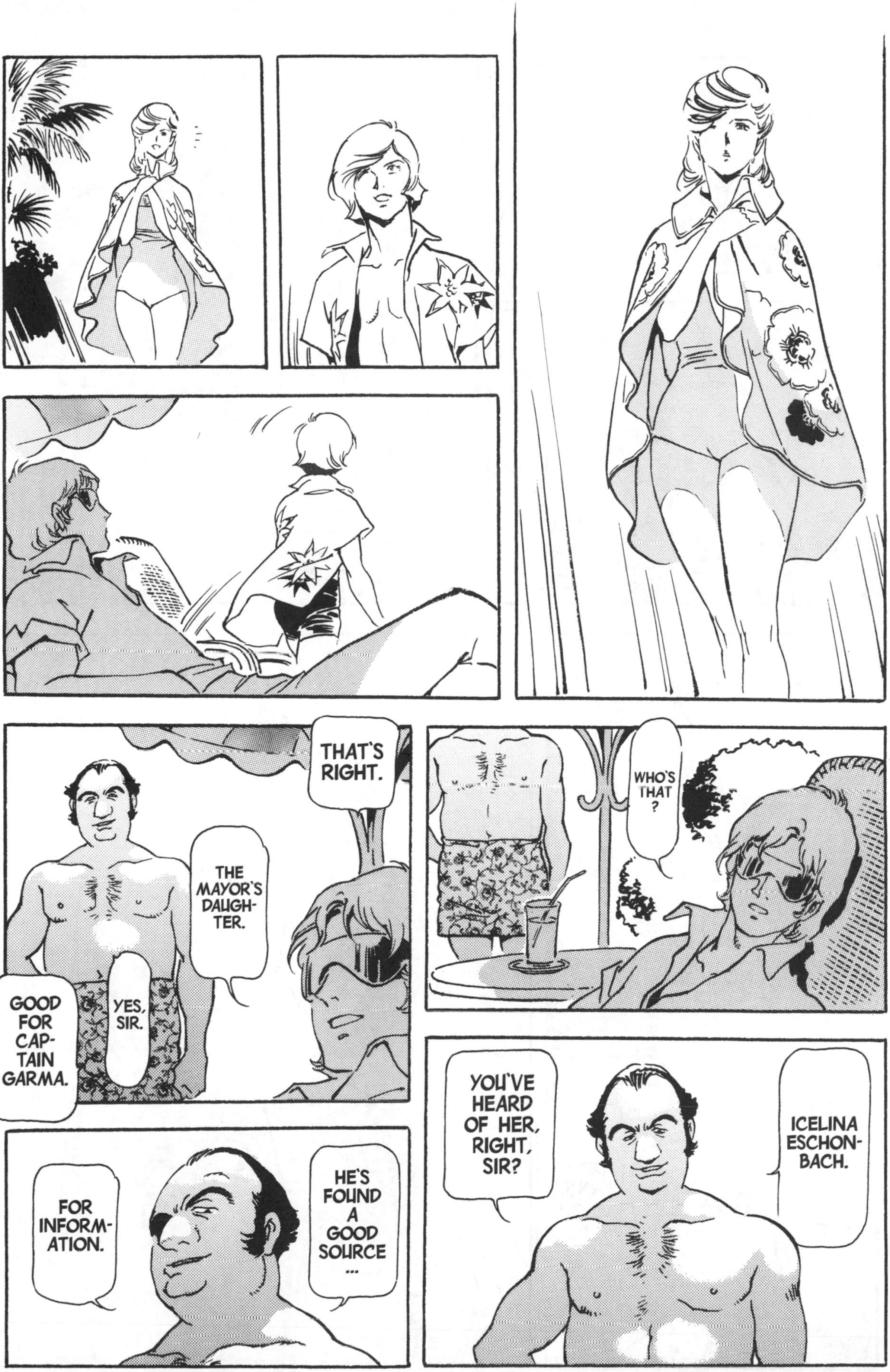
WHO'S THAT ?
ICELINA ESCHON-BACH.
YOU'VE HEARD OF HER, RIGHT, SIR?
THAT'S RIGHT.
THE MAYOR'S DAUGH-TER.
YES, SIR.
GOOD FOR CAP-TAIN GARMA.
HE'S FOUND A GOOD SOURCE ...
FOR INFORM-ATION.

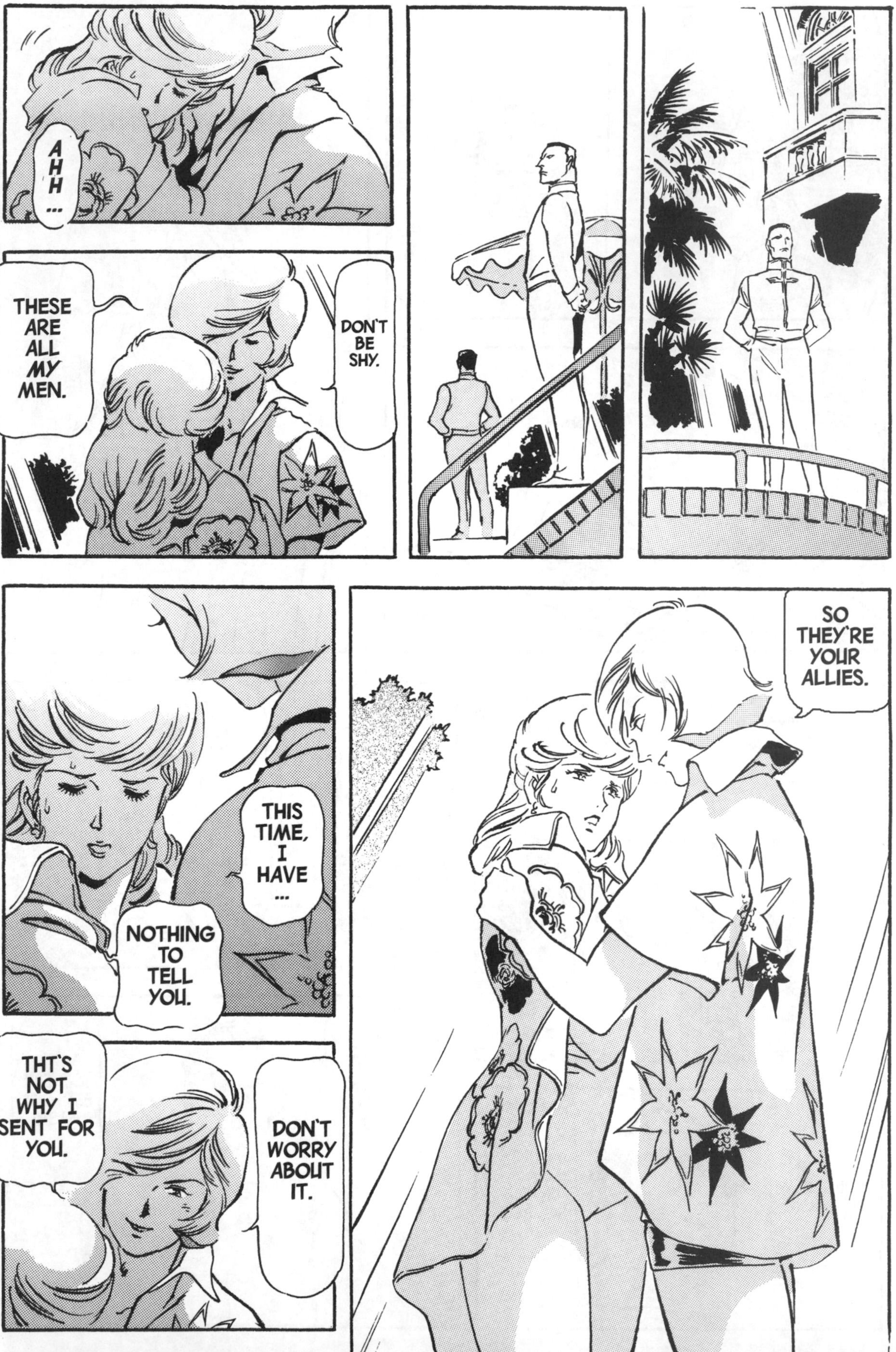
AHHH ...
DON'T BE SHY.
THESE ARE ALL MY MEN.
SO THEY'RE YOUR ALLIES.
THIS TIME, I HAVE ...
NOTHING TO TELL YOU.
DON'T WORRY ABOUT IT.
THT'S NOT WHY I SENT FOR YOU.

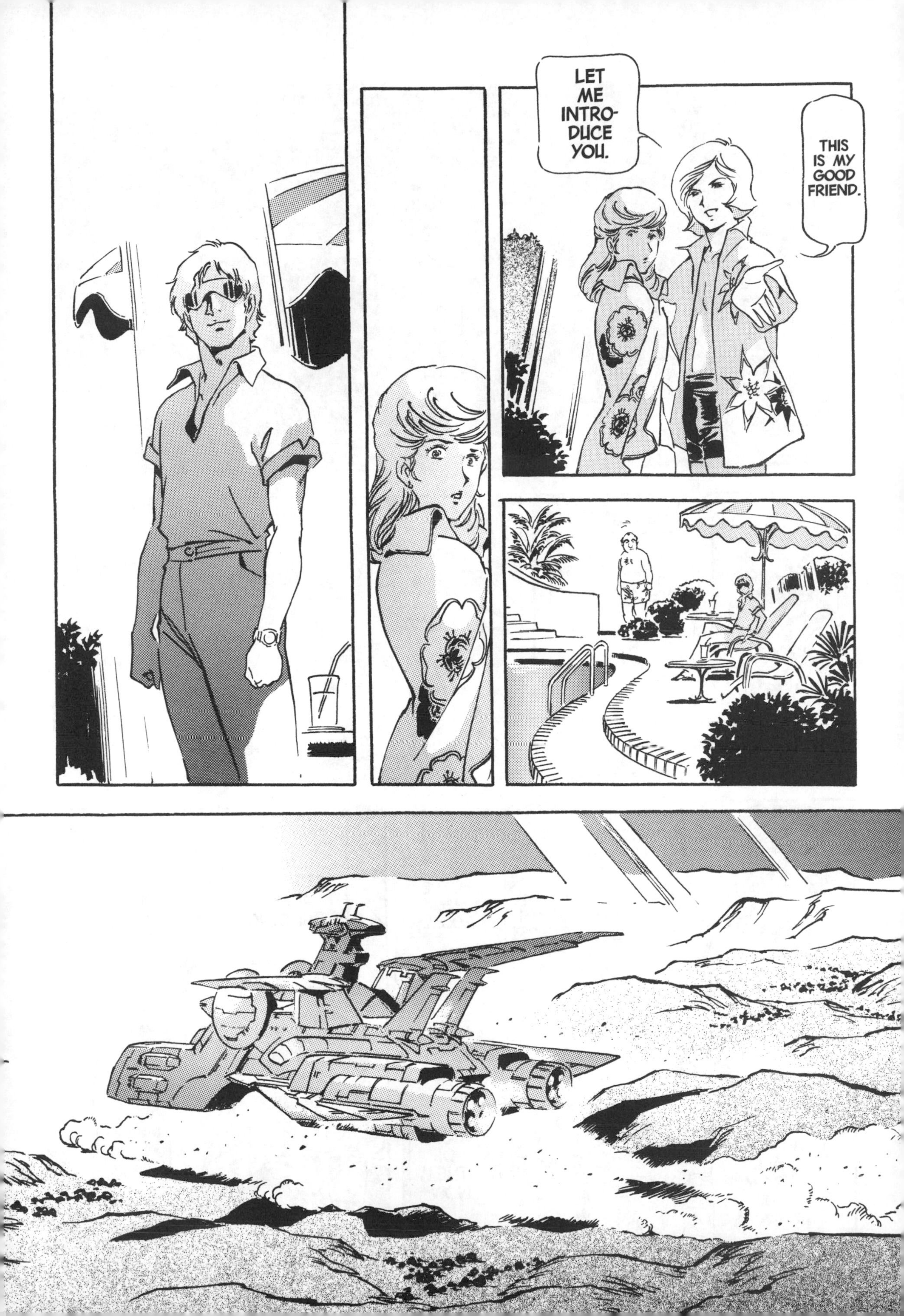
LET ME INTRO-DUCE YOU.
THIS IS MY GOOD FRIEND.

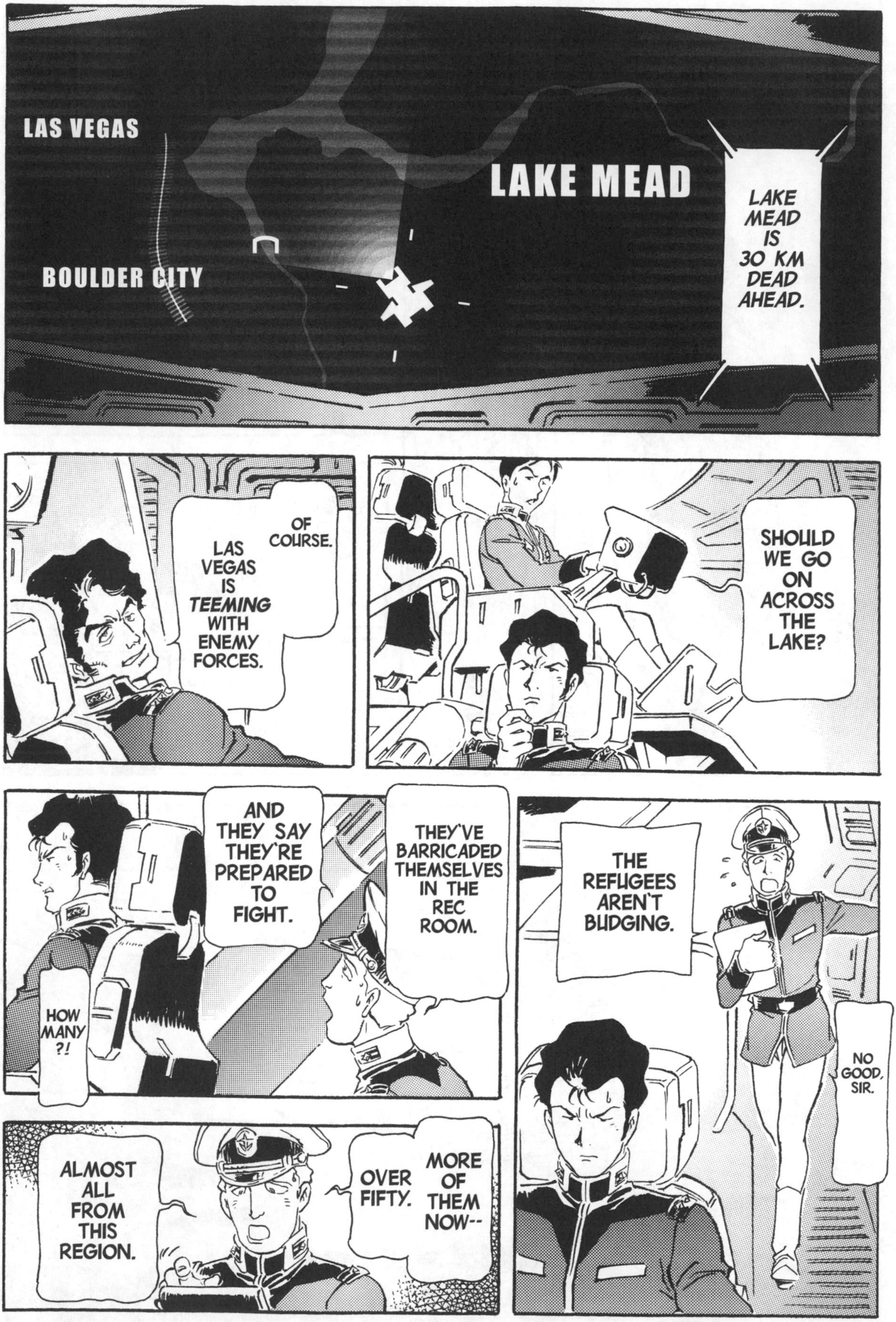
LAKE MEAD IS 30 KM DEAD AHEAD.
LAKE MEAD
LAS VEGAS
BOULDER CITY
SHOULD WE GO ON ACROSS THE LAKE?
OF COURSE.
LAS VEGAS IS *TEEMING* WITH ENEMY FORCES.
THE REFUGEES AREN'T BUDGING.
NO GOOD, SIR.
THEY'VE BARRICADED THEMSELVES IN THE REC ROOM.
AND THEY SAY THEY'RE PREPARED TO FIGHT.
HOW MANY?!
MORE OF THEM NOW--
OVER FIFTY.
ALMOST ALL FROM THIS REGION.

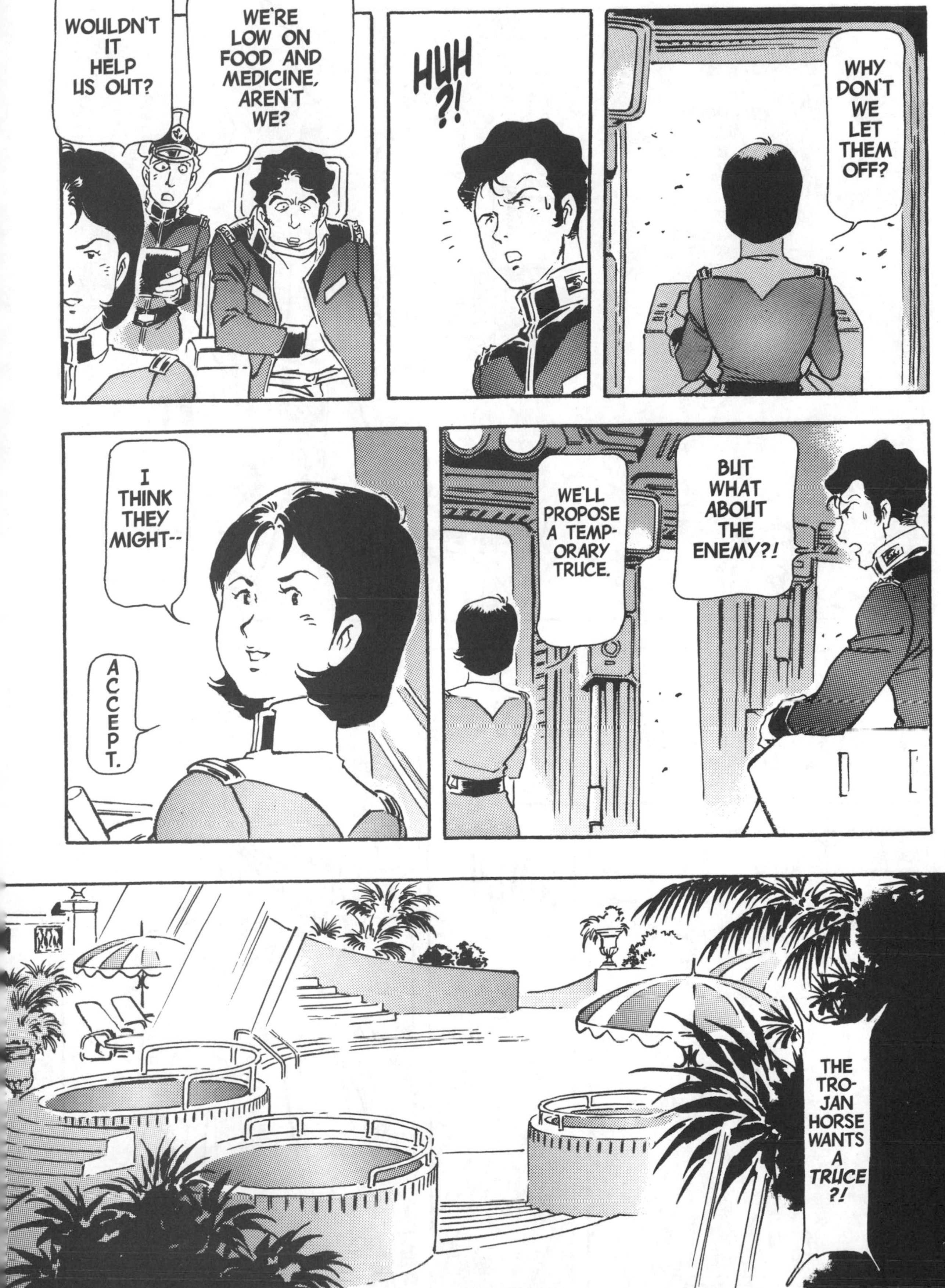
WHY DON'T WE LET THEM OFF?
HUH?!
WE'RE LOW ON FOOD AND MEDICINE, AREN'T WE?
WOULDN'T IT HELP US OUT?
BUT WHAT ABOUT THE ENEMY?!
WE'LL PROPOSE A TEMPORARY TRUCE.
I THINK THEY MIGHT--
ACCEPT.
THE TROJAN HORSE WANTS A *TRUCE*?!

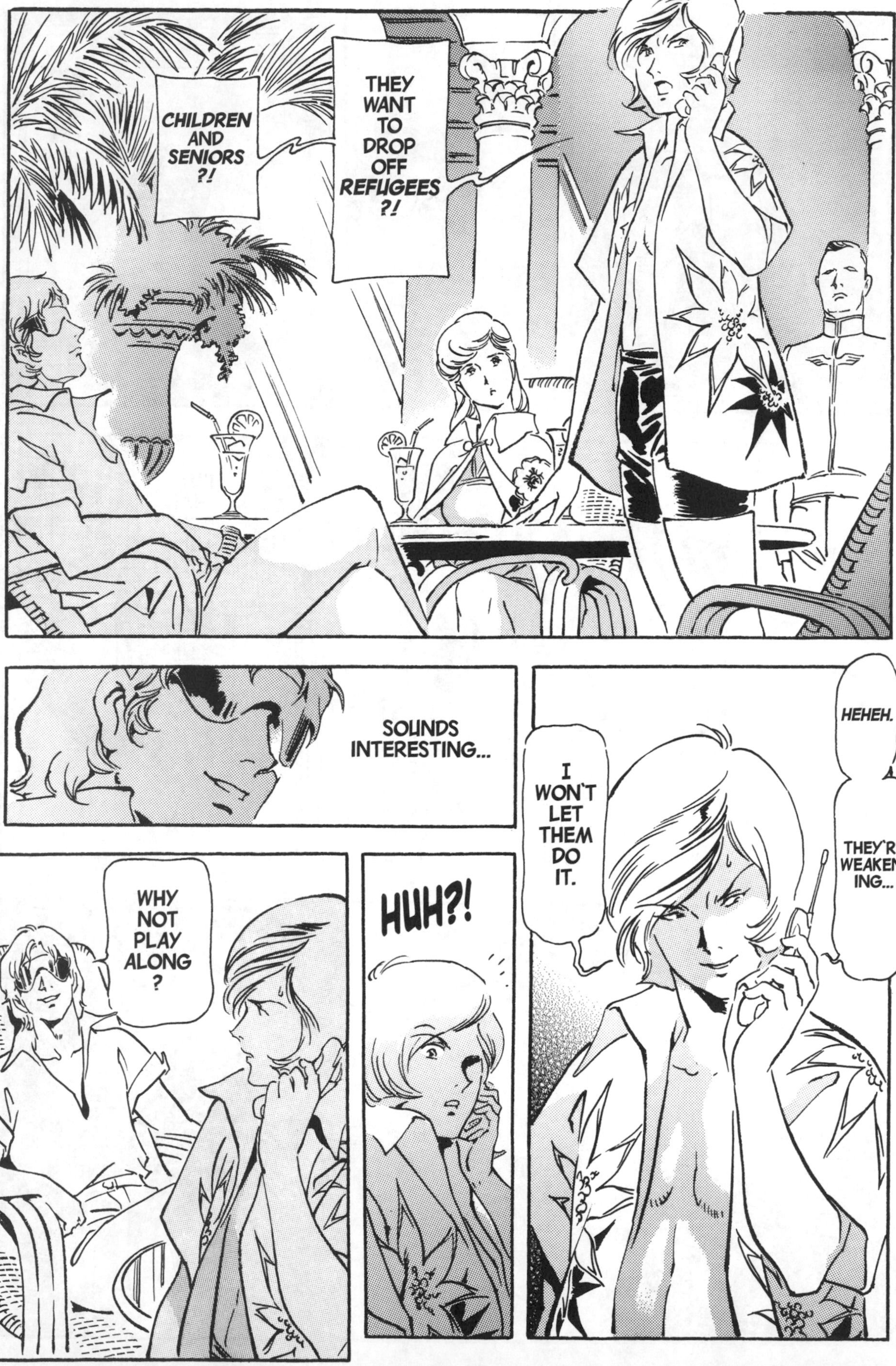
THEY WANT TO DROP OFF REFUGEES ?!
CHILDREN AND SENIORS ?!
HEHEH.
THEY'RE WEAKEN-ING...
I WON'T LET THEM DO IT.
SOUNDS INTERESTING...
HUH?!
WHY NOT PLAY ALONG ?

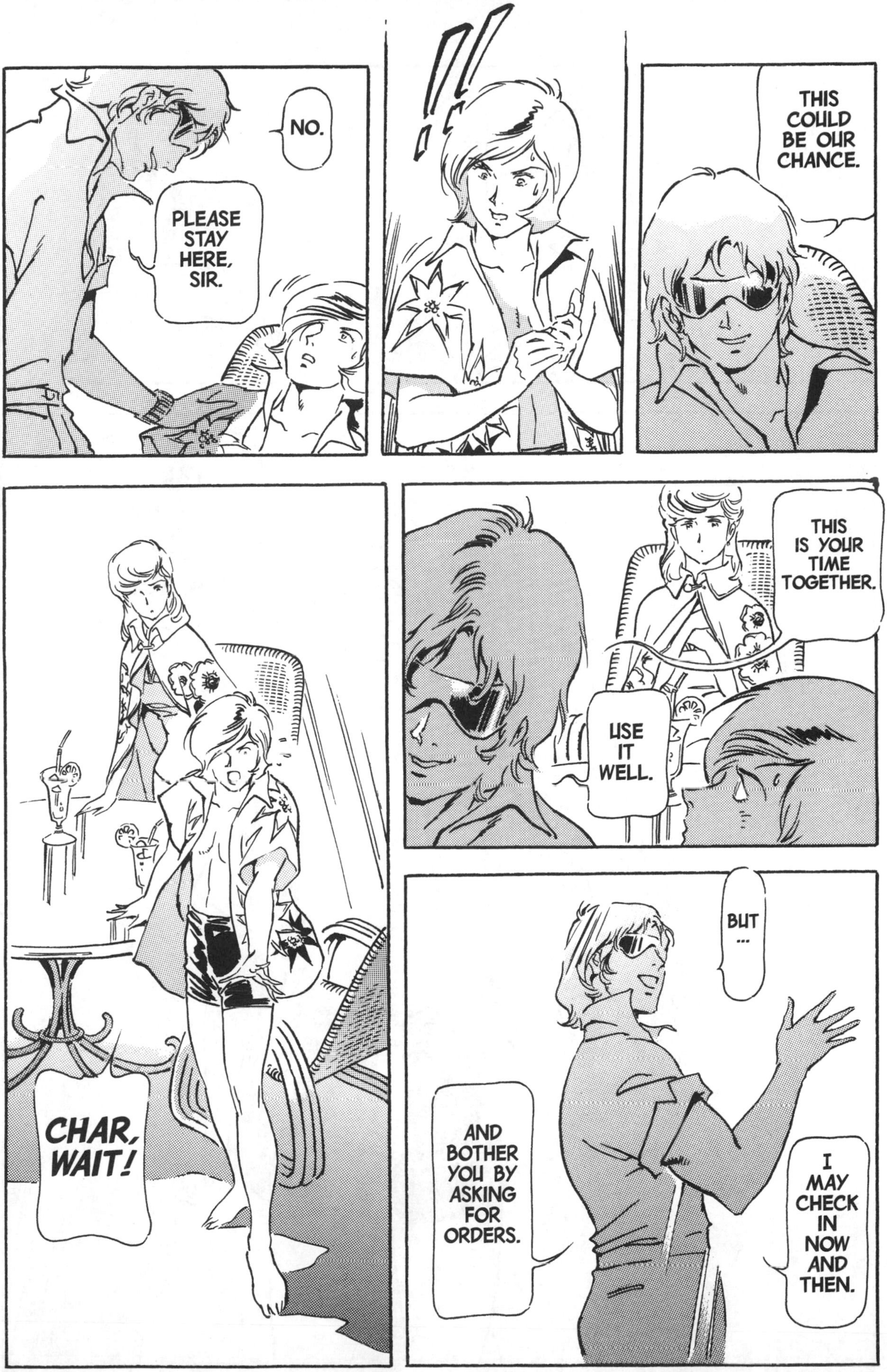
THIS COULD BE OUR CHANCE.
NO.
PLEASE STAY HERE, SIR.
THIS IS YOUR TIME TOGETHER.
USE IT WELL.
BUT ...
I MAY CHECK IN NOW AND THEN.
AND BOTHER YOU BY ASKING FOR ORDERS.
CHAR, WAIT!

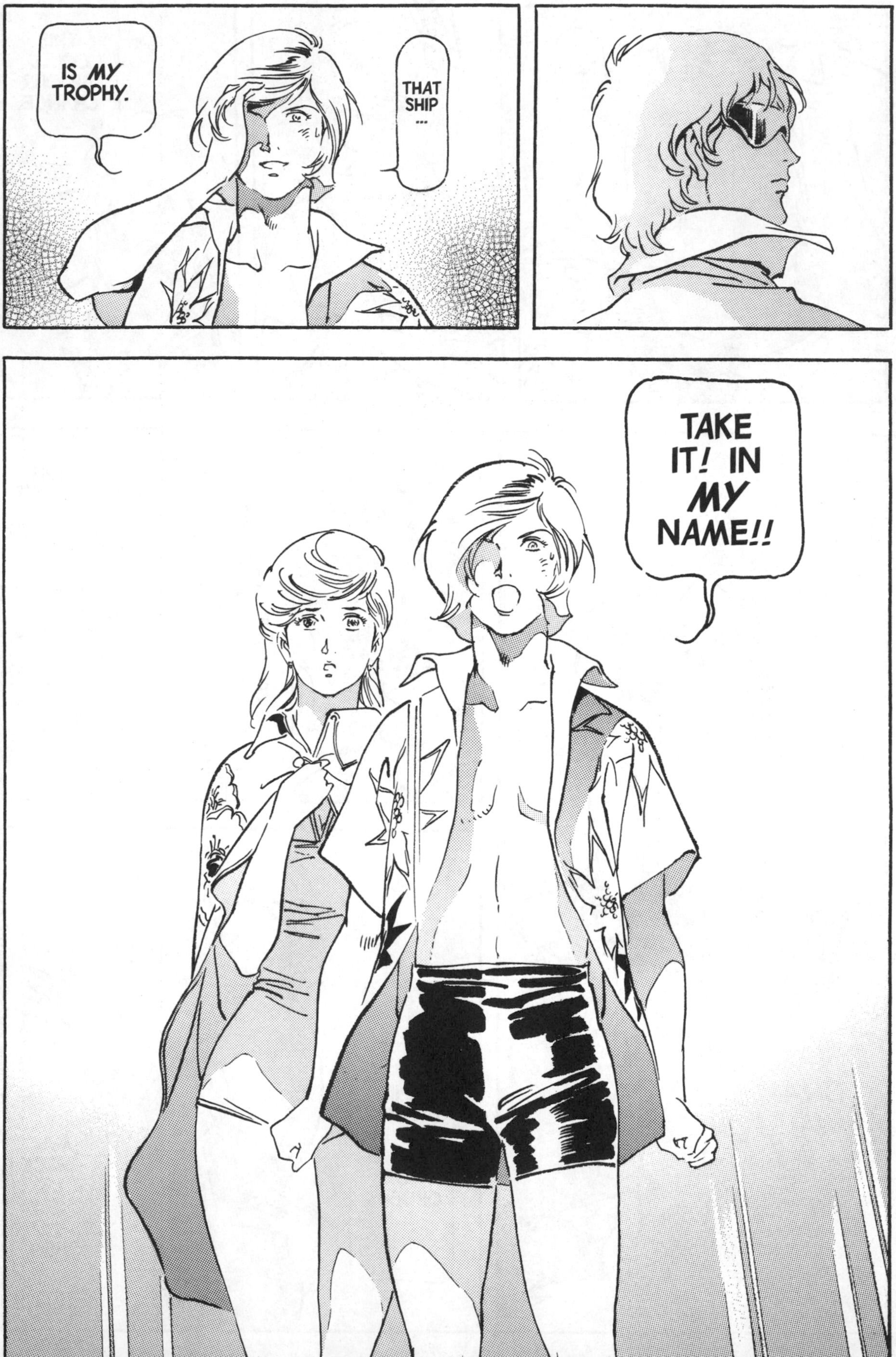
THAT SHIP ...
IS MY TROPHY.
TAKE IT! IN MY NAME!!

GARMA

SECTION IV

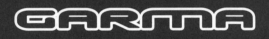

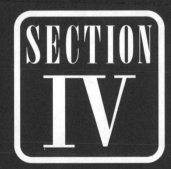

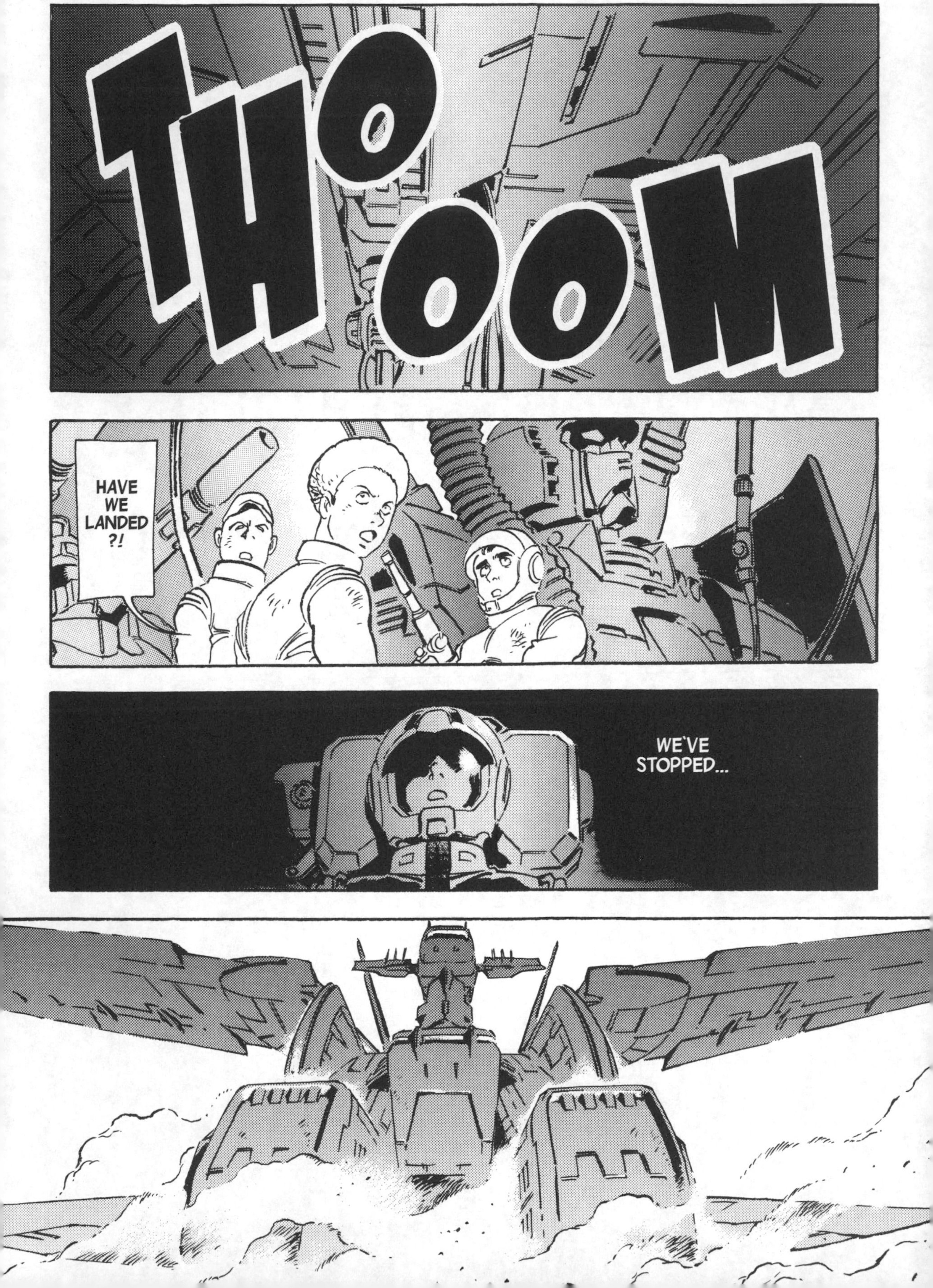
THOOM
HAVE WE LANDED ?!
WE'VE STOPPED...

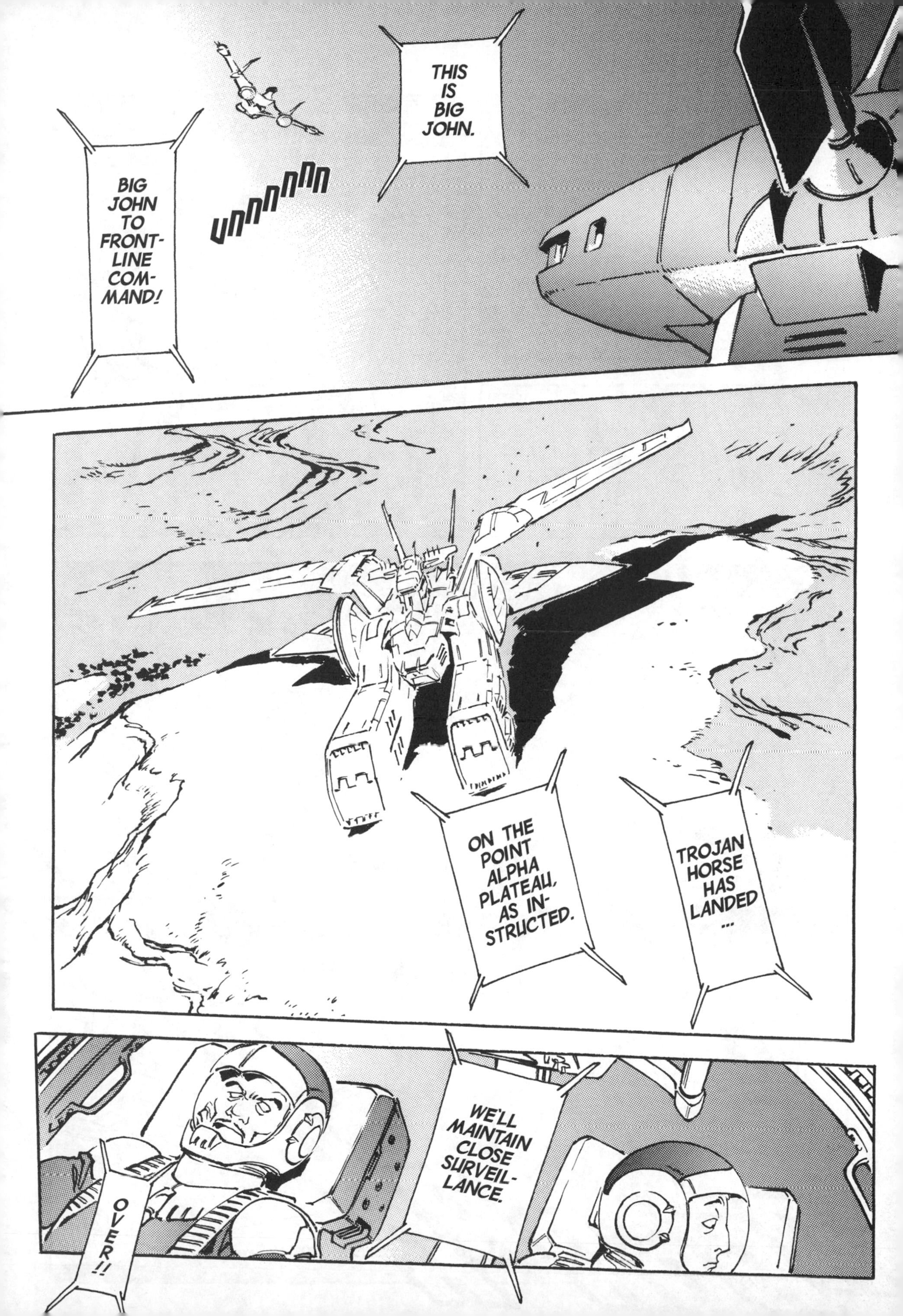
THIS IS BIG JOHN.
BIG JOHN TO FRONT-LINE COM-MAND!
UNNNNNN
TROJAN HORSE HAS LANDED ...
ON THE POINT ALPHA PLATEAU, AS IN-STRUCTED.
WE'LL MAINTAIN CLOSE SURVEIL-LANCE.
OVER!!

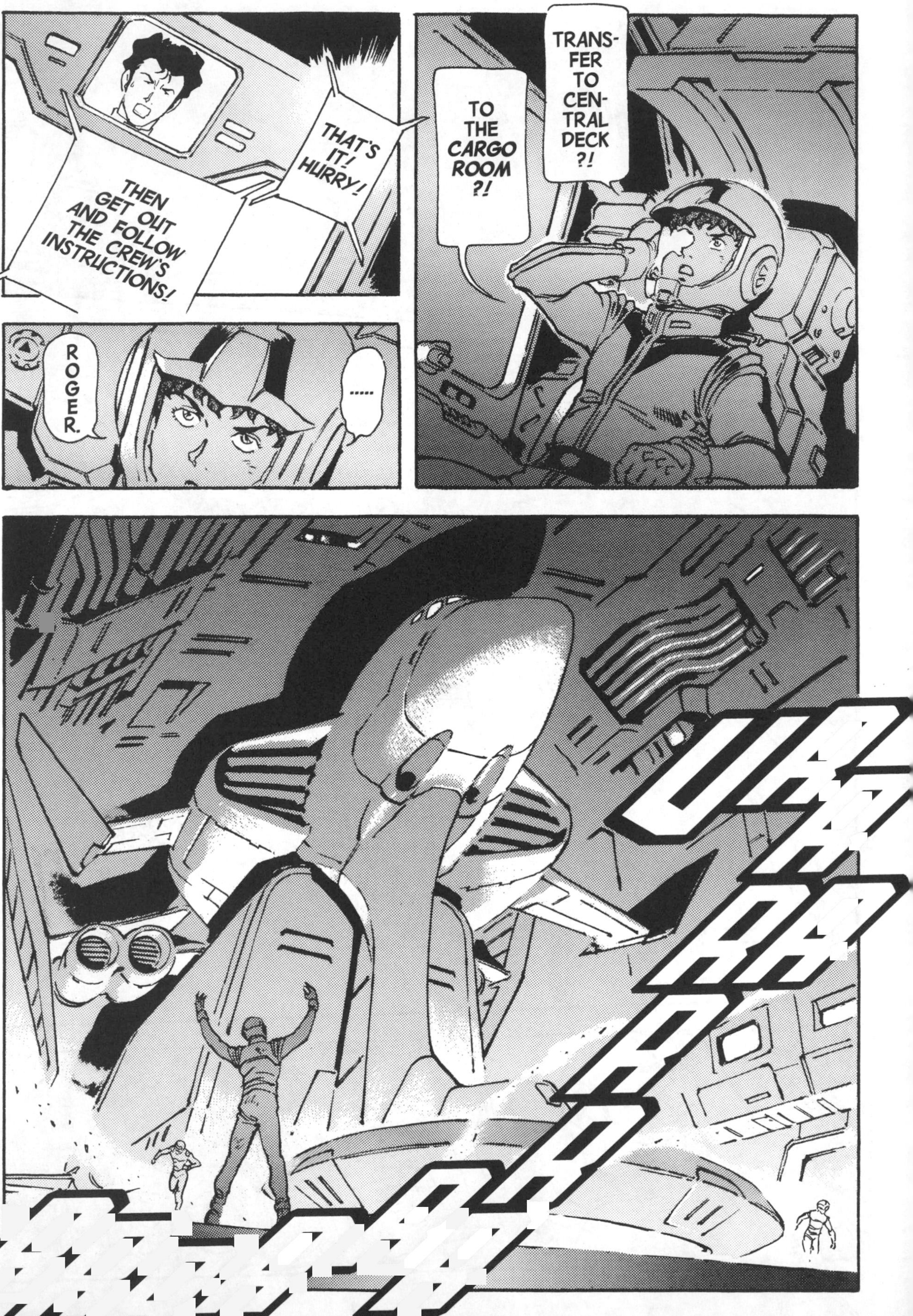
TRANSFER TO CENTRAL DECK?!
TO THE CARGO ROOM?!
THAT'S IT! HURRY!
THEN GET OUT AND FOLLOW THE CREW'S INSTRUCTIONS!
......
ROGER.

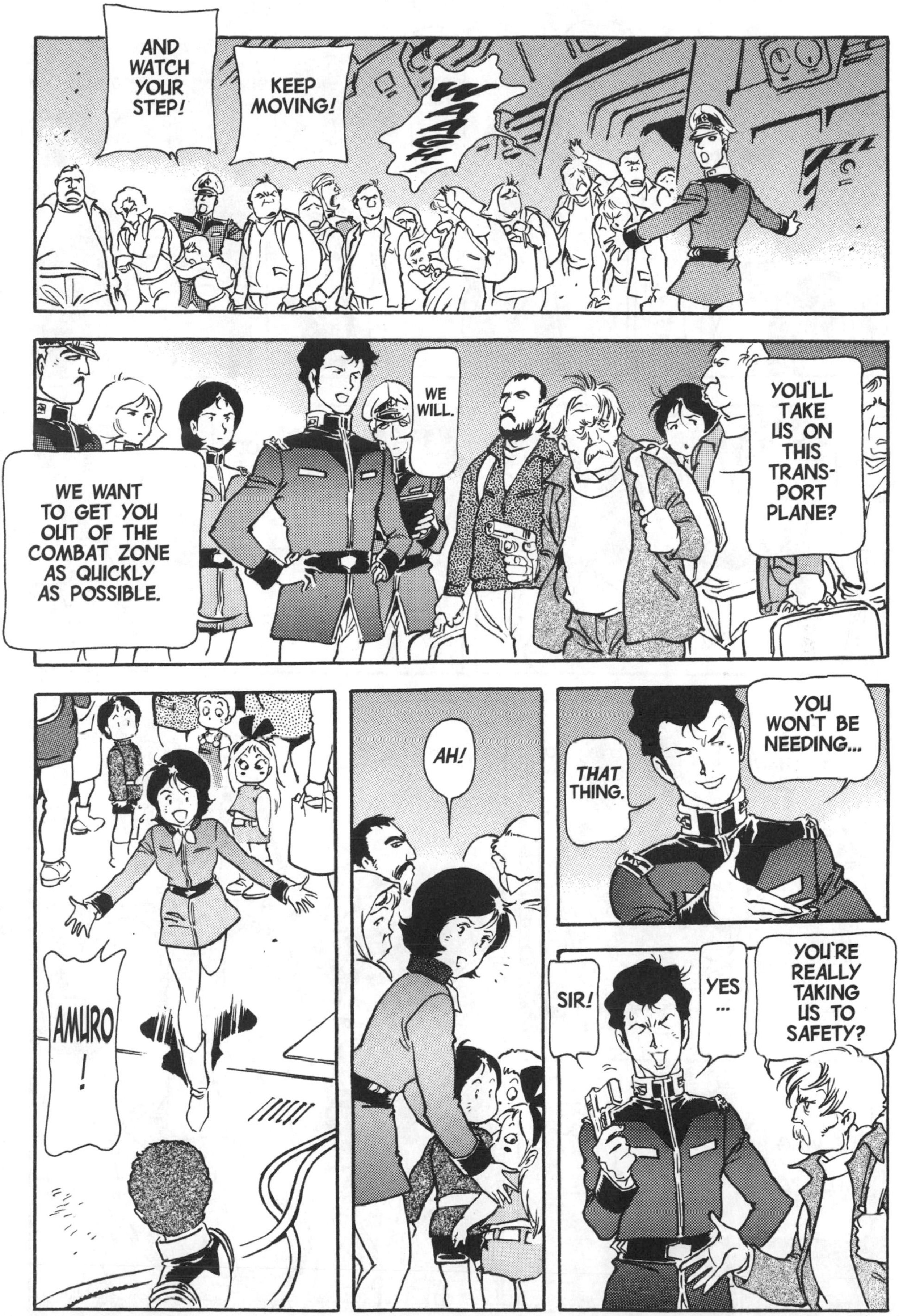
WAAGH!
KEEP MOVING!
AND WATCH YOUR STEP!
YOU'LL TAKE US ON THIS TRANSPORT PLANE?
WE WILL.
WE WANT TO GET YOU OUT OF THE COMBAT ZONE AS QUICKLY AS POSSIBLE.
YOU WON'T BE NEEDING...
THAT THING.
YOU'RE REALLY TAKING US TO SAFETY?
YES...
SIR!
AH!
AMURO!

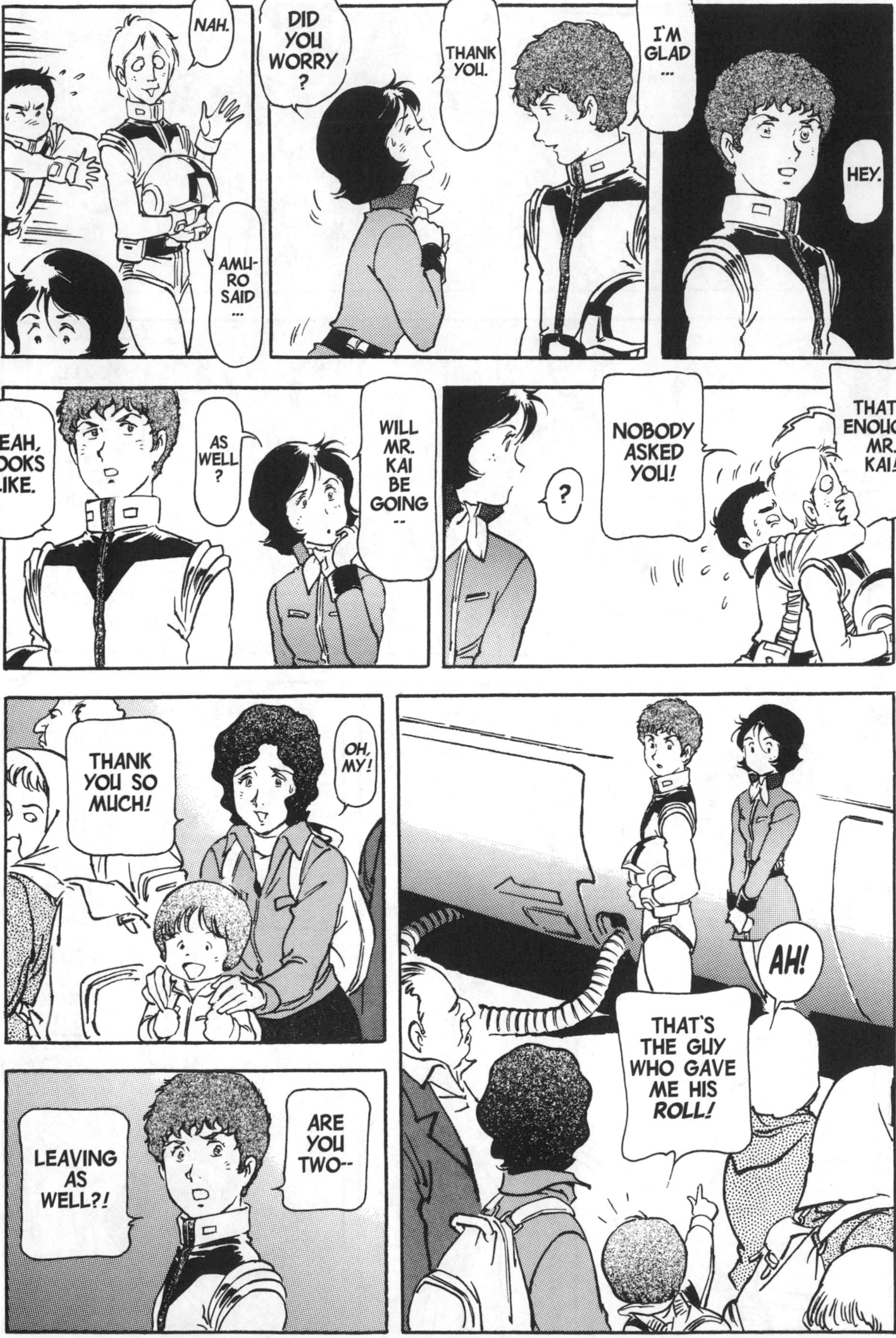

I'M GLAD ...
HEY.
THANK YOU.
DID YOU WORRY ?
NAH.
AMU-RO SAID ...
THAT'S ENOUGH, MR. KAI!
NOBODY ASKED YOU!
?
WILL MR. KAI BE GOING --
AS WELL ?
YEAH, LOOKS LIKE.
AH!
THAT'S THE GUY WHO GAVE ME HIS ROLL!
OH, MY!
THANK YOU SO MUCH!
ARE YOU TWO--
LEAVING AS WELL?!

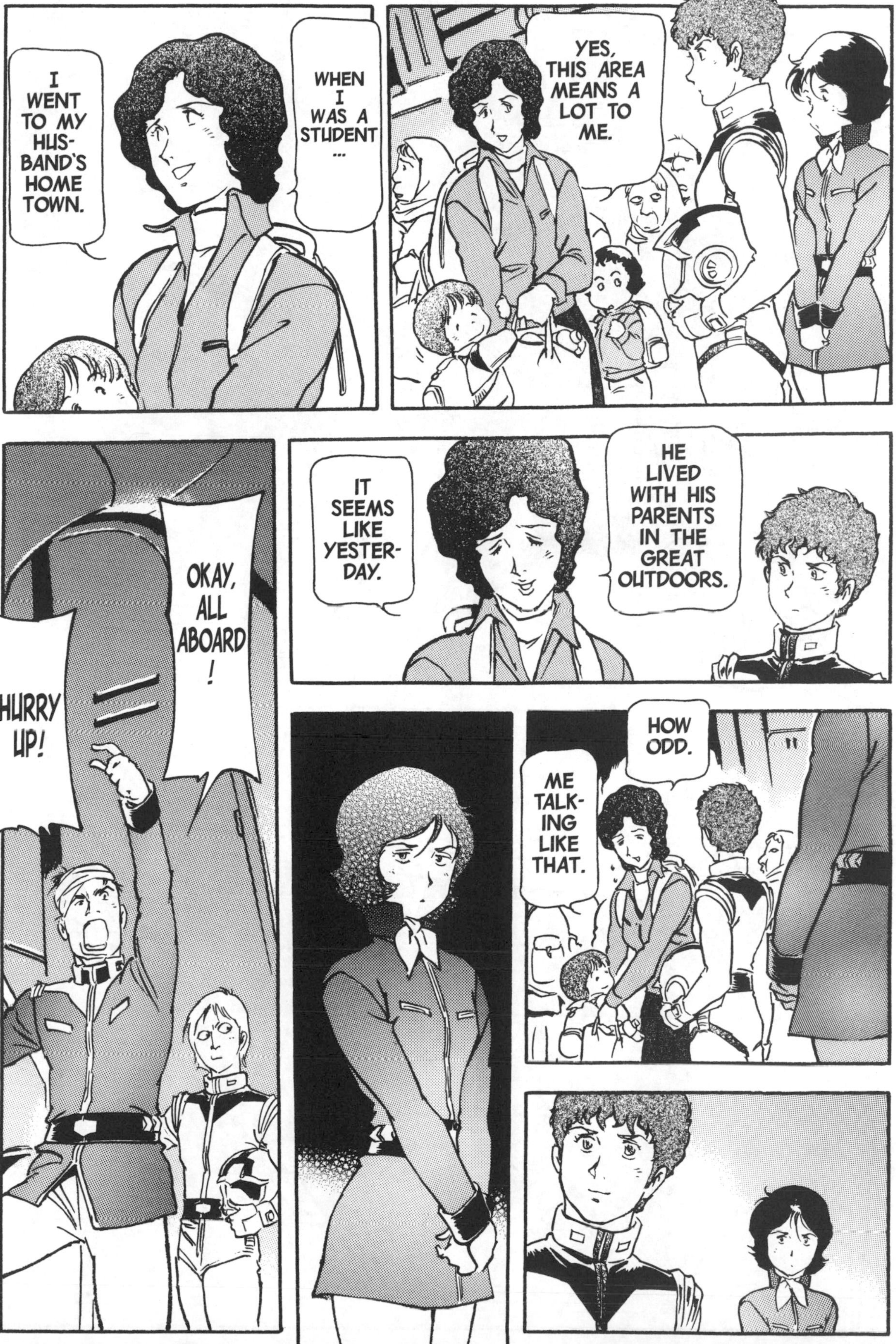
YES, THIS AREA MEANS A LOT TO ME.
WHEN I WAS A STUDENT ...
I WENT TO MY HUS-BAND'S HOME TOWN.
HE LIVED WITH HIS PARENTS IN THE GREAT OUTDOORS.
IT SEEMS LIKE YESTER-DAY.
HOW ODD.
ME TALK-ING LIKE THAT.
OKAY, ALL ABOARD!
HURRY UP!

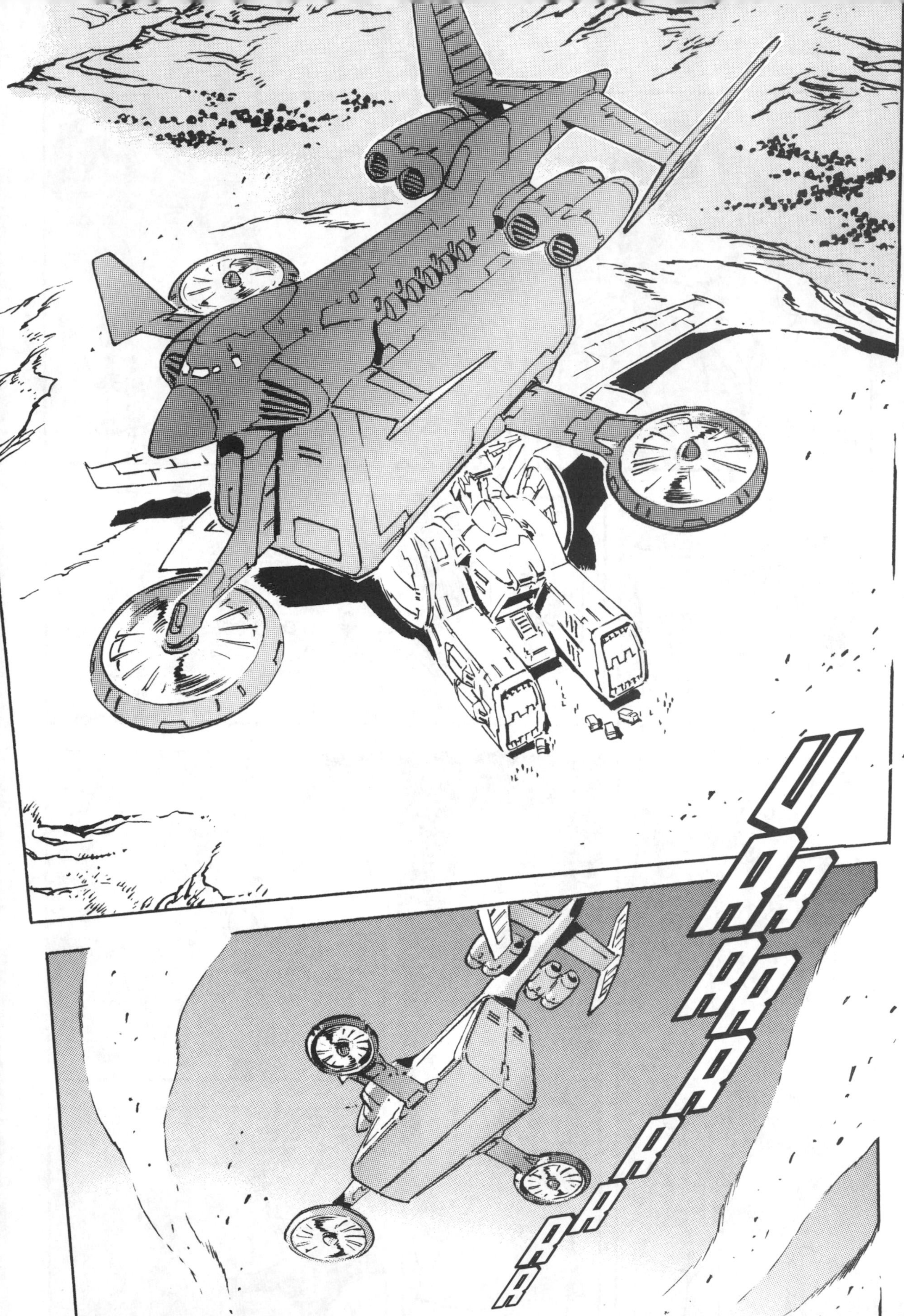
VRRRRRRRRRR

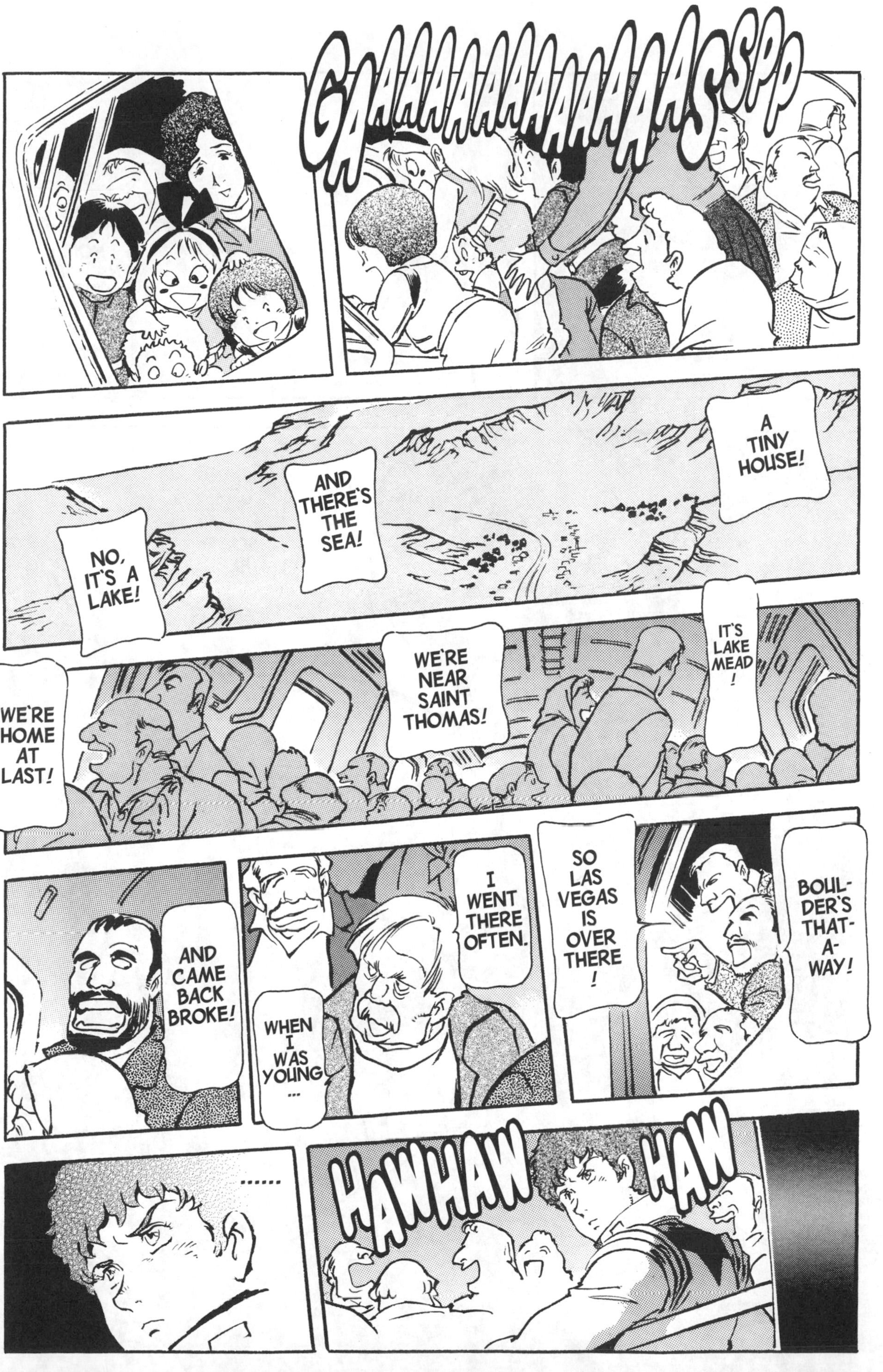
GAAAAAAAAAAAASPP
A TINY HOUSE!
AND THERE'S THE SEA!
NO, IT'S A LAKE!
IT'S LAKE MEAD!
WE'RE NEAR SAINT THOMAS!
WE'RE HOME AT LAST!
BOULDER'S THAT-A-WAY!
SO LAS VEGAS IS OVER THERE!
I WENT THERE OFTEN.
WHEN I WAS YOUNG ...
AND CAME BACK BROKE!
HAWHAW HAW
......

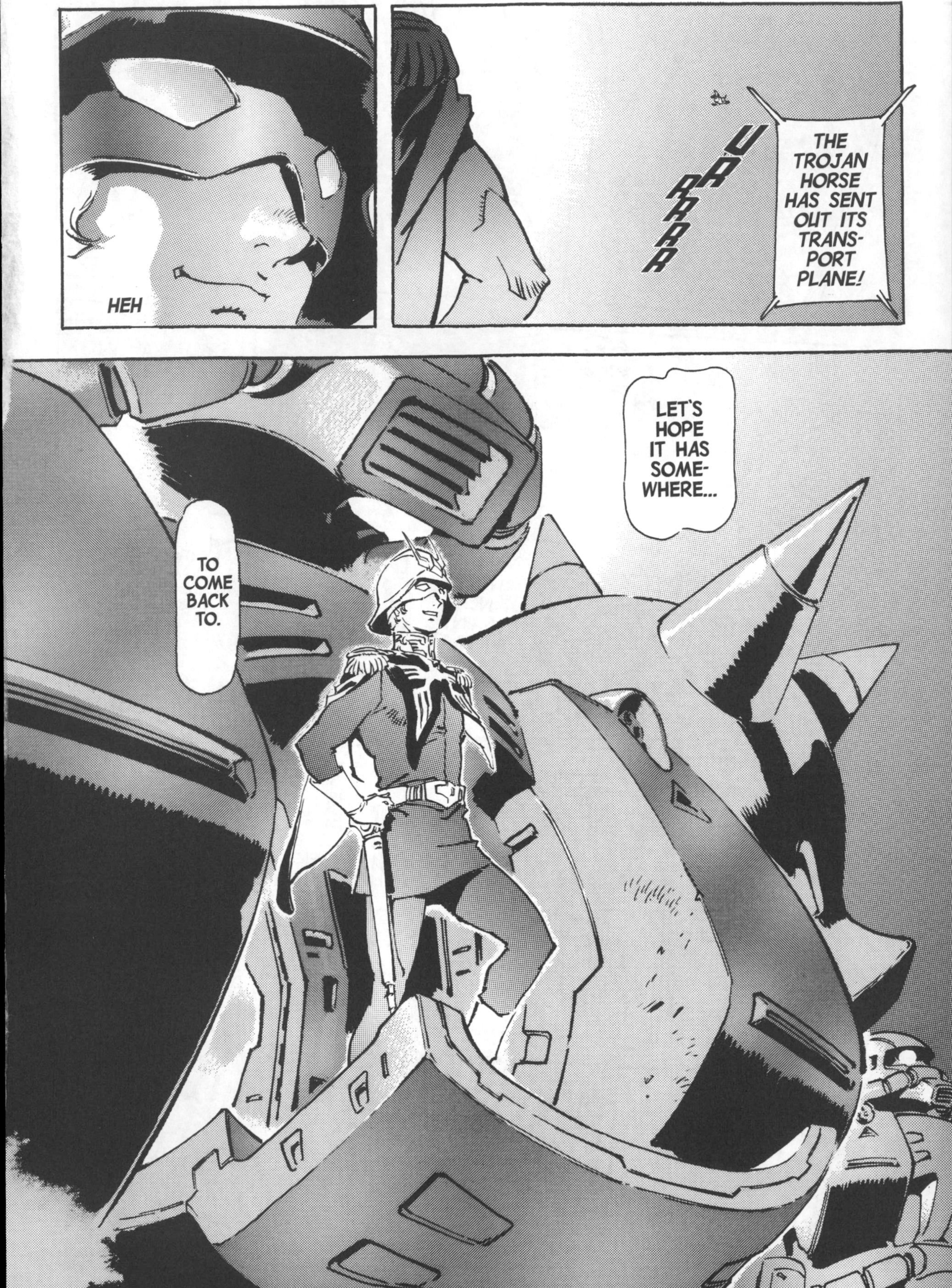
URRRRR
THE TROJAN HORSE HAS SENT OUT ITS TRANS-PORT PLANE!
HEH
LET'S HOPE IT HAS SOME-WHERE...
TO COME BACK TO.

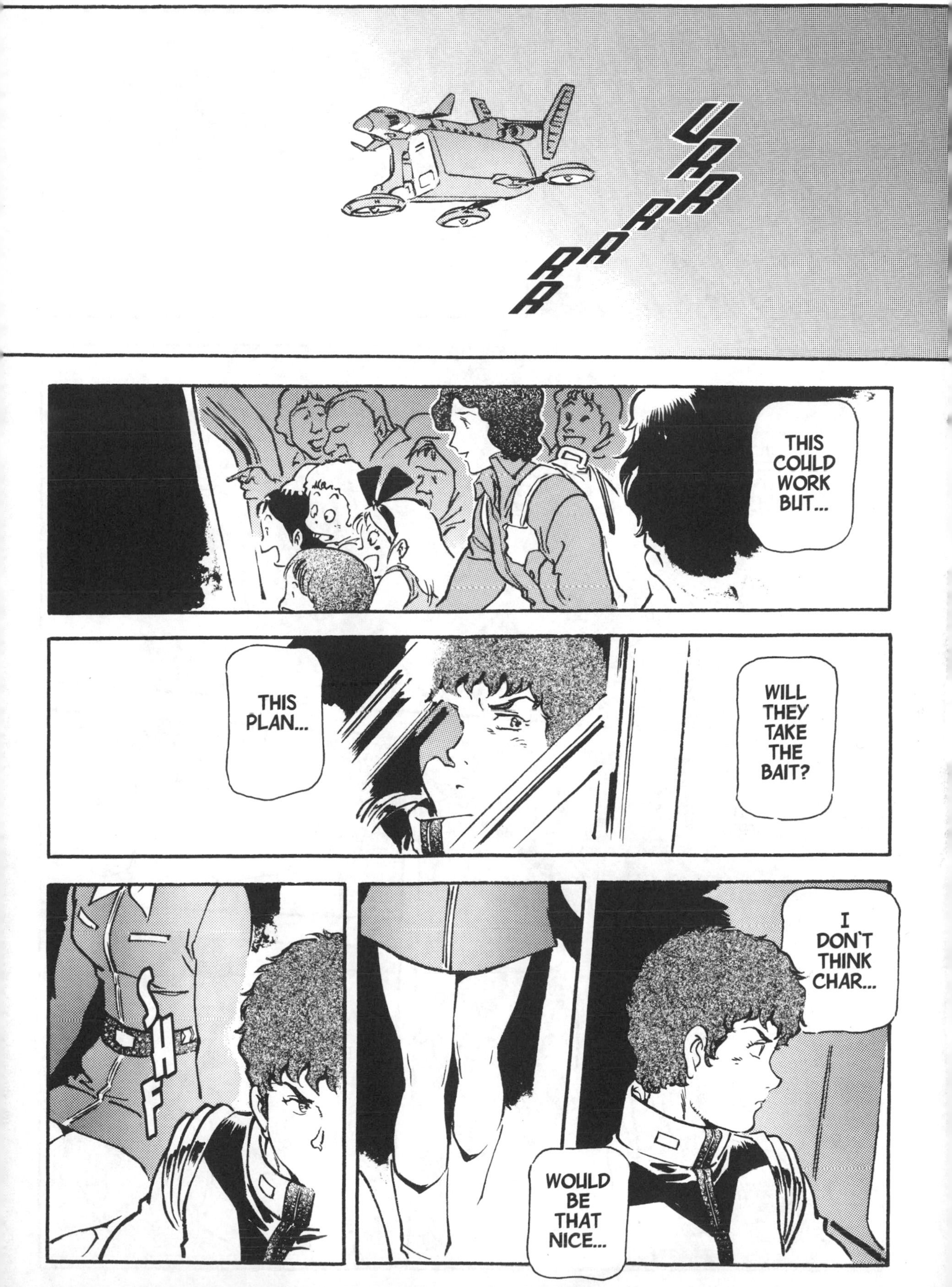
URRRRR
THIS COULD WORK BUT...
WILL THEY TAKE THE BAIT?
THIS PLAN...
I DON'T THINK CHAR...
WOULD BE THAT NICE...
SHF

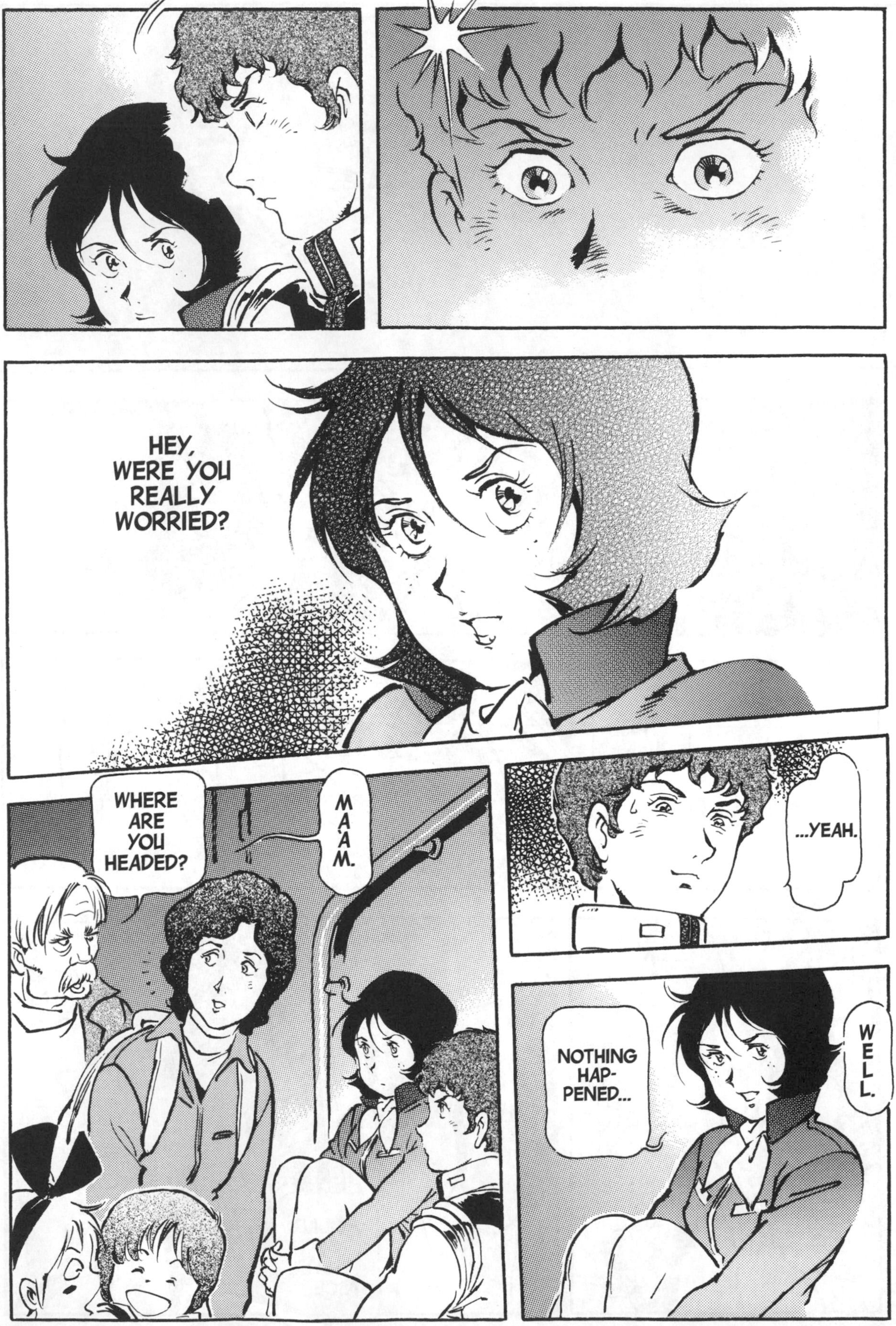
HEY, WERE YOU REALLY WORRIED?
...YEAH.
WELL.
NOTHING HAP-PENED...
MA'AM.
WHERE ARE YOU HEADED?

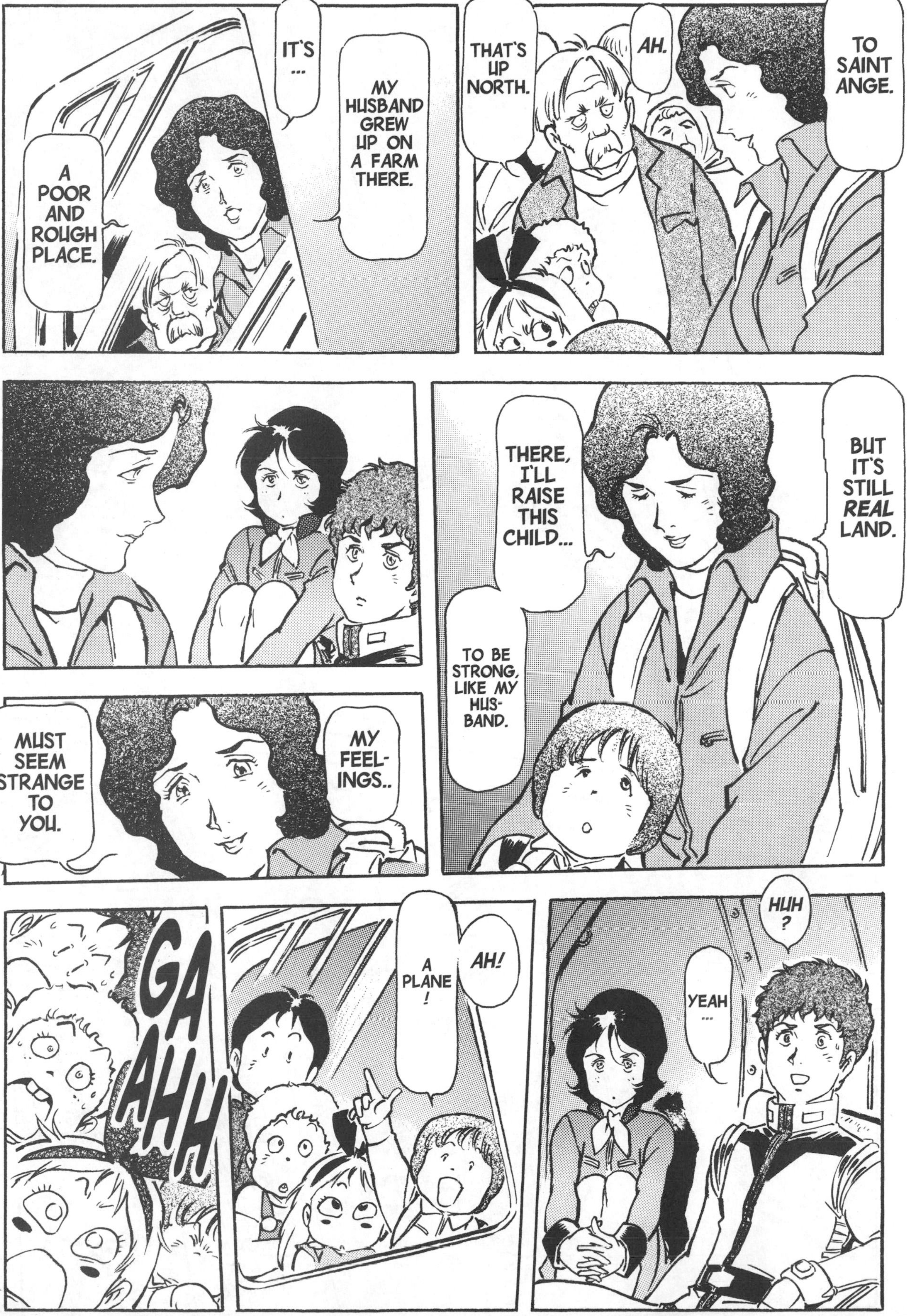
TO SAINT ANGE.
AH.
THAT'S UP NORTH.
IT'S ...
MY HUSBAND GREW UP ON A FARM THERE.
A POOR AND ROUGH PLACE.
BUT IT'S STILL *REAL* LAND.
THERE, I'LL RAISE THIS CHILD...
TO BE STRONG, LIKE MY HUS- BAND.
MY FEEL- INGS..
MUST SEEM STRANGE TO YOU.
HUH?
YEAH ...
AH!
A PLANE!
GAAHH

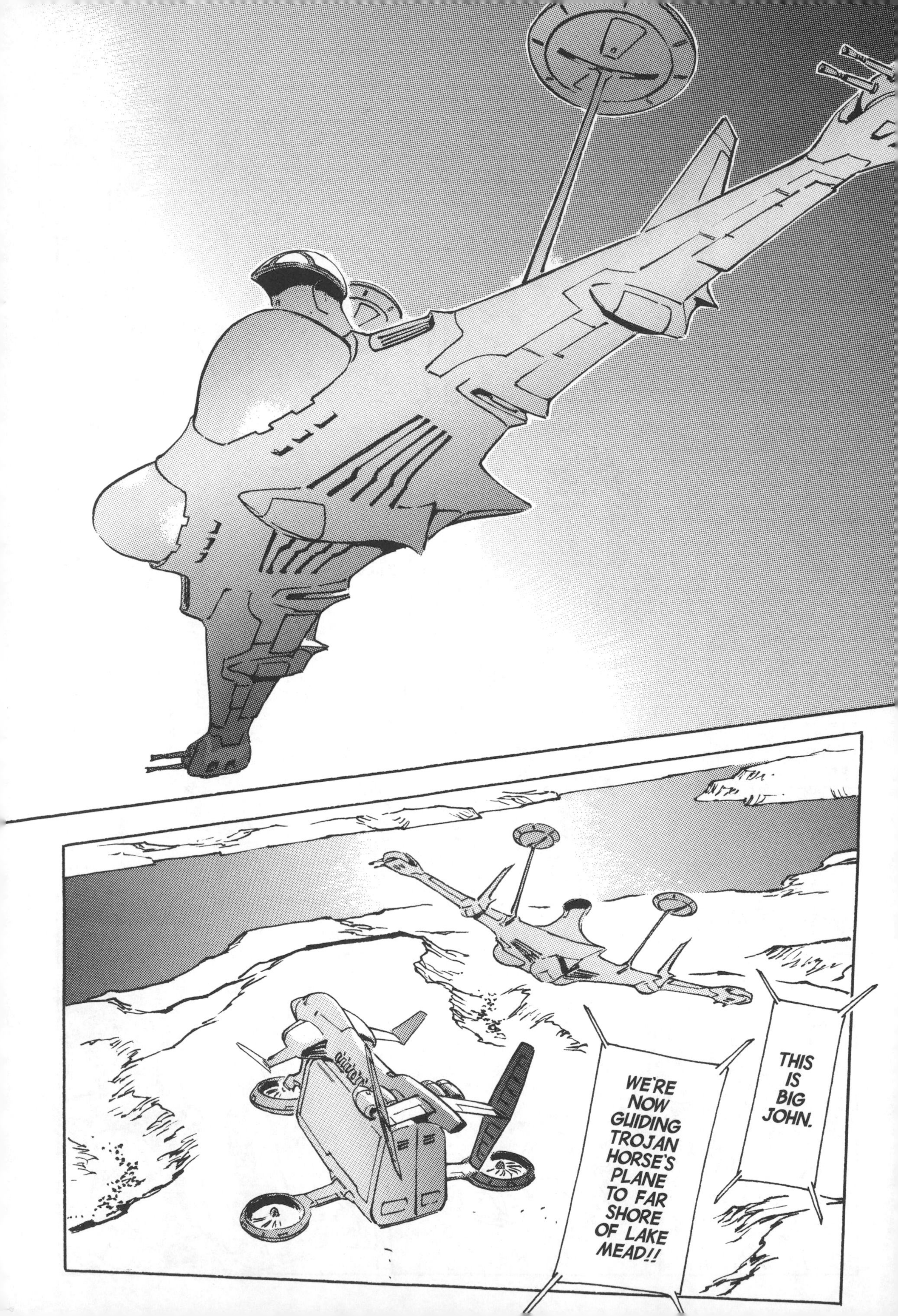
THIS IS BIG JOHN.
WE'RE NOW GUIDING TROJAN HORSE'S PLANE TO FAR SHORE OF LAKE MEAD!!

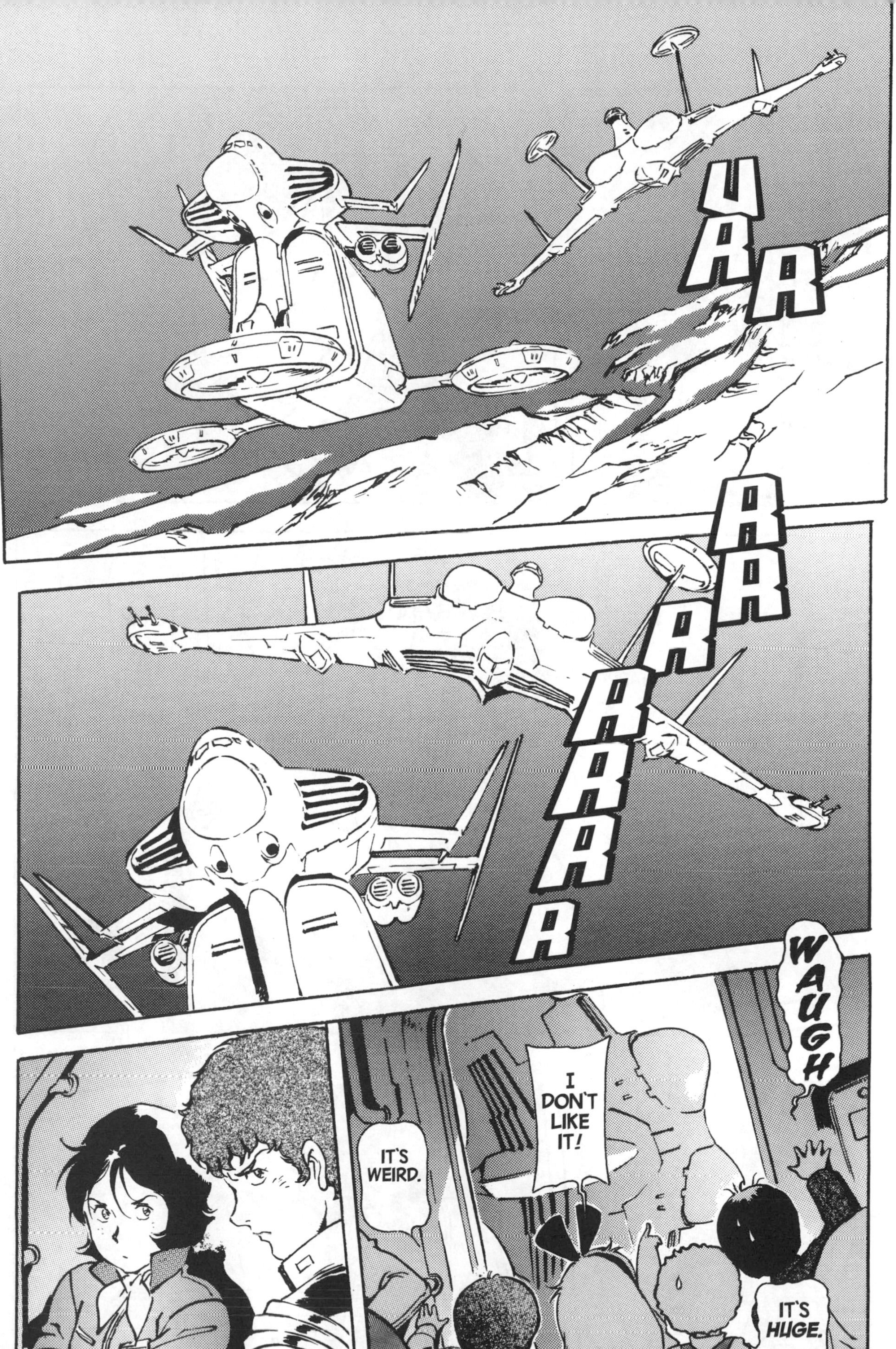
URR
RRRRRRRR
WAUGH
I DON'T LIKE IT!
IT'S WEIRD.
IT'S *HUGE*.

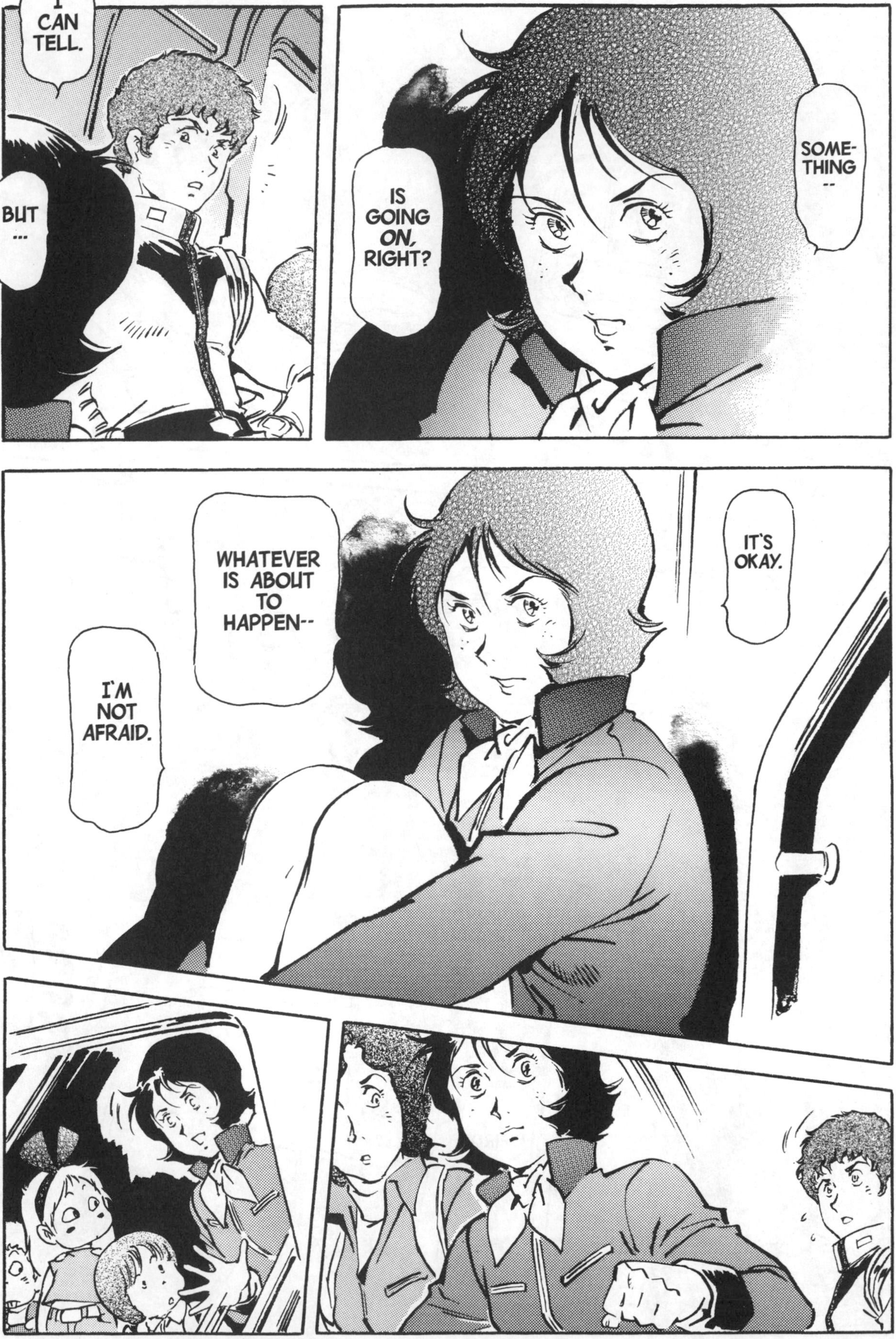
SOME-THING--
IS GOING ON, RIGHT?
I CAN TELL.
BUT...
IT'S OKAY.
WHATEVER IS ABOUT TO HAPPEN--
I'M NOT AFRAID.

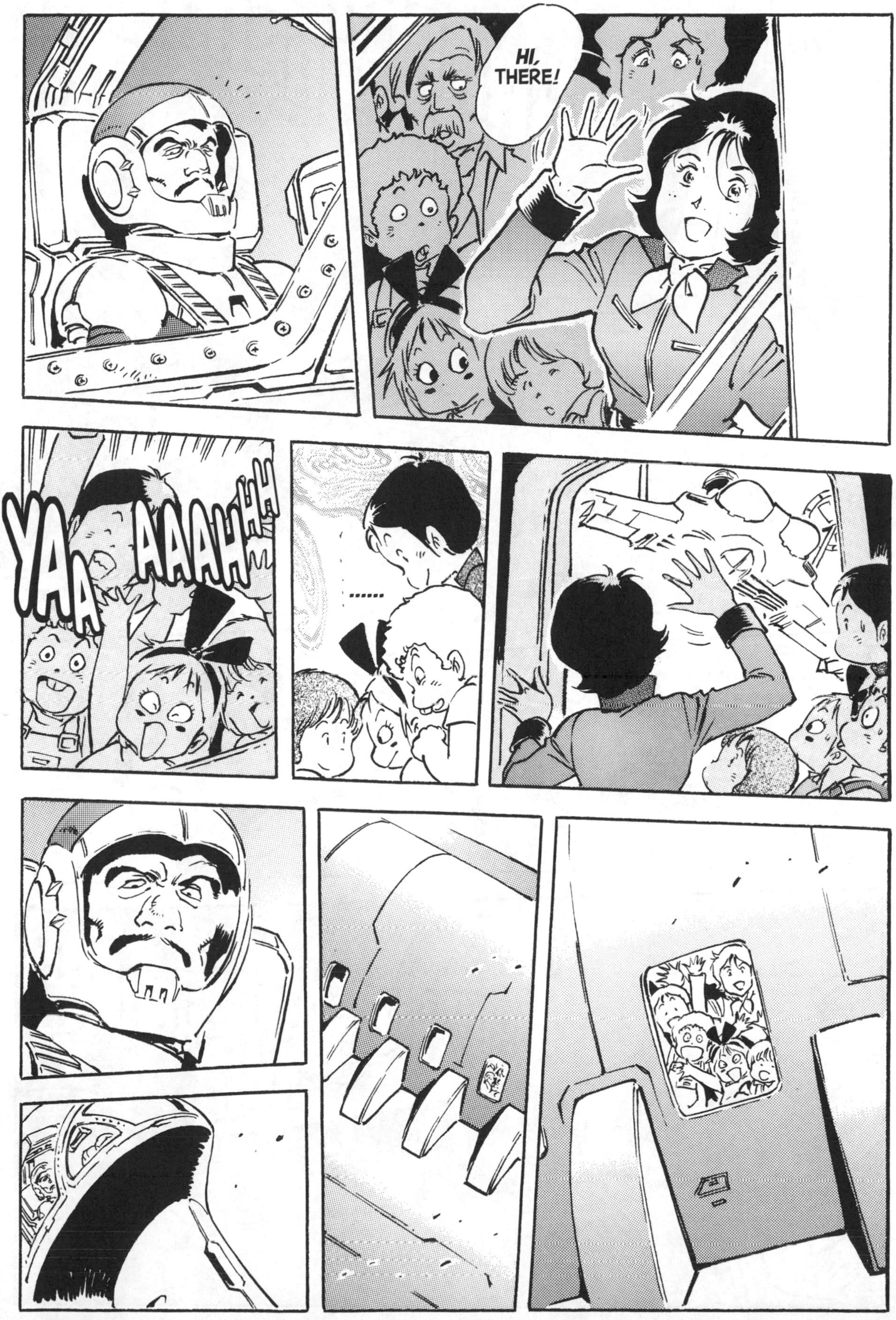
HI, THERE!
YAAAAAHHH
......

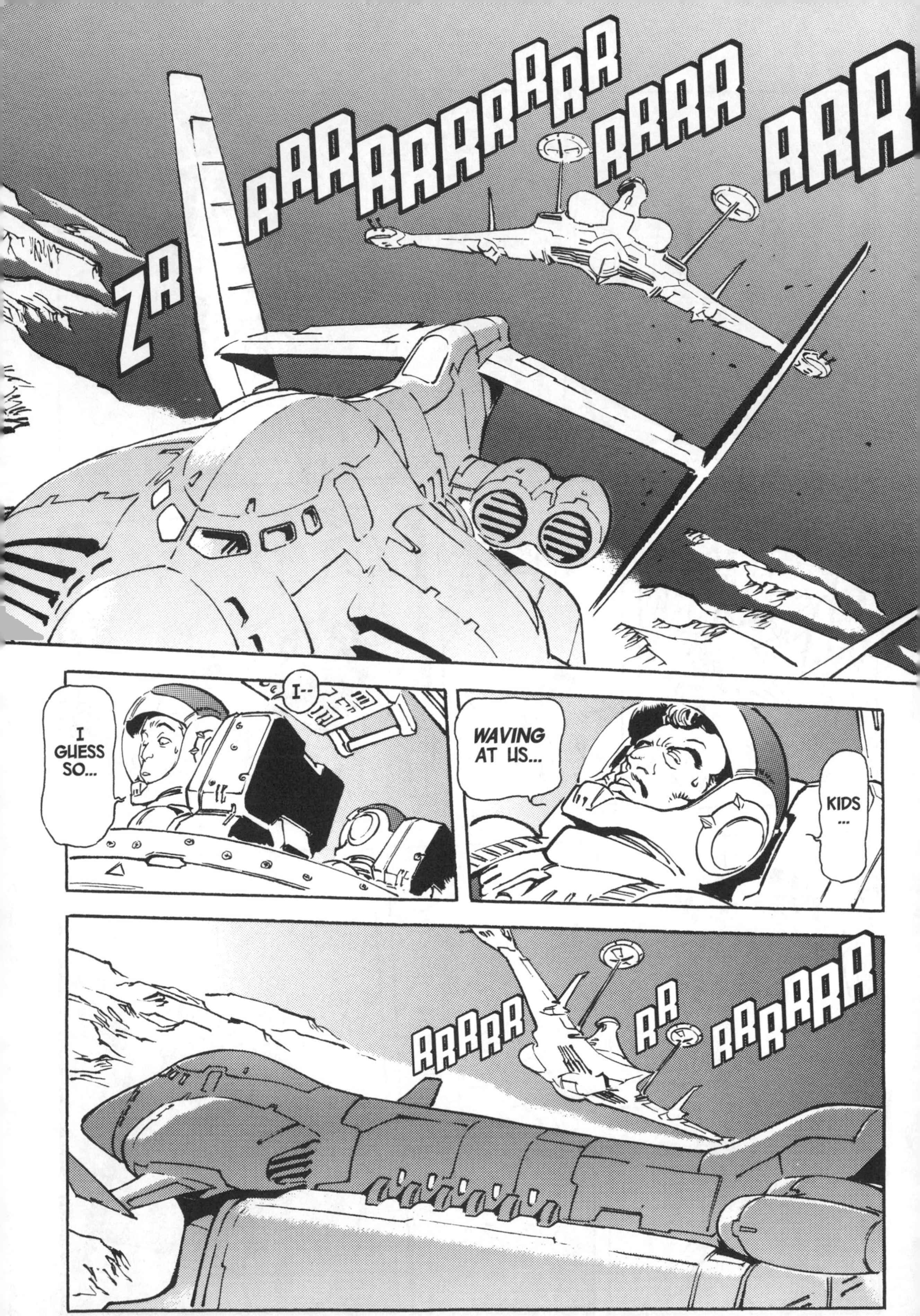
ZRRRRRRRRRRRR RRRR RRR
KIDS ...
WAVING AT US...
I--
I GUESS SO...
RRRRR RR RRRRRR

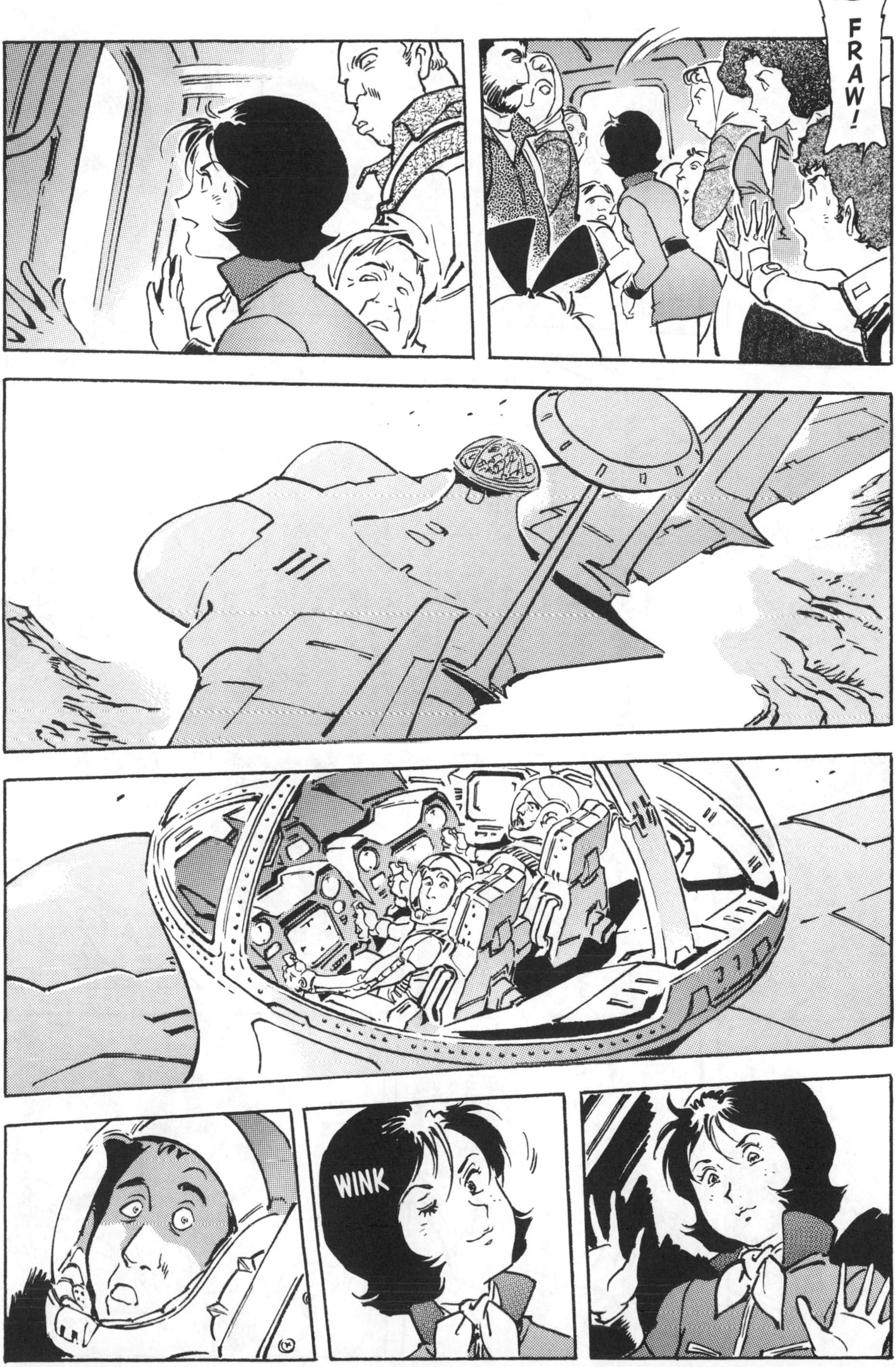
FRAW!
WINK

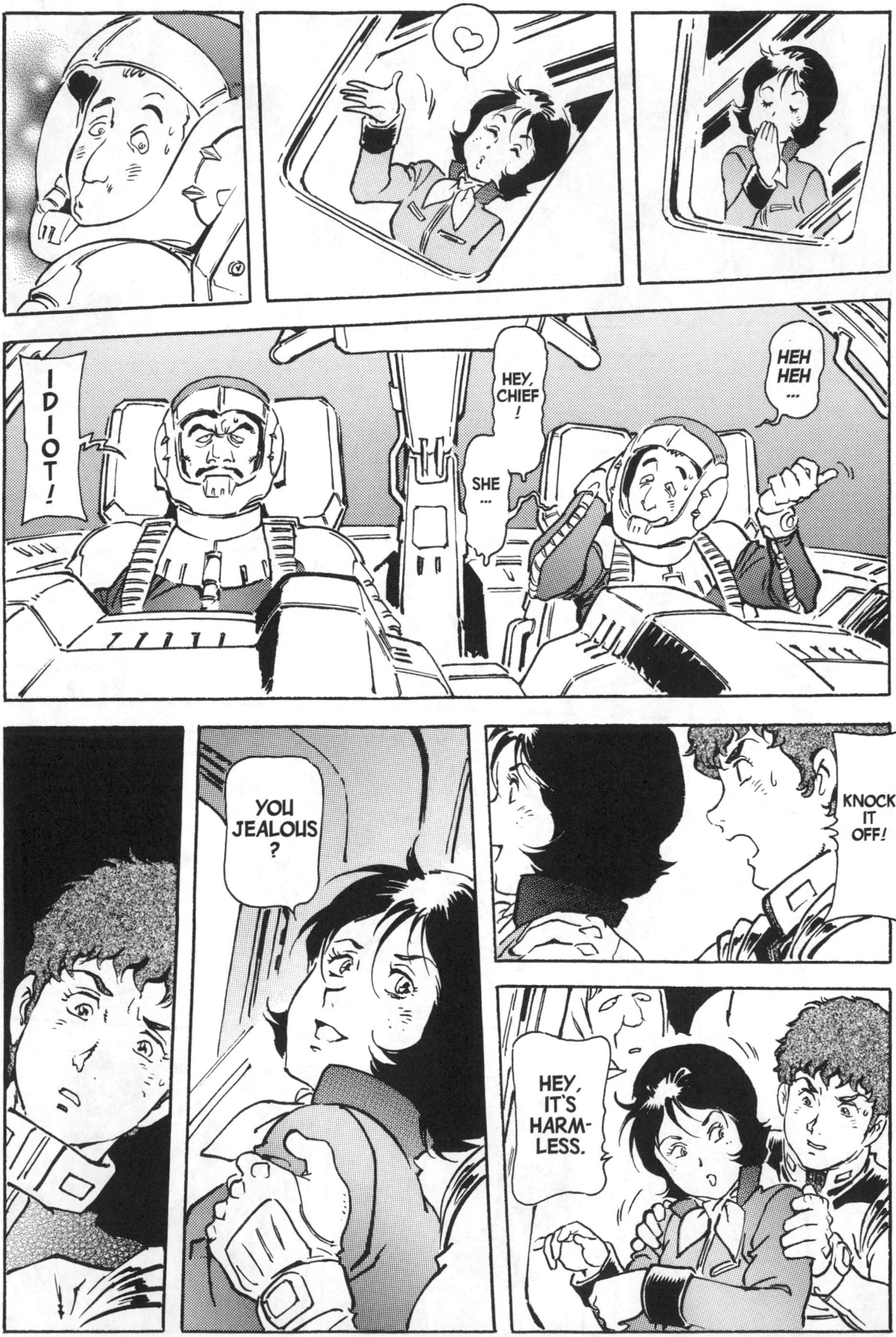
HEH HEH ...
HEY, CHIEF!
SHE ...
IDIOT!
KNOCK IT OFF!
HEY, IT'S HARMLESS.
YOU JEALOUS?

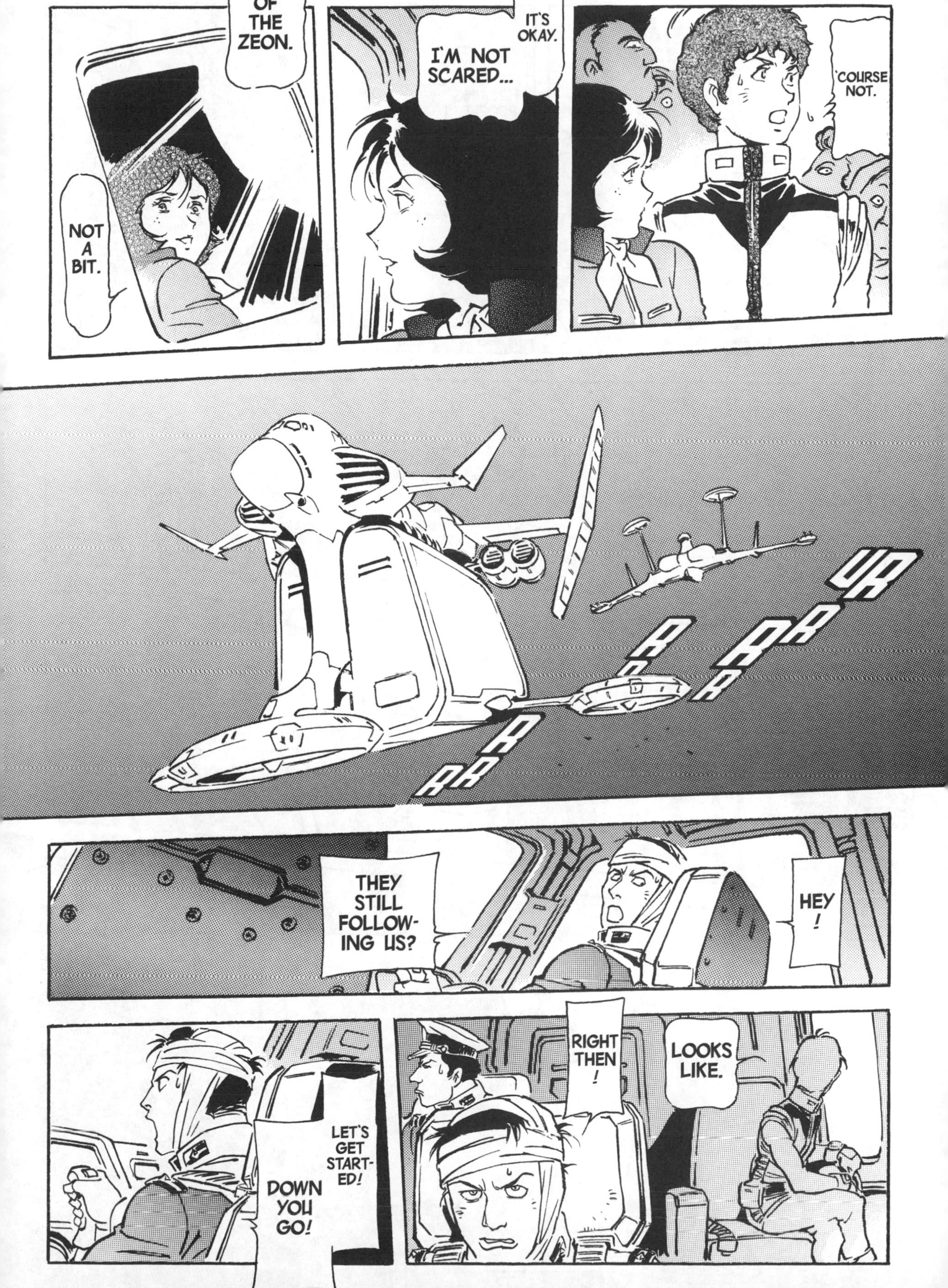
'COURSE NOT.
IT'S OKAY.
I'M NOT SCARED...
OF THE ZEON.
NOT A BIT.
VRRRRR
RRRR
HEY!
THEY STILL FOLLOWING US?
LOOKS LIKE.
RIGHT THEN!
LET'S GET STARTED!
DOWN YOU GO!

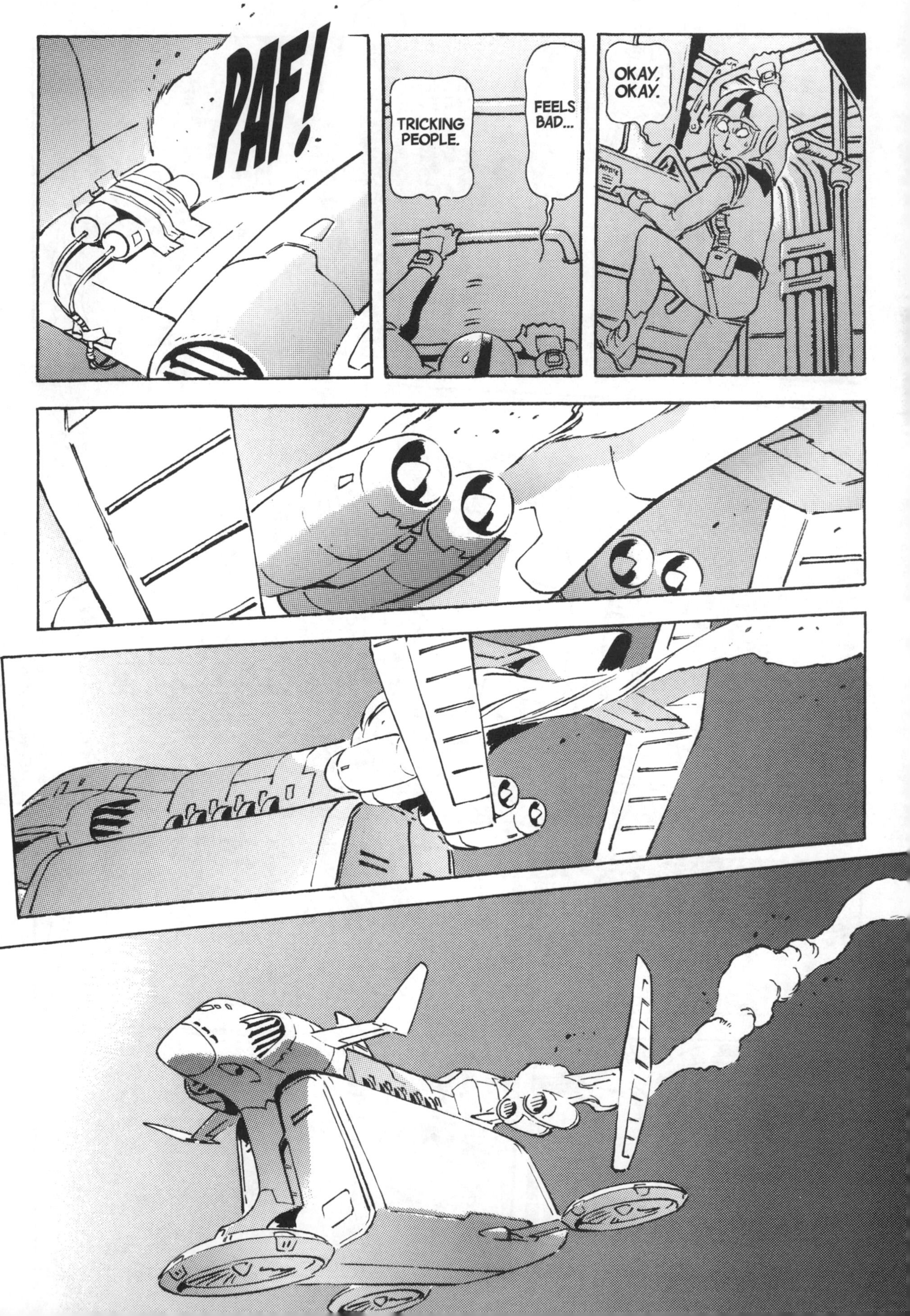

OKAY, OKAY.
FEELS BAD...
TRICKING PEOPLE.
PAF!

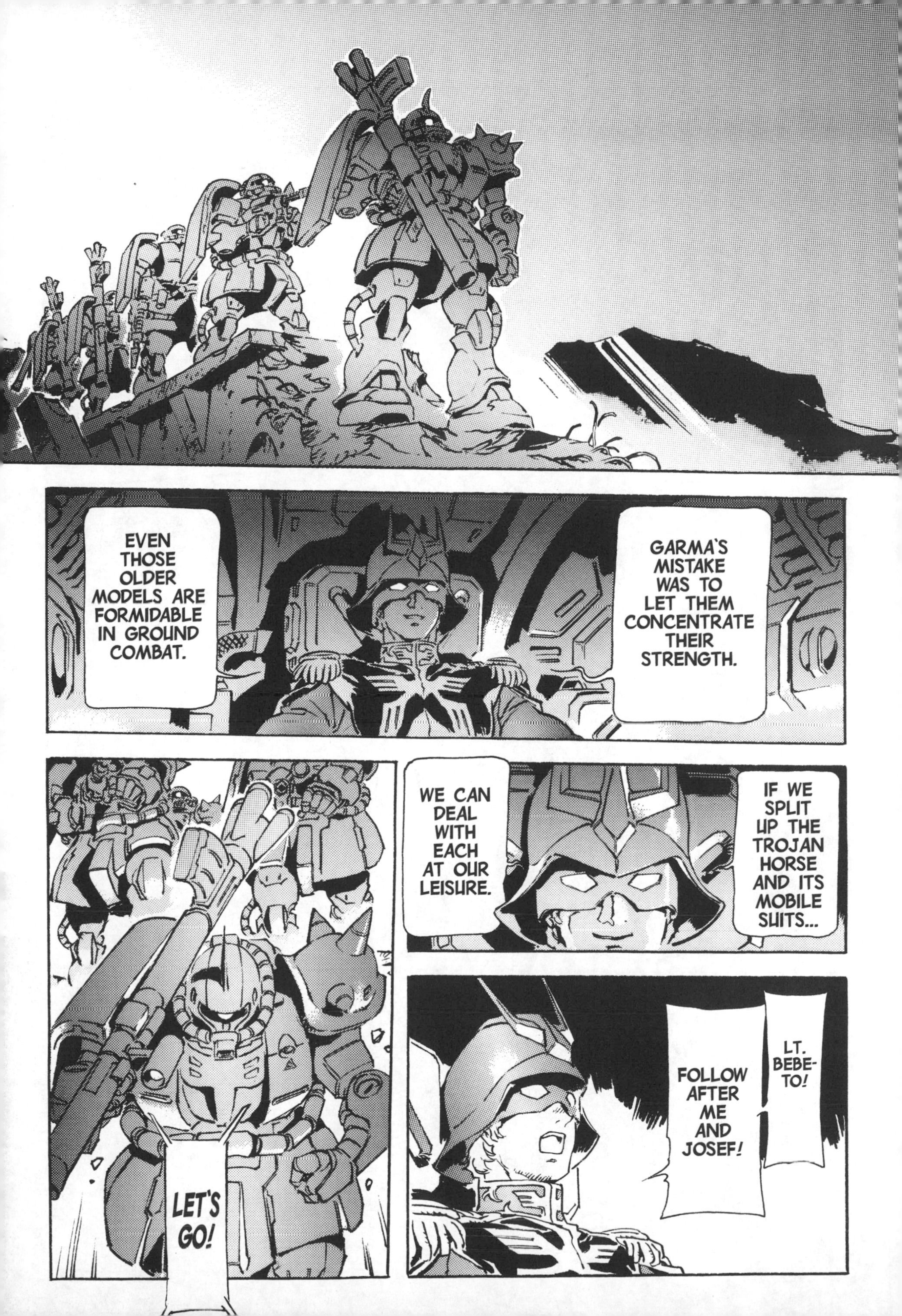
GARMA'S MISTAKE WAS TO LET THEM CONCENTRATE THEIR STRENGTH.
EVEN THOSE OLDER MODELS ARE FORMIDABLE IN GROUND COMBAT.
IF WE SPLIT UP THE TROJAN HORSE AND ITS MOBILE SUITS...
WE CAN DEAL WITH EACH AT OUR LEISURE.
LT. BEBE-TO!
FOLLOW AFTER ME AND JOSEF!
LET'S GO!

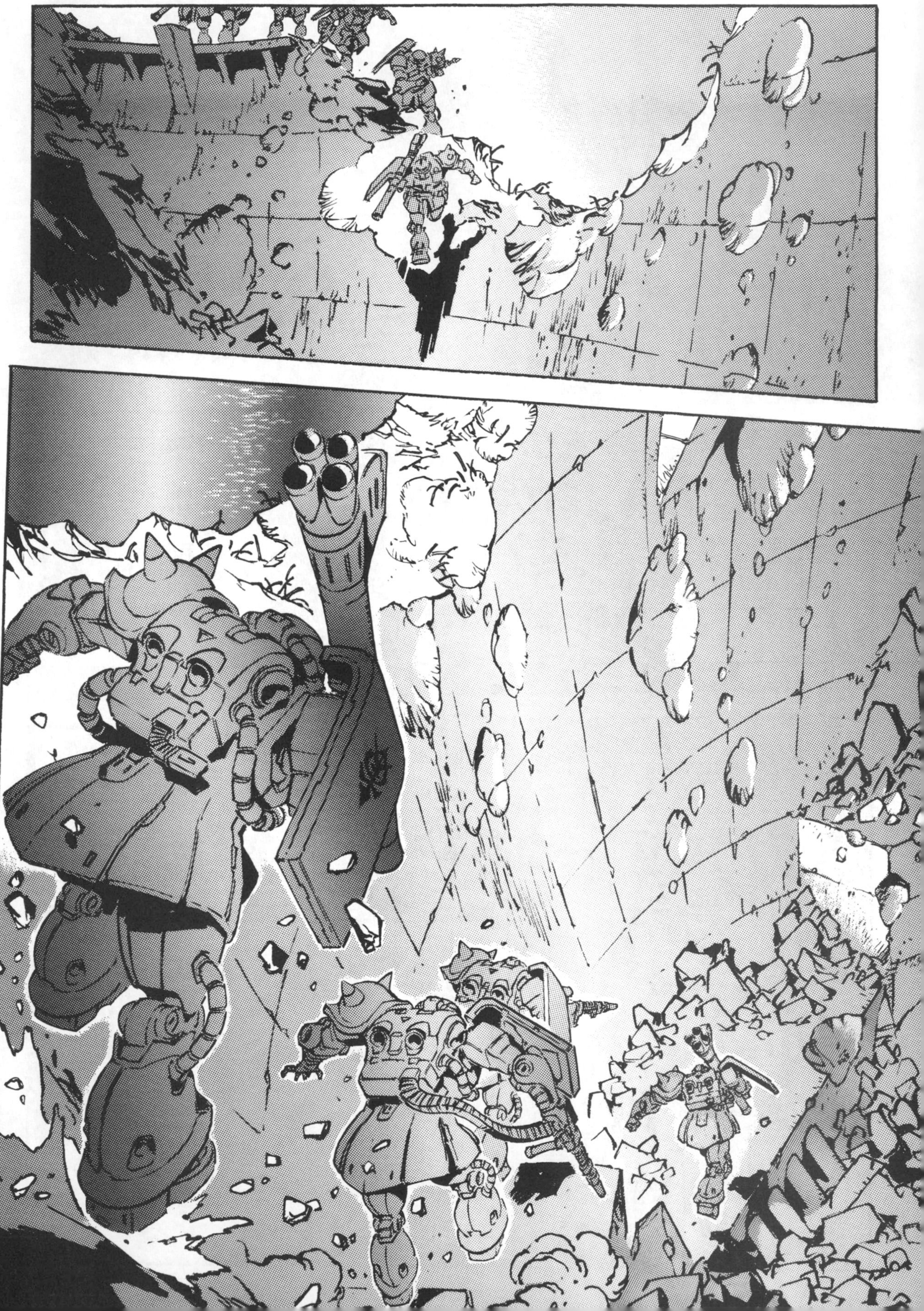

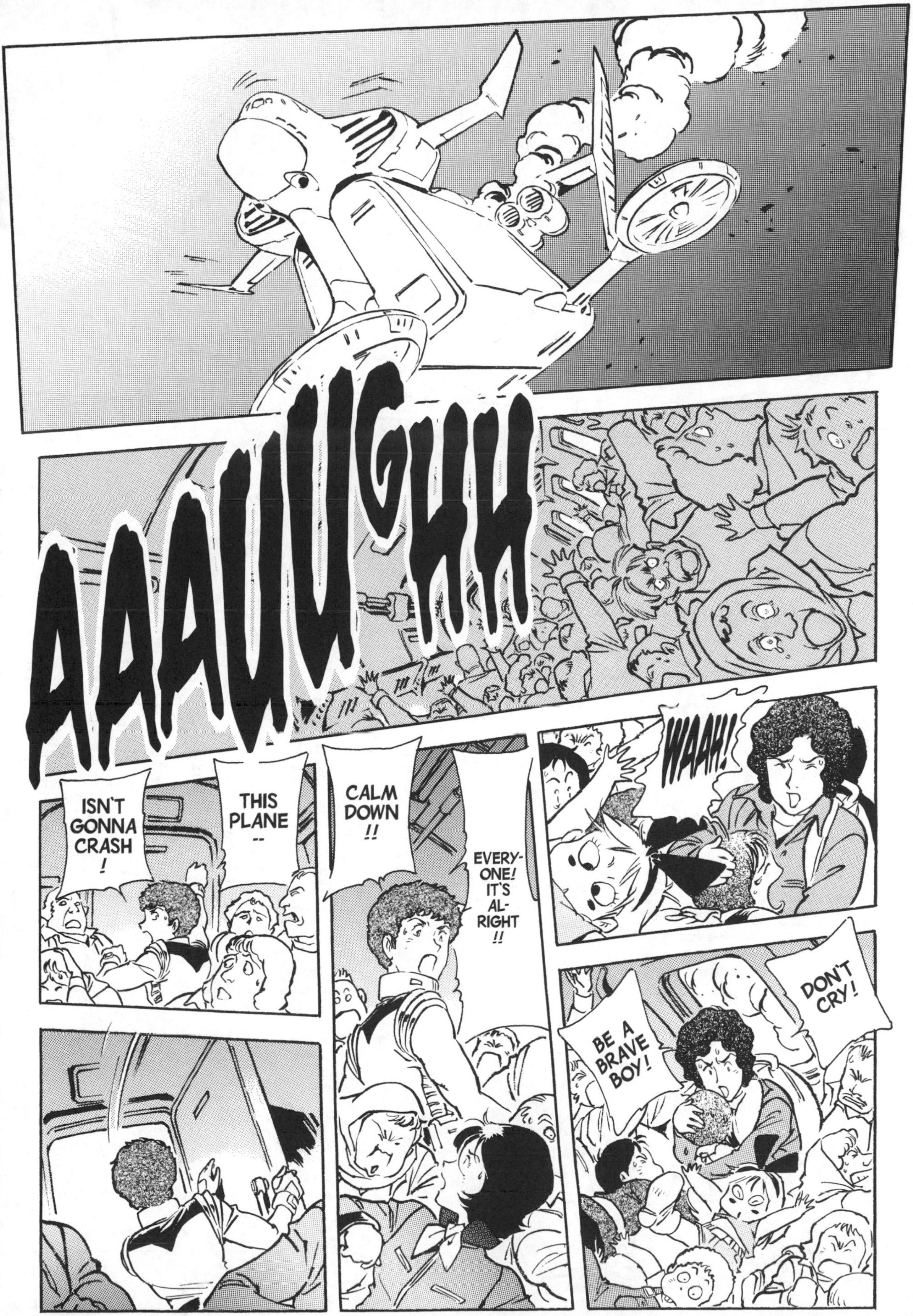
AAAUUGHH
WAAH!
DON'T CRY!
BE A BRAVE BOY!
EVERY-ONE! IT'S AL-RIGHT!!
CALM DOWN!!
THIS PLANE --
ISN'T GONNA CRASH!

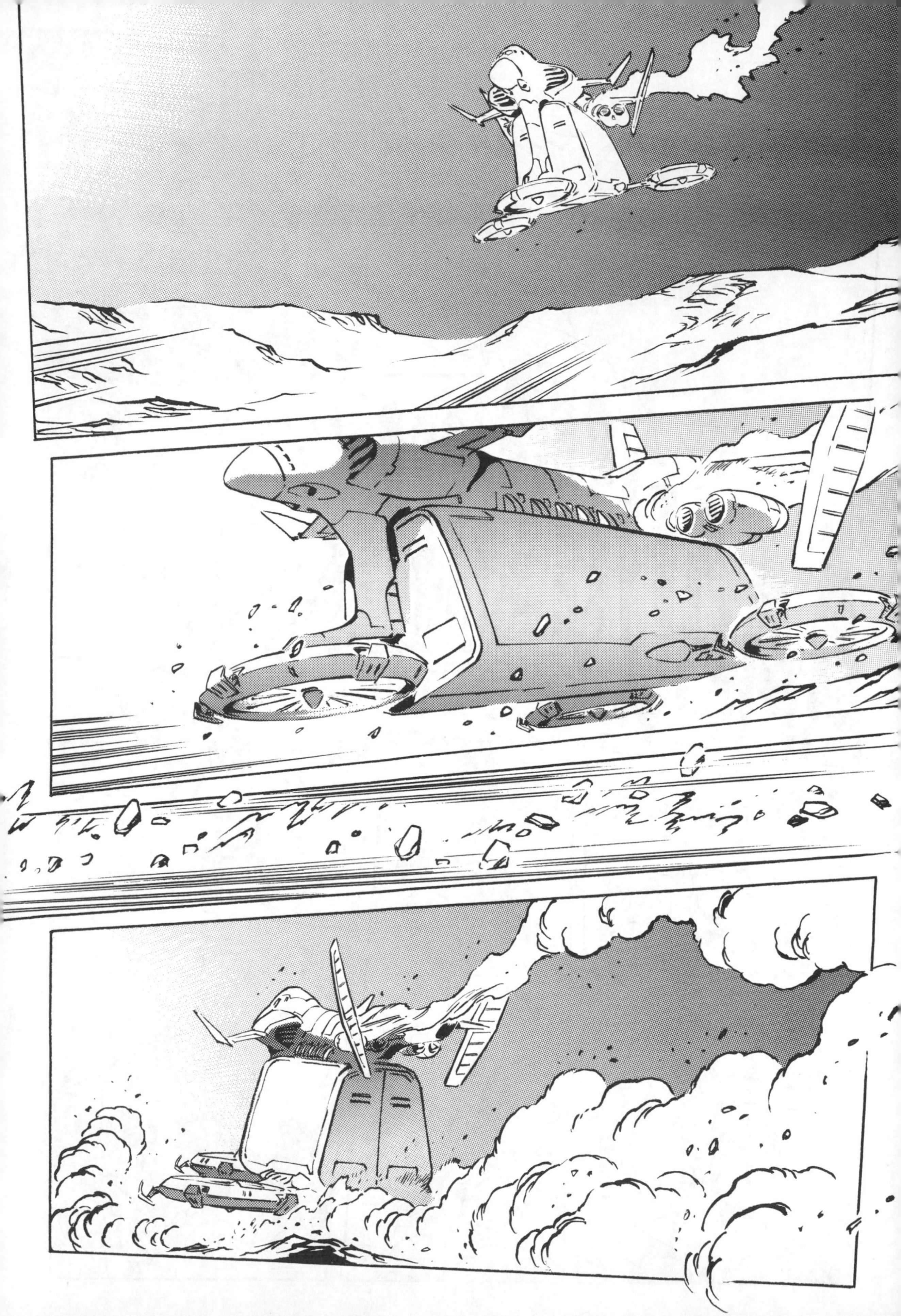

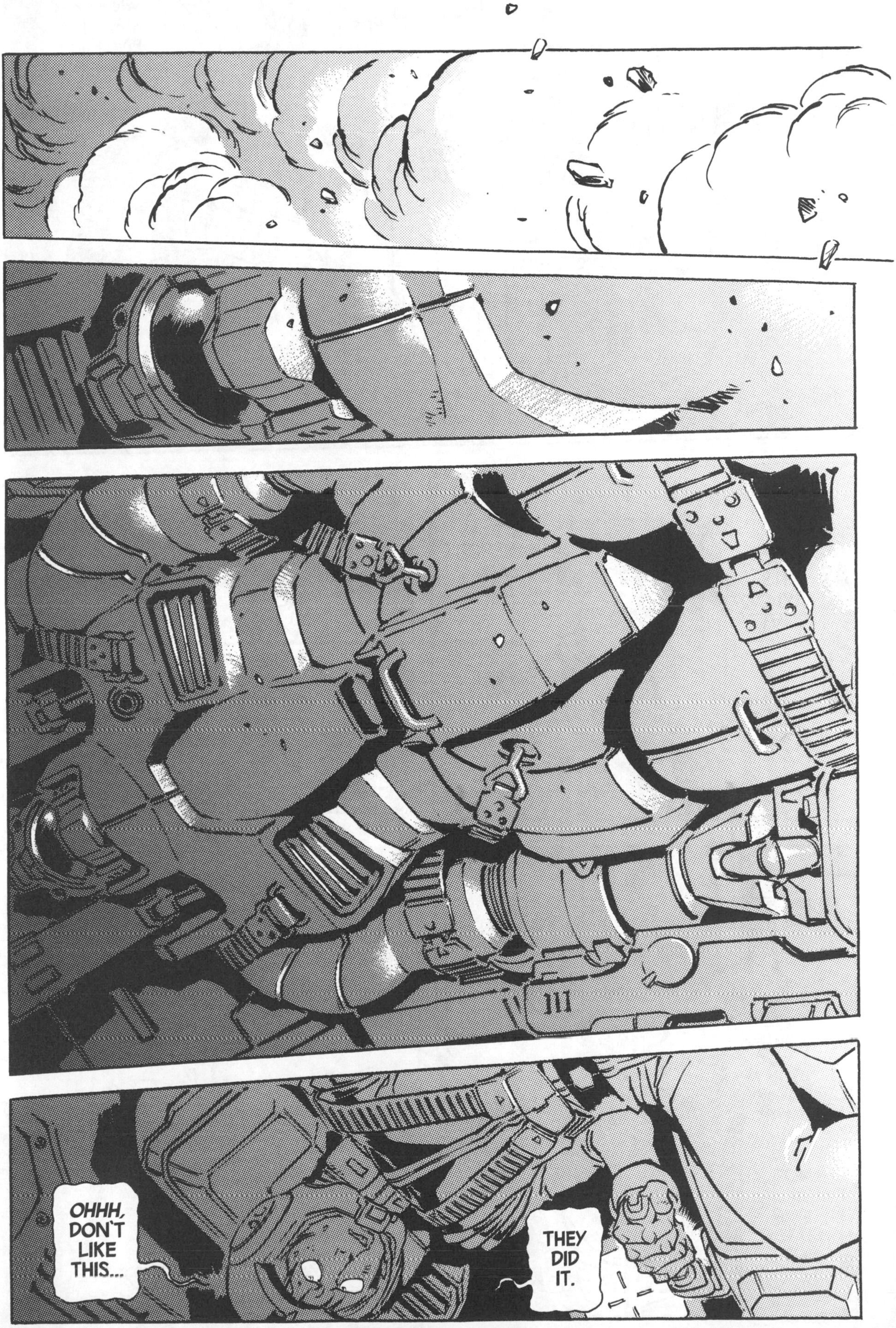
THEY DID IT.
OHHH, DON'T LIKE THIS...

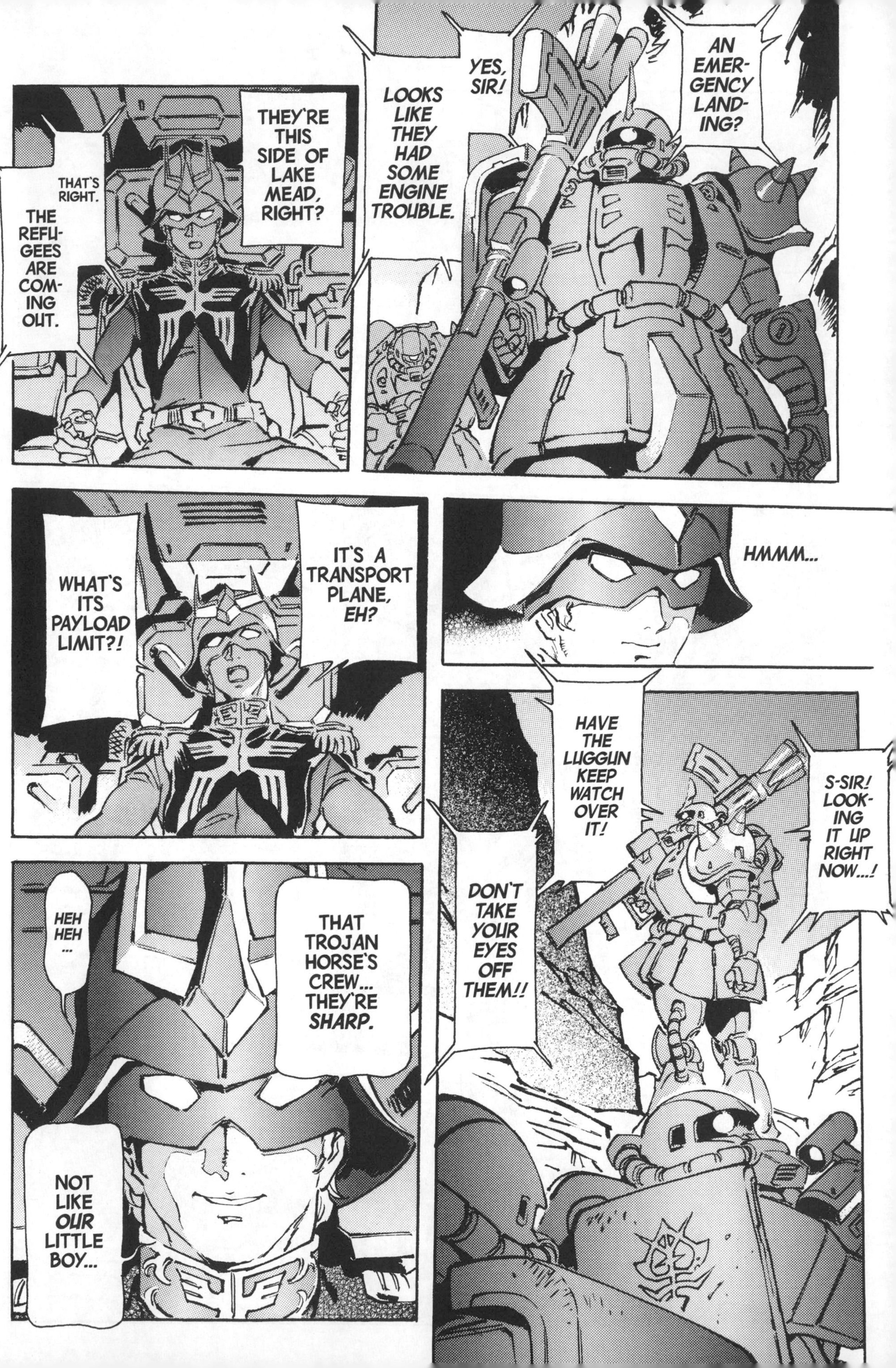
AN EMERGENCY LANDING?
YES, SIR!
LOOKS LIKE THEY HAD SOME ENGINE TROUBLE.
THEY'RE THIS SIDE OF LAKE MEAD, RIGHT?
THAT'S RIGHT.
THE REFUGEES ARE COMING OUT.
HMMM...
IT'S A TRANSPORT PLANE, EH?
WHAT'S ITS PAYLOAD LIMIT?!
S-SIR! LOOKING IT UP RIGHT NOW...!
HAVE THE LUGGUN KEEP WATCH OVER IT!
DON'T TAKE YOUR EYES OFF THEM!!
THAT TROJAN HORSE'S CREW... THEY'RE SHARP.
HEH HEH ...
NOT LIKE OUR LITTLE BOY...

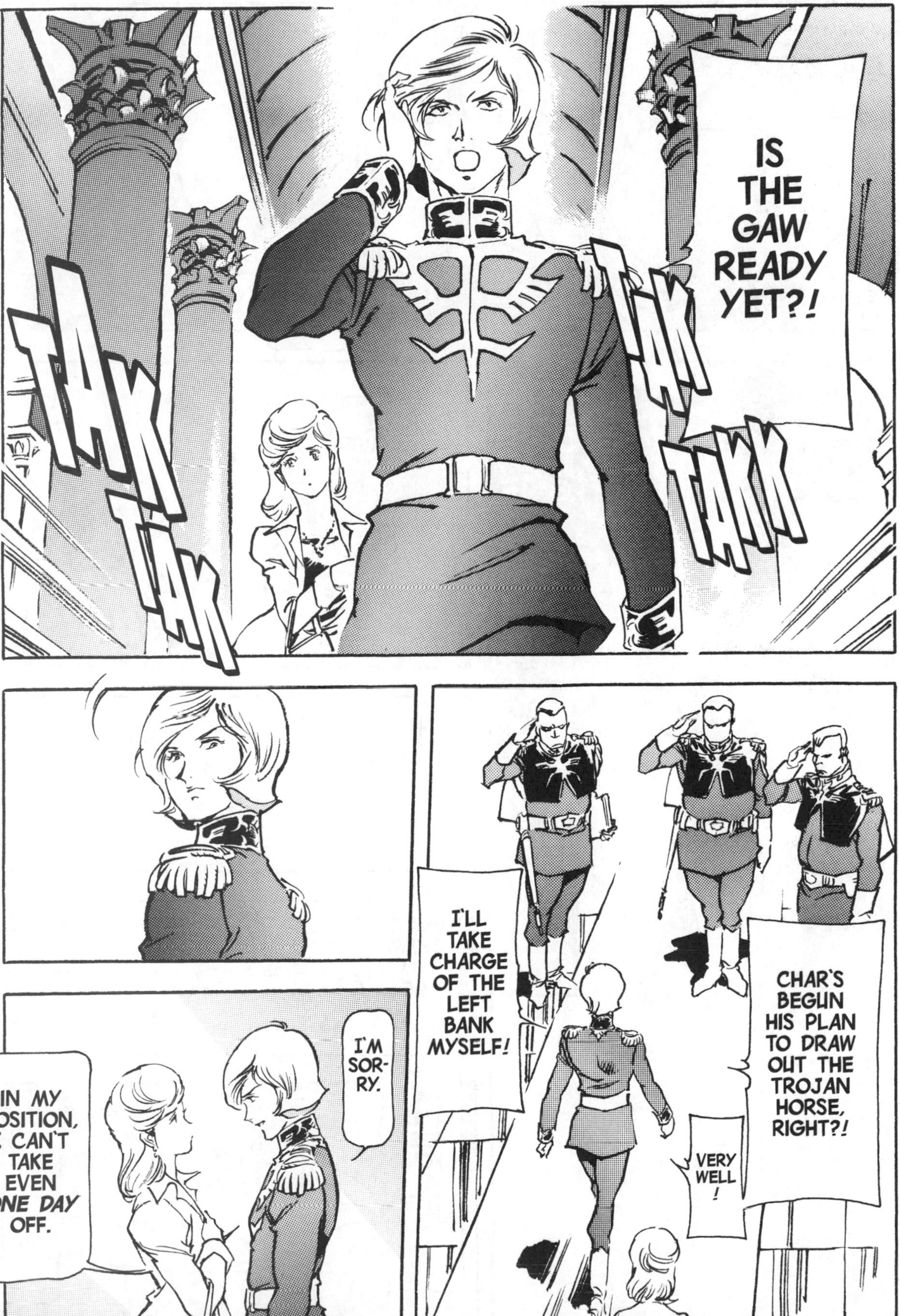
TAK TAK TAK
IS THE GAW READY YET?!
TAK TAKK
I'M SORRY.
IN MY POSITION, I CAN'T TAKE EVEN ONE DAY OFF.
I'LL TAKE CHARGE OF THE LEFT BANK MYSELF!
CHAR'S BEGUN HIS PLAN TO DRAW OUT THE TROJAN HORSE, RIGHT?!
VERY WELL!

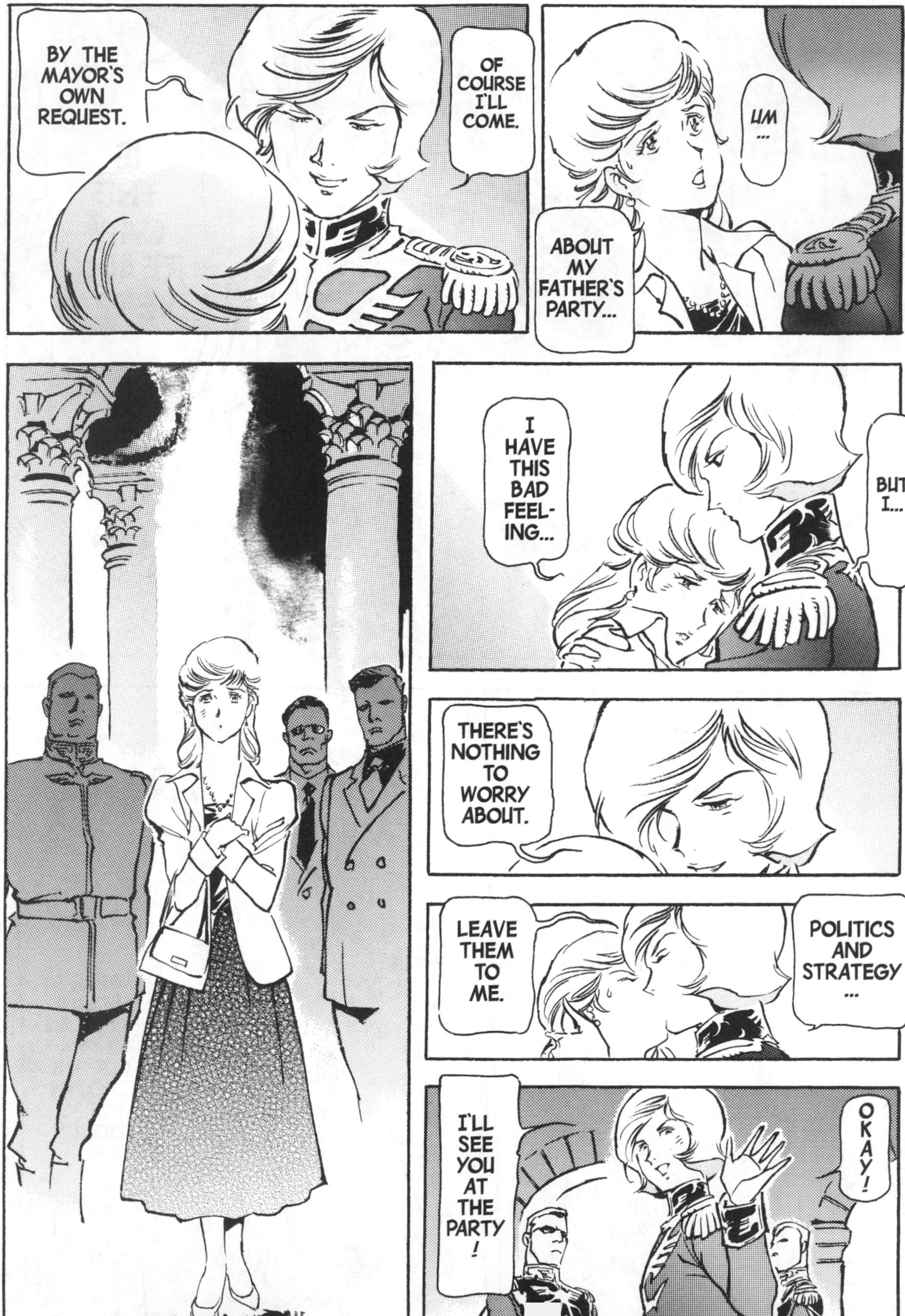
UM ...
ABOUT MY FATHER'S PARTY...
OF COURSE I'LL COME.
BY THE MAYOR'S OWN REQUEST.
BUT I...
I HAVE THIS BAD FEEL-ING...
THERE'S NOTHING TO WORRY ABOUT.
POLITICS AND STRATEGY ...
LEAVE THEM TO ME.
OKAY!
I'LL SEE YOU AT THE PARTY!

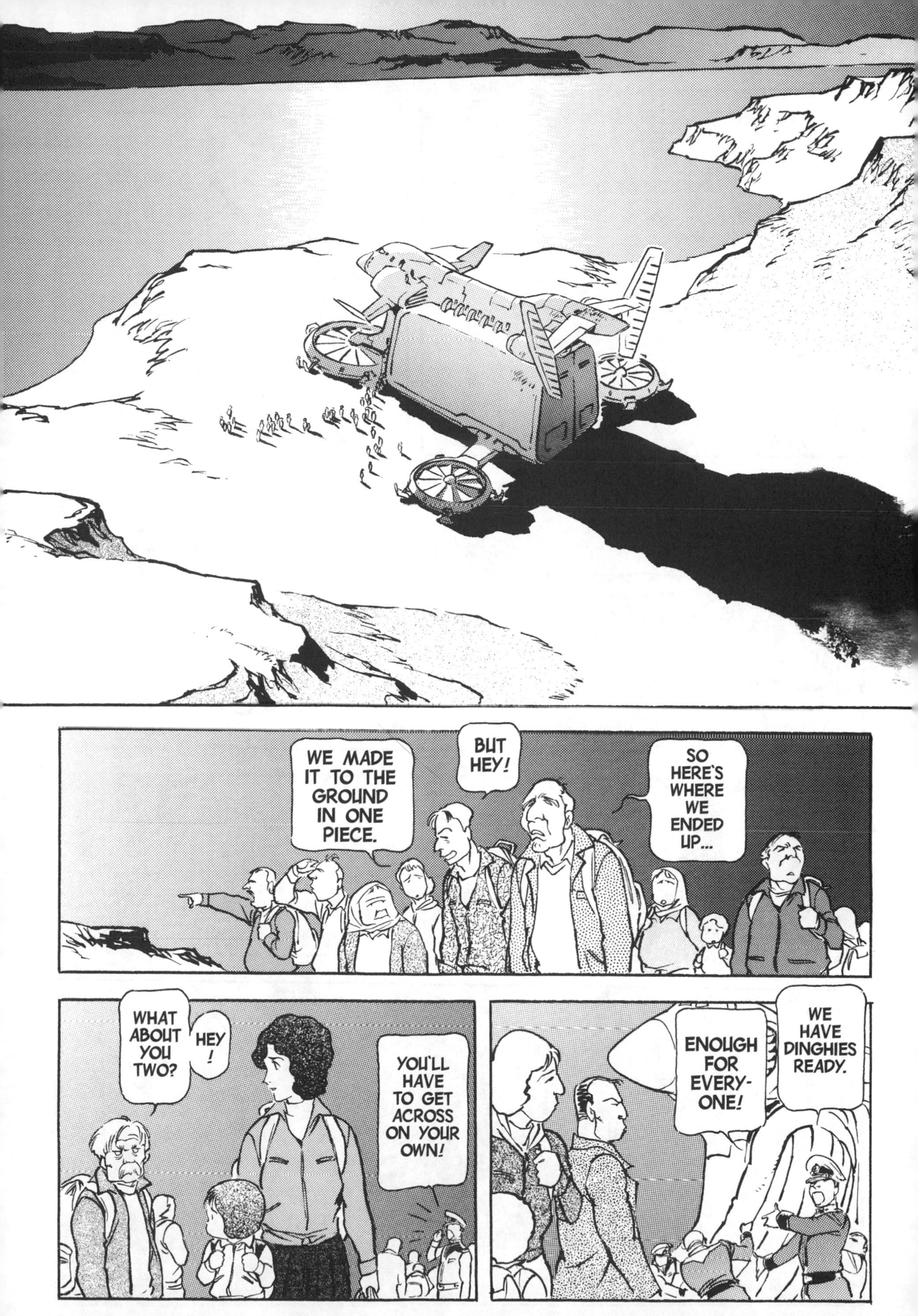
SO HERE'S WHERE WE ENDED UP...
BUT HEY!
WE MADE IT TO THE GROUND IN ONE PIECE.
WE HAVE DINGHIES READY.
ENOUGH FOR EVERY-ONE!
YOU'LL HAVE TO GET ACROSS ON YOUR OWN!
HEY!
WHAT ABOUT YOU TWO?

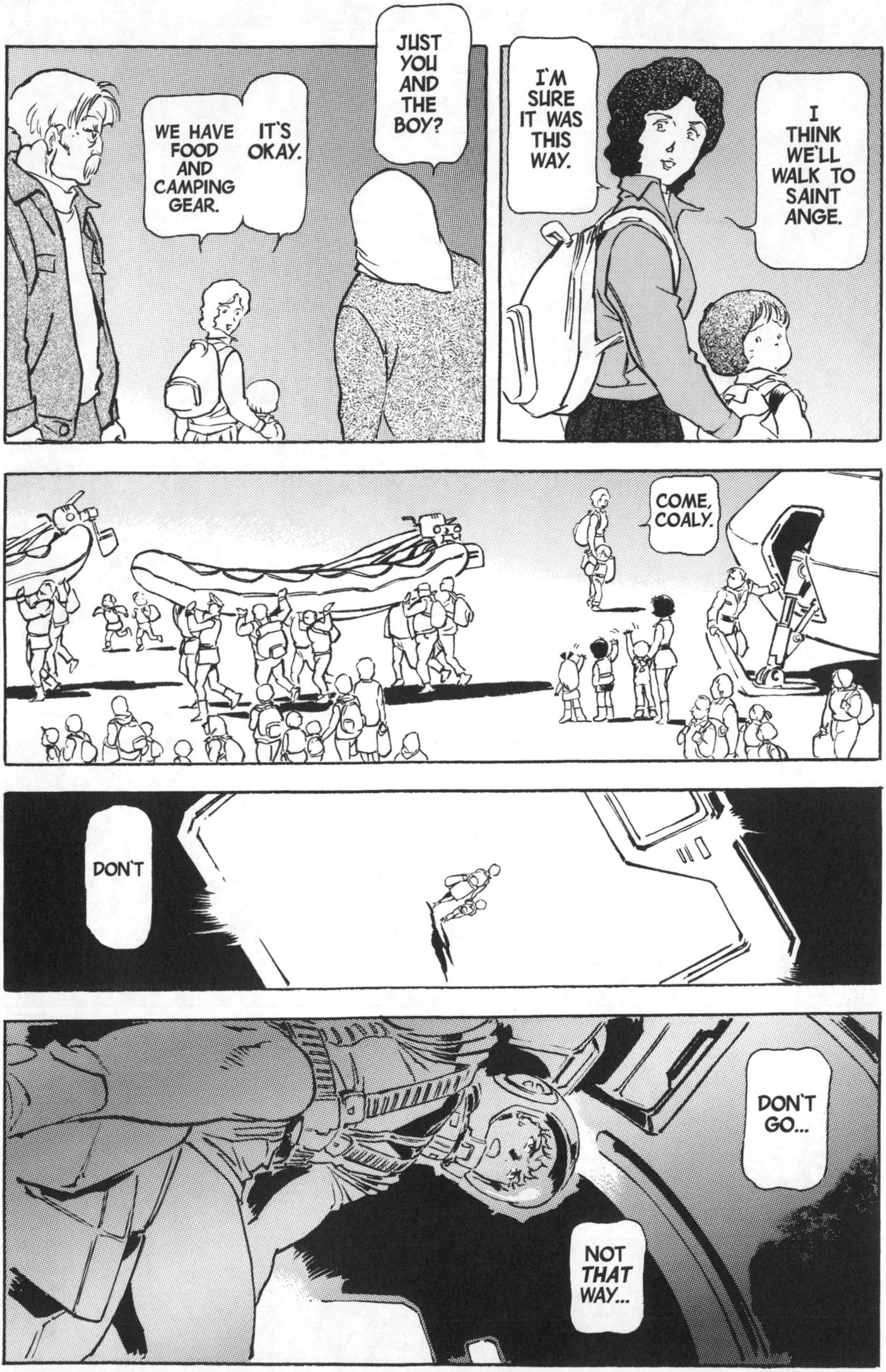
I THINK WE'LL WALK TO SAINT ANGE.
I'M SURE IT WAS THIS WAY.
JUST YOU AND THE BOY?
IT'S OKAY.
WE HAVE FOOD AND CAMPING GEAR.
COME, COALY.
DON'T
DON'T GO...
NOT *THAT* WAY...

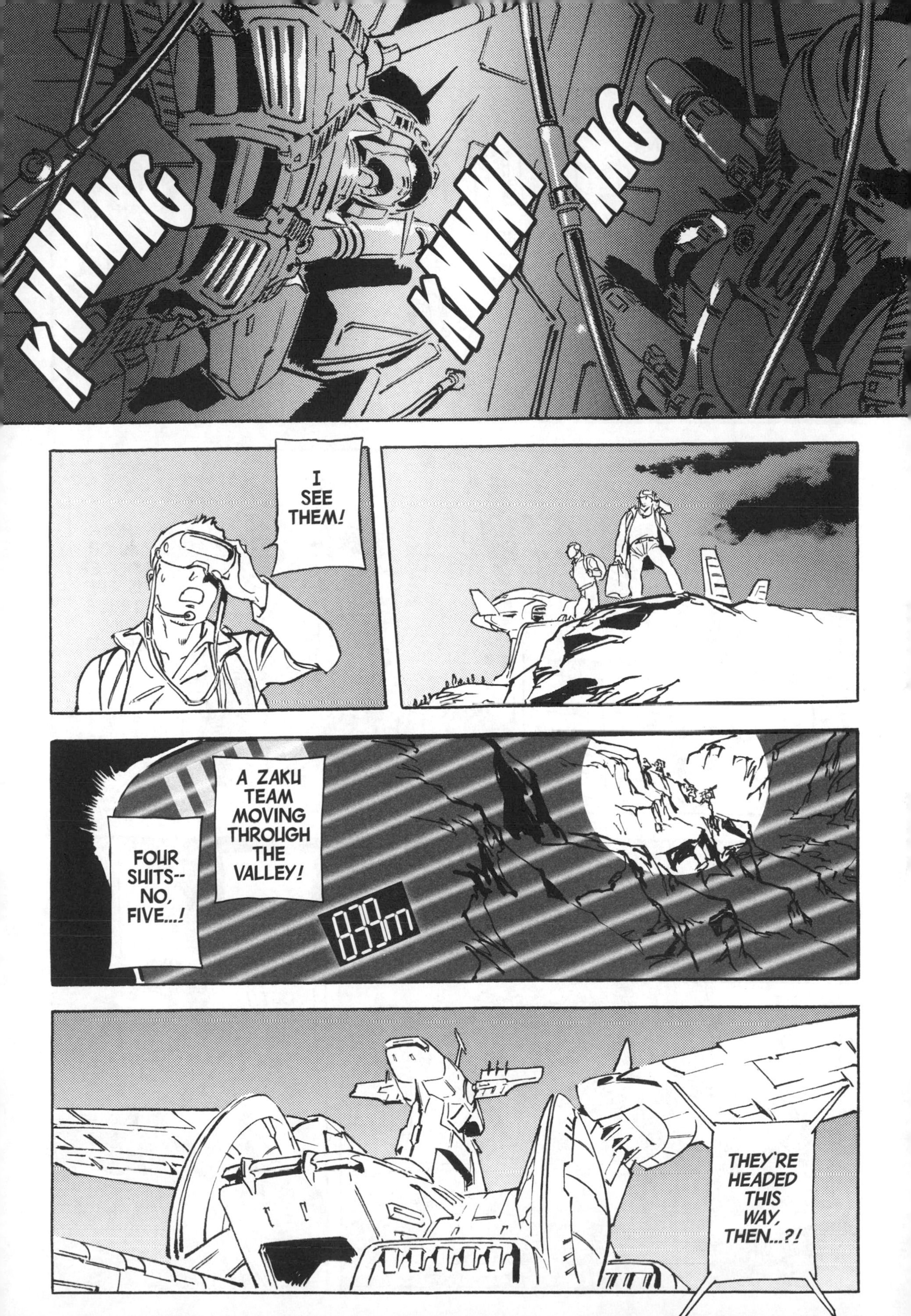
K'WNNN NG
K'WNNG
I SEE THEM!
A ZAKU TEAM MOVING THROUGH THE VALLEY!
FOUR SUITS-- NO, FIVE...!
839m
THEY'RE HEADED THIS WAY, THEN...?!

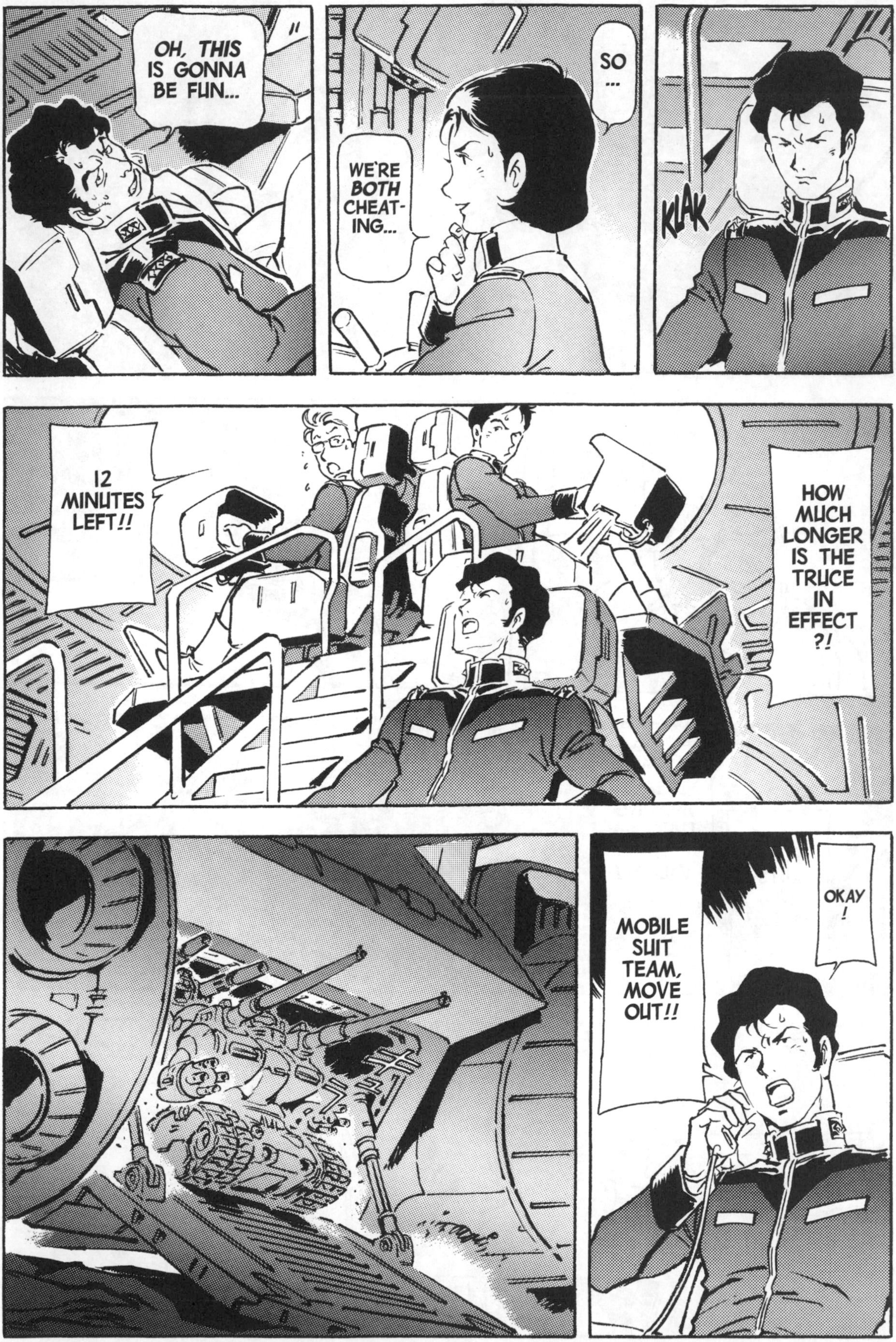
KLAK
SO ...
WE'RE *BOTH* CHEATING...
OH, THIS IS GONNA BE FUN...
HOW MUCH LONGER IS THE TRUCE IN EFFECT?!
12 MINUTES LEFT!!
OKAY!
MOBILE SUIT TEAM, MOVE OUT!!

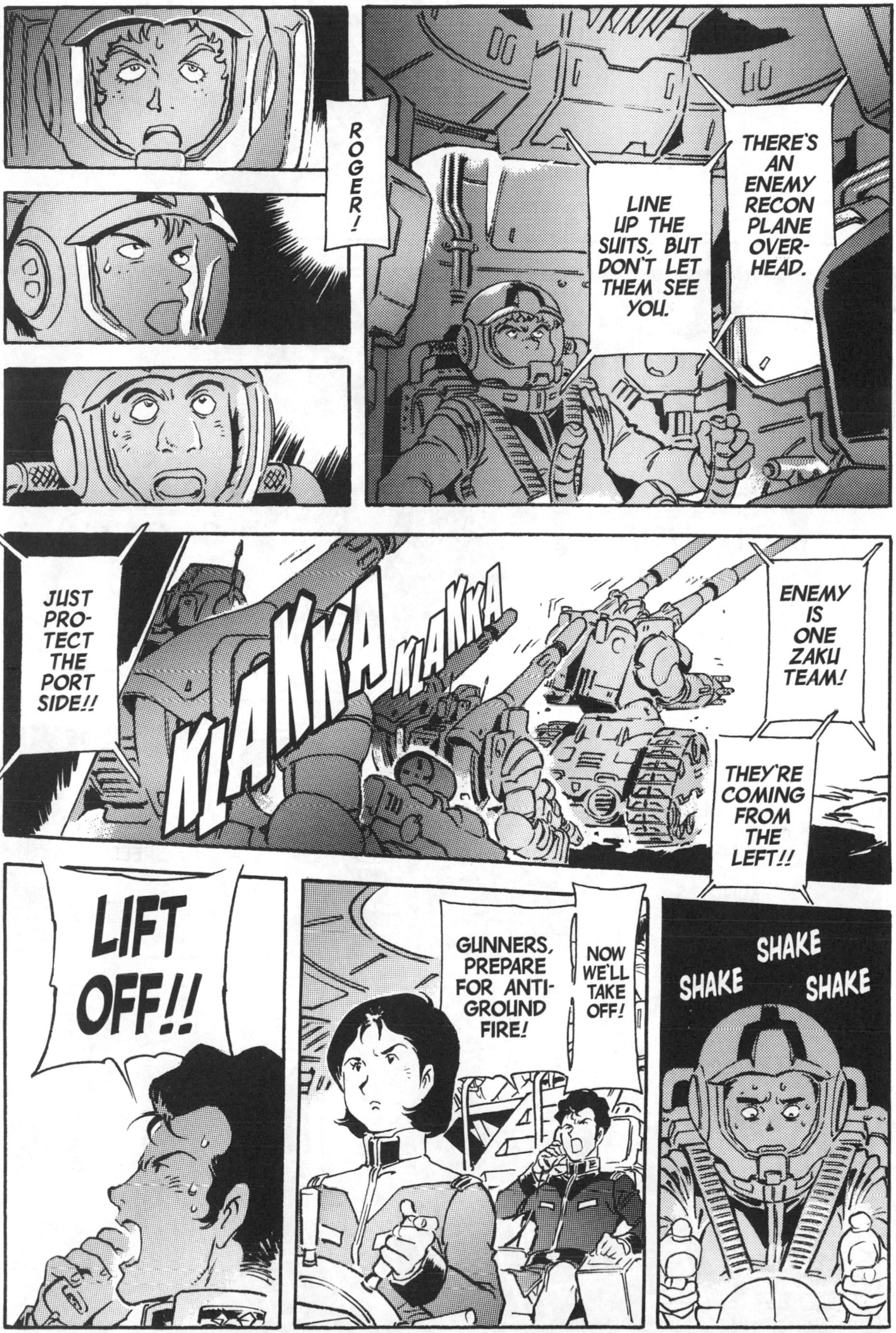
THERE'S AN ENEMY RECON PLANE OVER-HEAD.
LINE UP THE SUITS, BUT DON'T LET THEM SEE YOU.
ROGER!
ENEMY IS ONE ZAKU TEAM!
THEY'RE COMING FROM THE LEFT!!
JUST PRO-TECT THE PORT SIDE!!
KLAKKA KLAKKA
LIFT OFF!!
NOW WE'LL TAKE OFF!
GUNNERS, PREPARE FOR ANTI-GROUND FIRE!
SHAKE SHAKE SHAKE

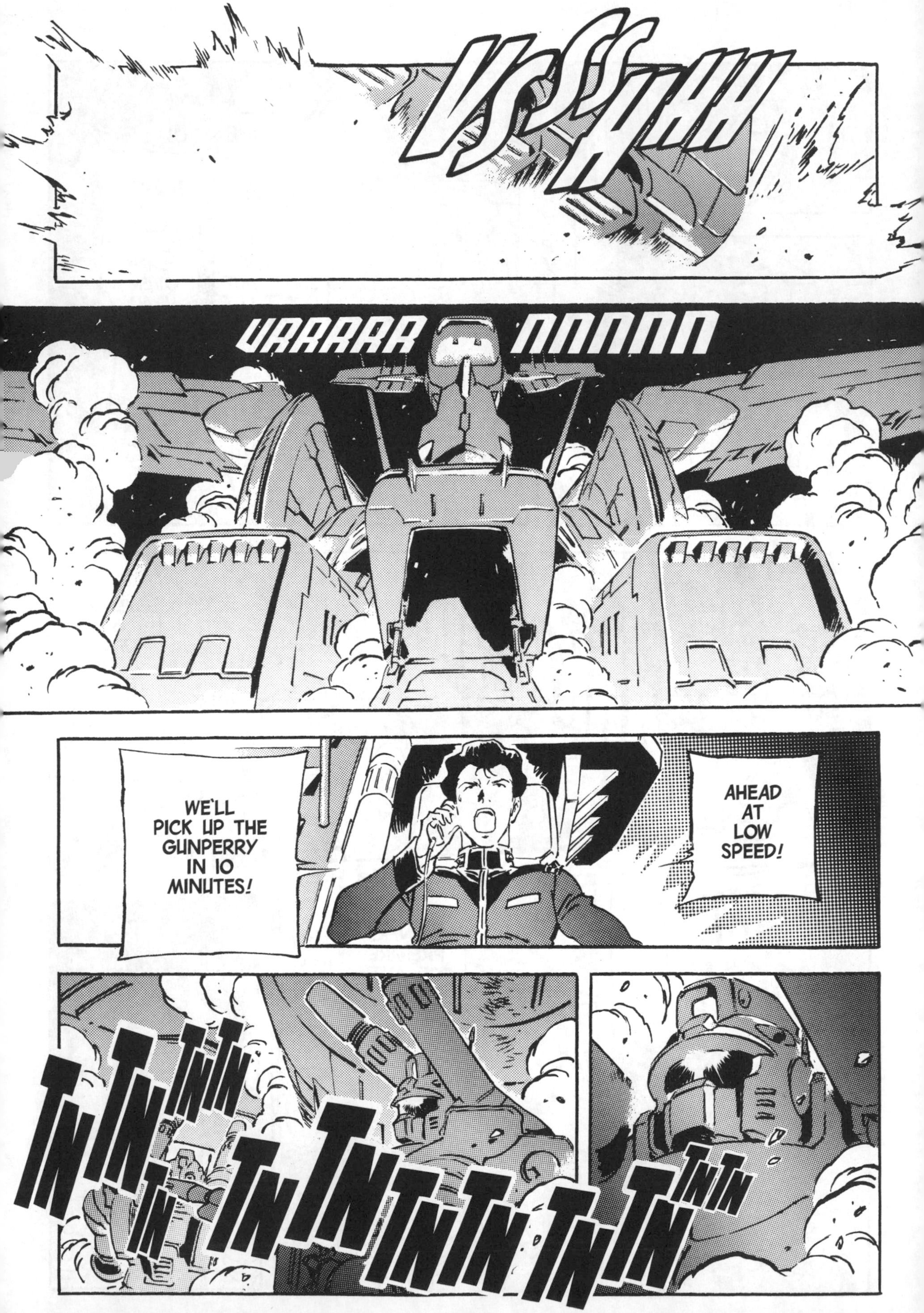
VSSHHH
URRRRR NNNNNN
AHEAD AT LOW SPEED!
WE'LL PICK UP THE GUNPERRY IN 10 MINUTES!
TN TN TN TN TN TN TN TN TN TN TN TN TN TN TN TN

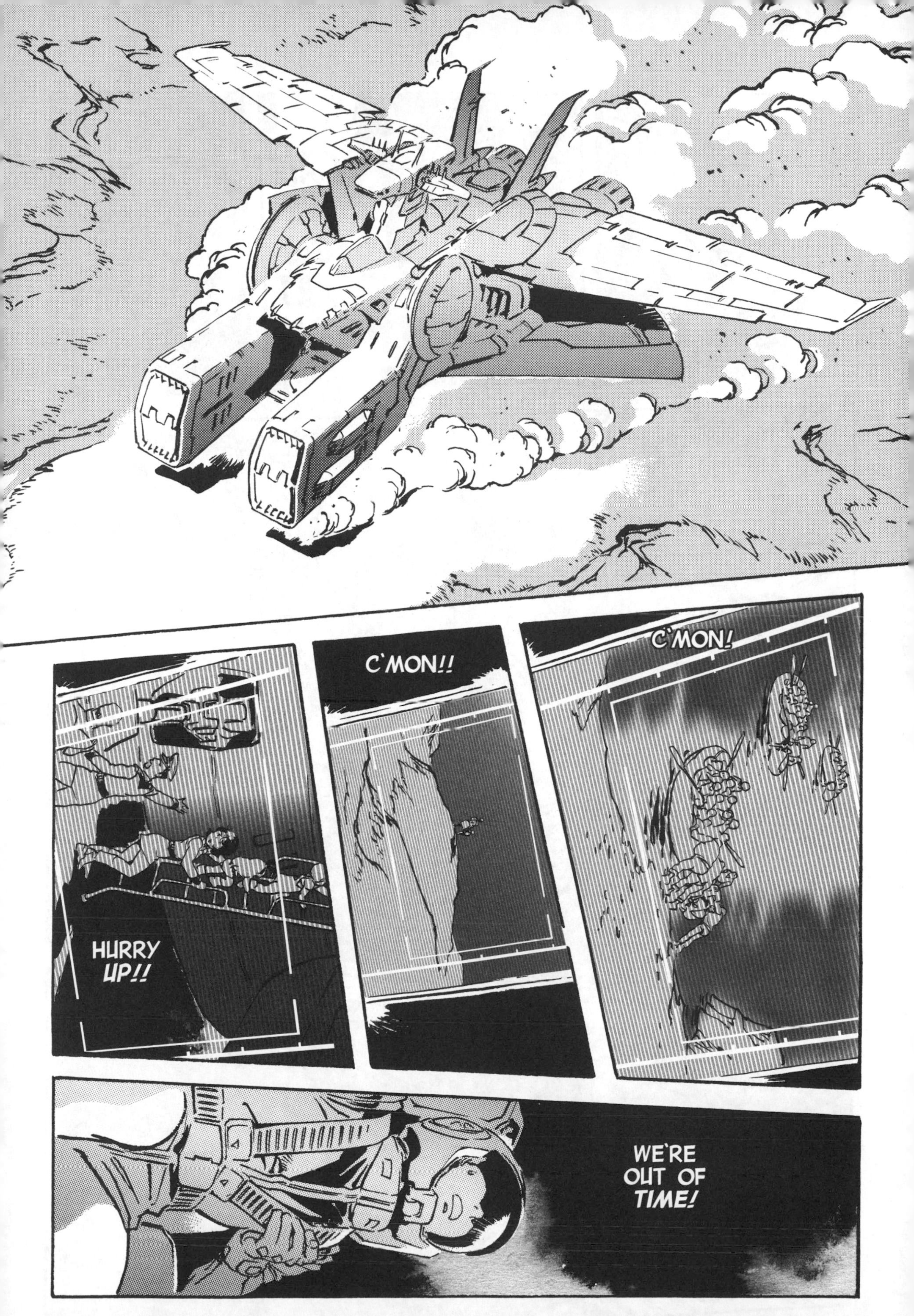
C'MON!
C'MON!!
HURRY UP!!
WE'RE OUT OF TIME!

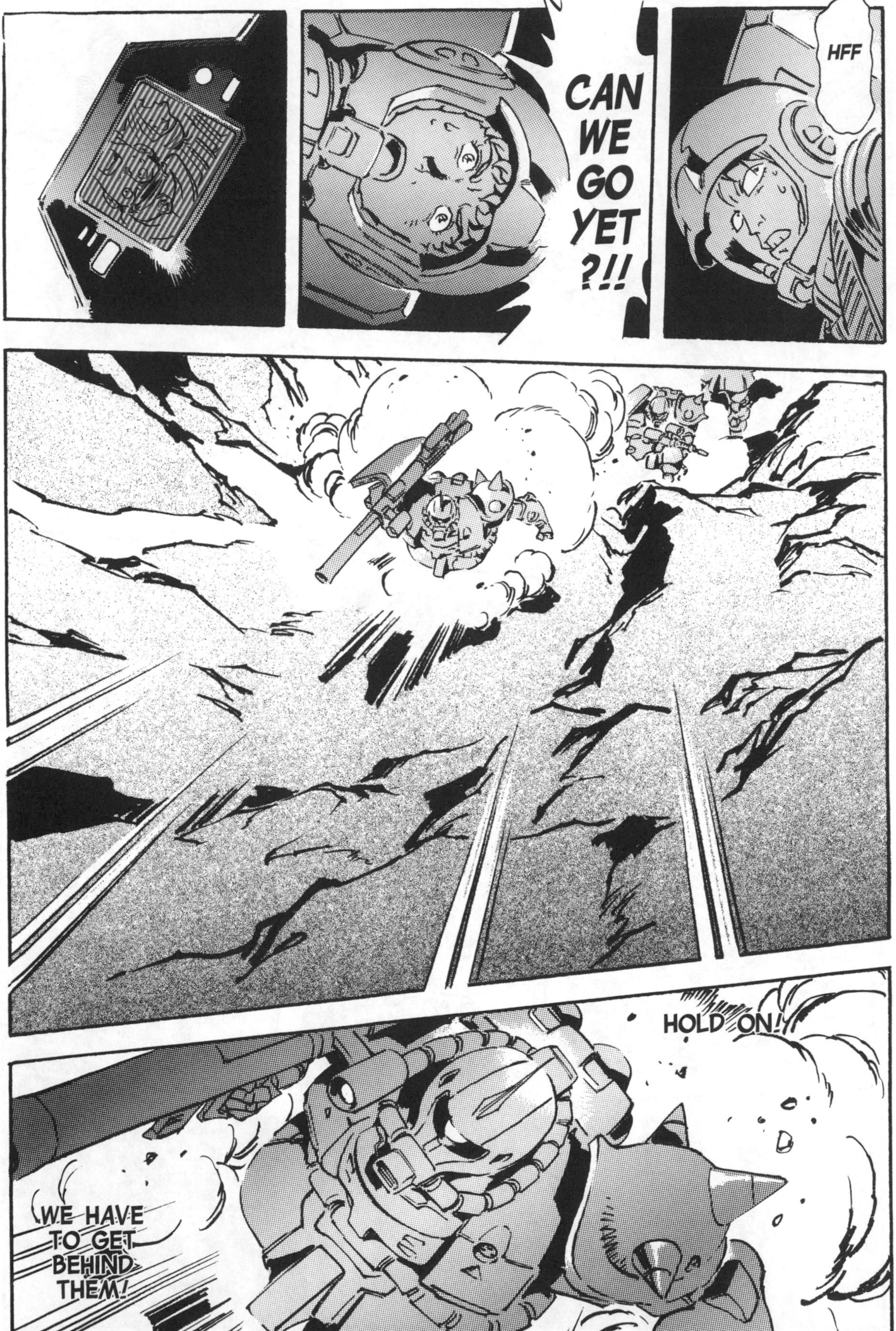
HFF
CAN WE GO YET?!!
HOLD ON!
WE HAVE TO GET BEHIND THEM!

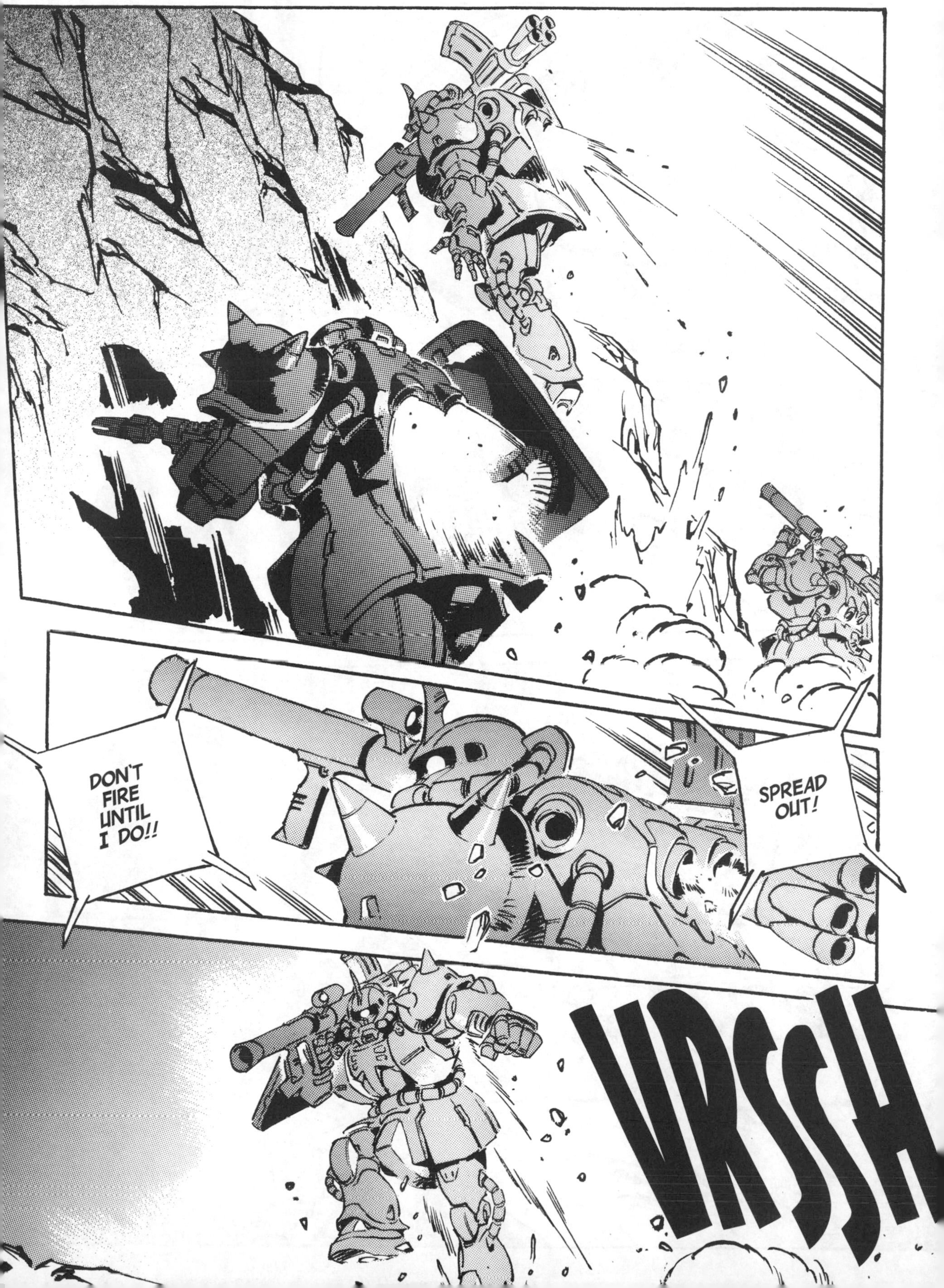
SPREAD OUT!
DON'T FIRE UNTIL I DO!!
VRSSH

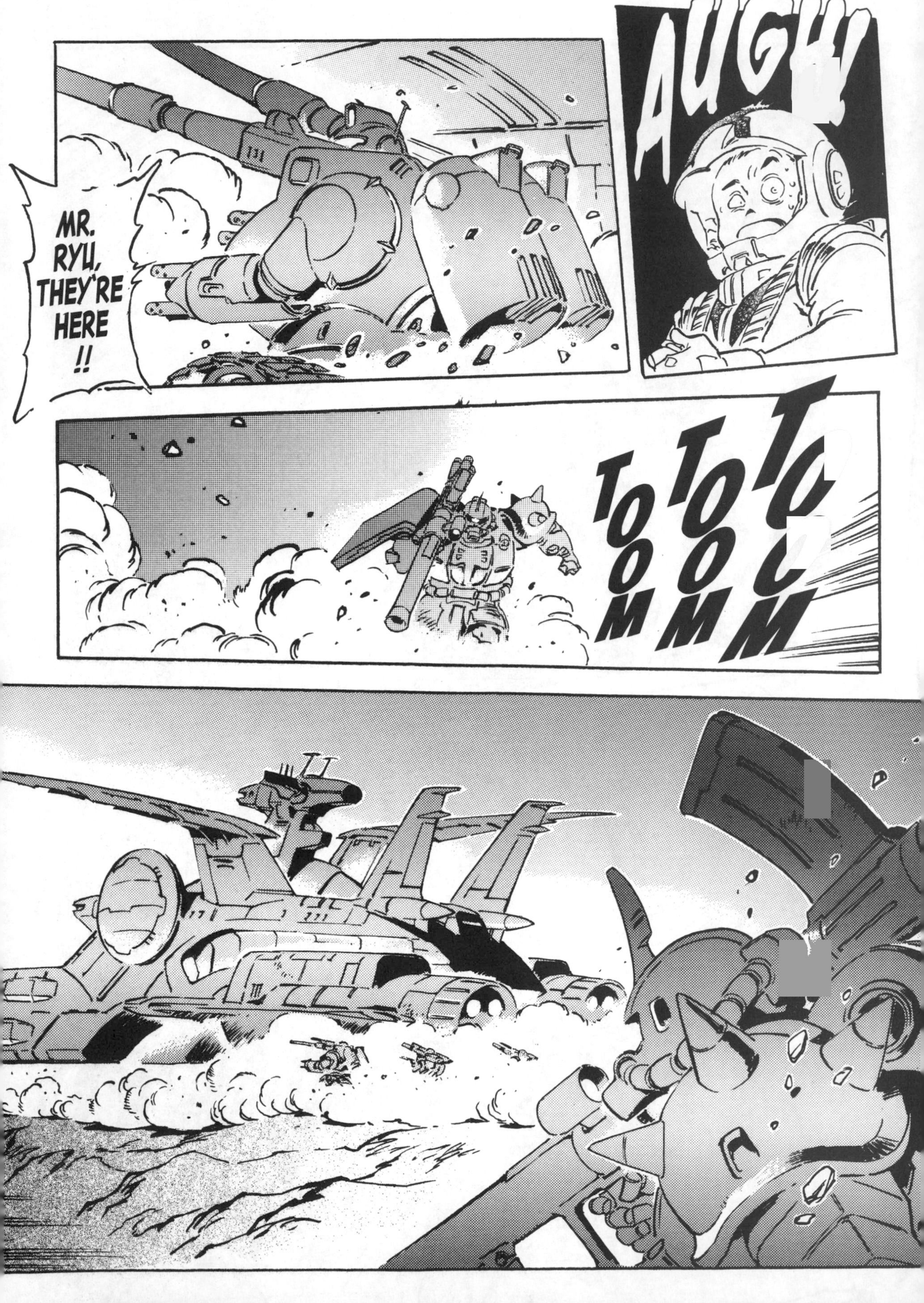
AUGH!
MR. RYU, THEY'RE HERE !!
TOOM
TOOM
TOOM

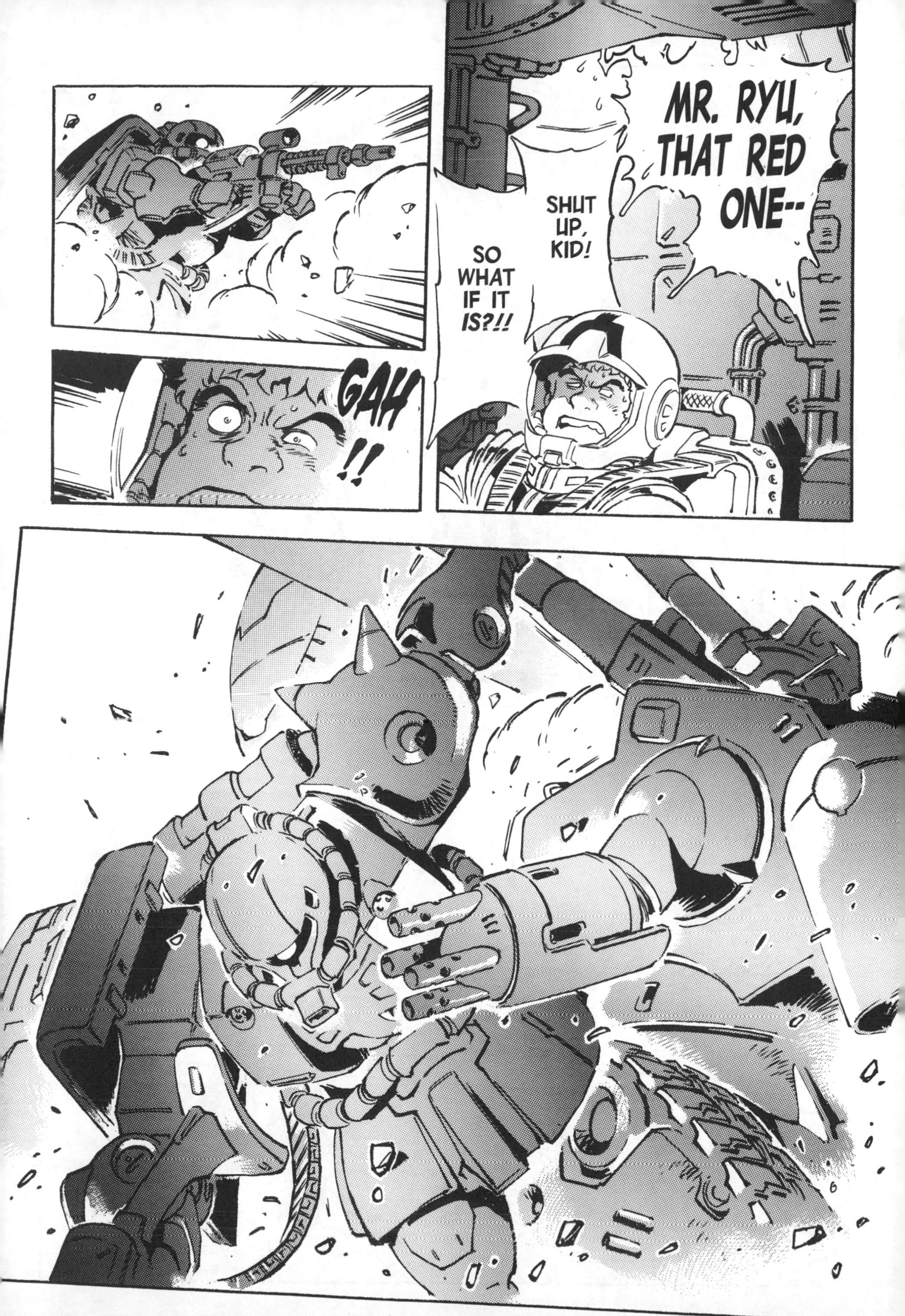
MR. RYU, THAT RED ONE--
SHUT UP, KID!
SO WHAT IF IT IS?!!
GAH!!

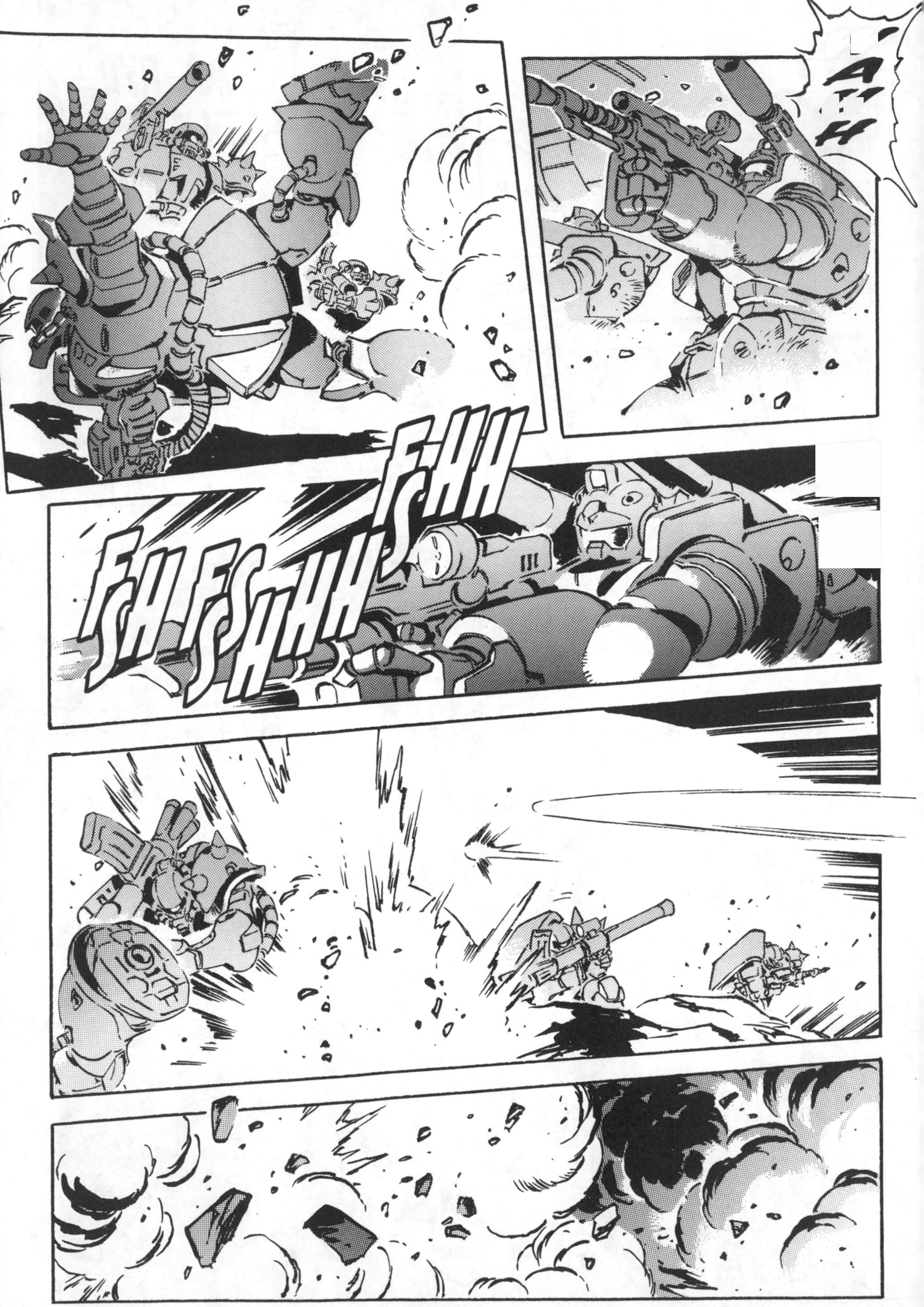
FSH FSHHH FSHH

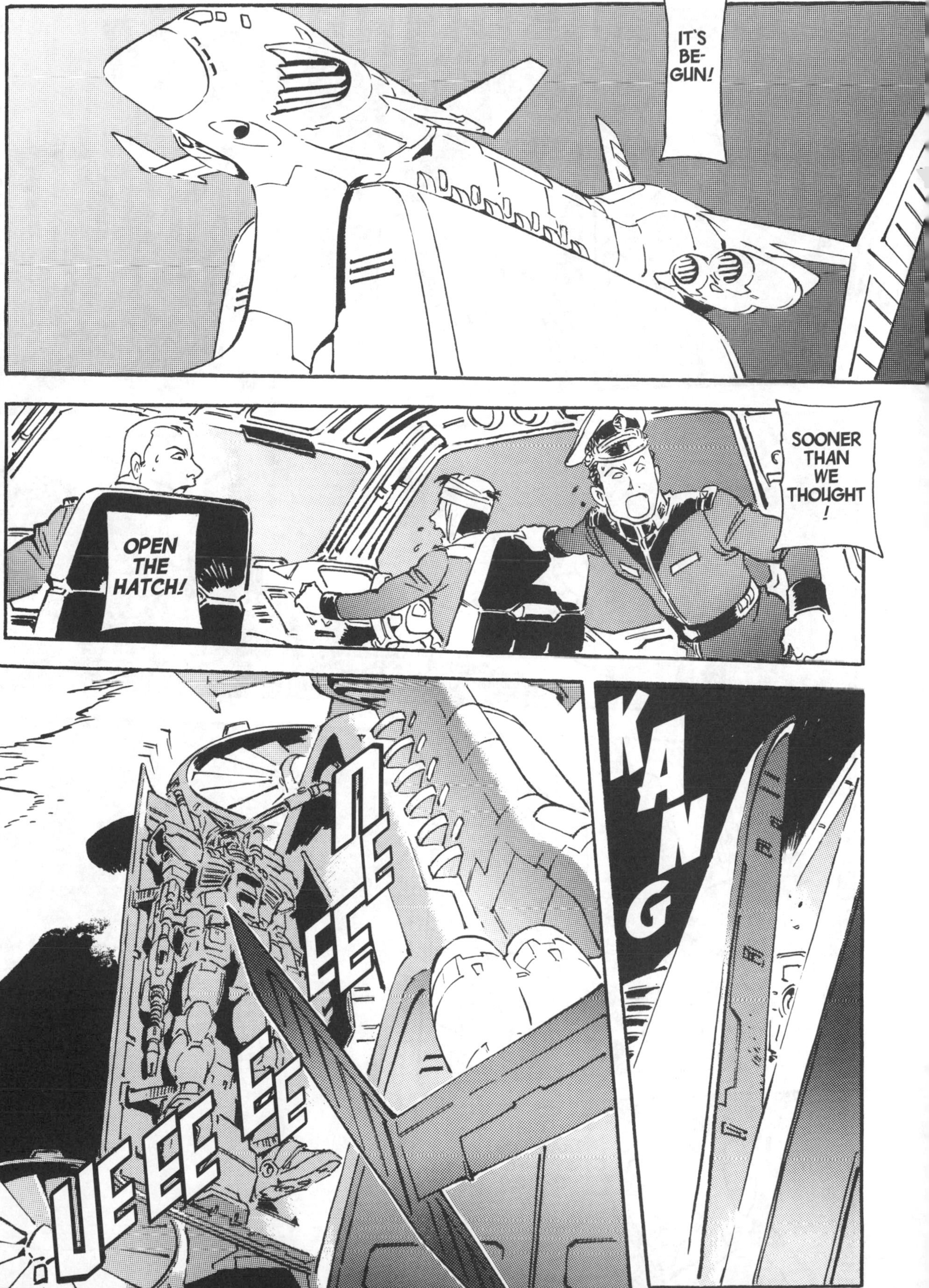
IT'S BE-GUN!
SOONER THAN WE THOUGHT!
OPEN THE HATCH!
KANG
NEEEE
UEEEEE

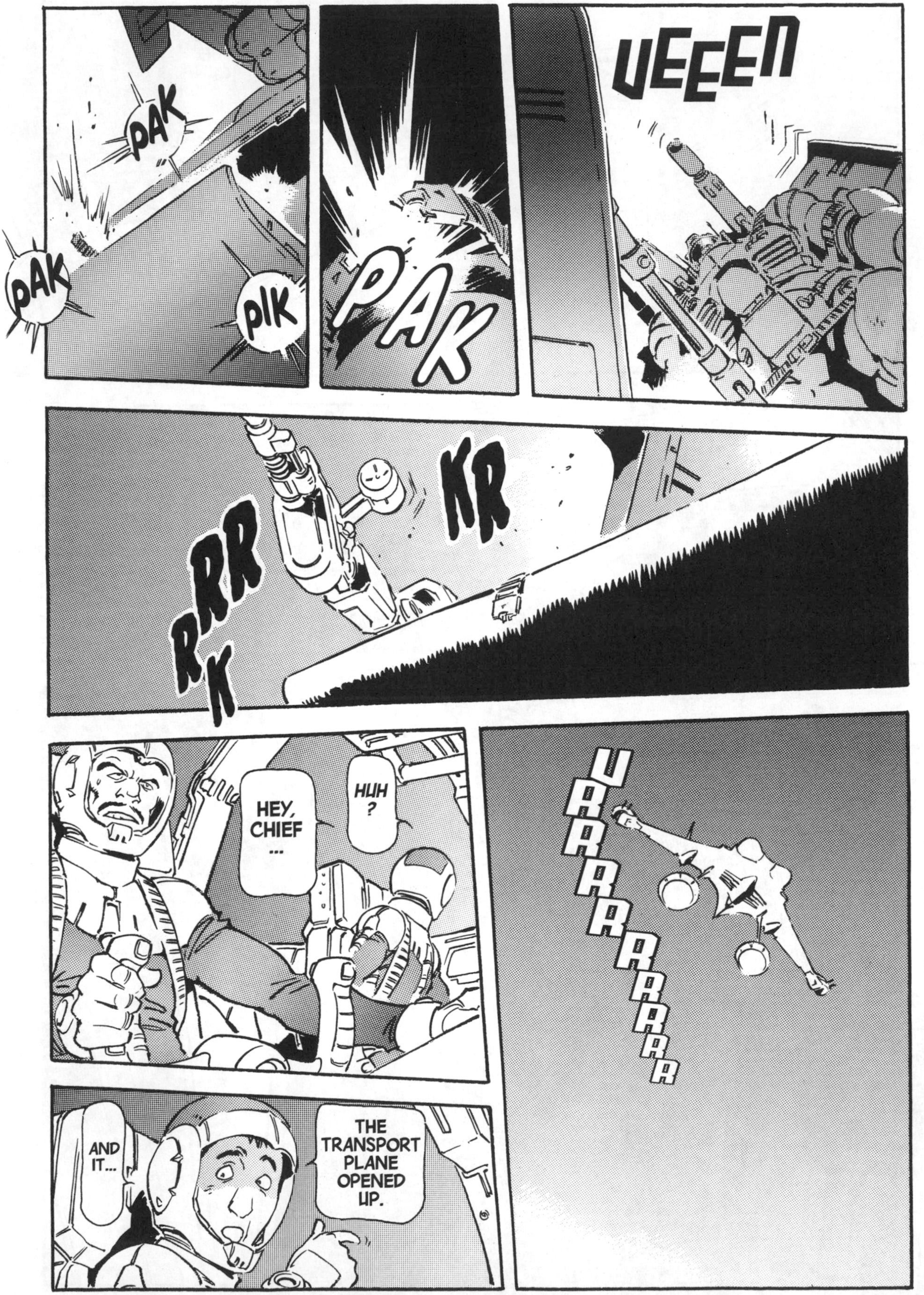
UEEEN
PAK
PAK
PAK
PIK
KR
RRR
K
URRRRRRRRRR
HUH ?
HEY, CHIEF ...
THE TRANSPORT PLANE OPENED UP.
AND IT...

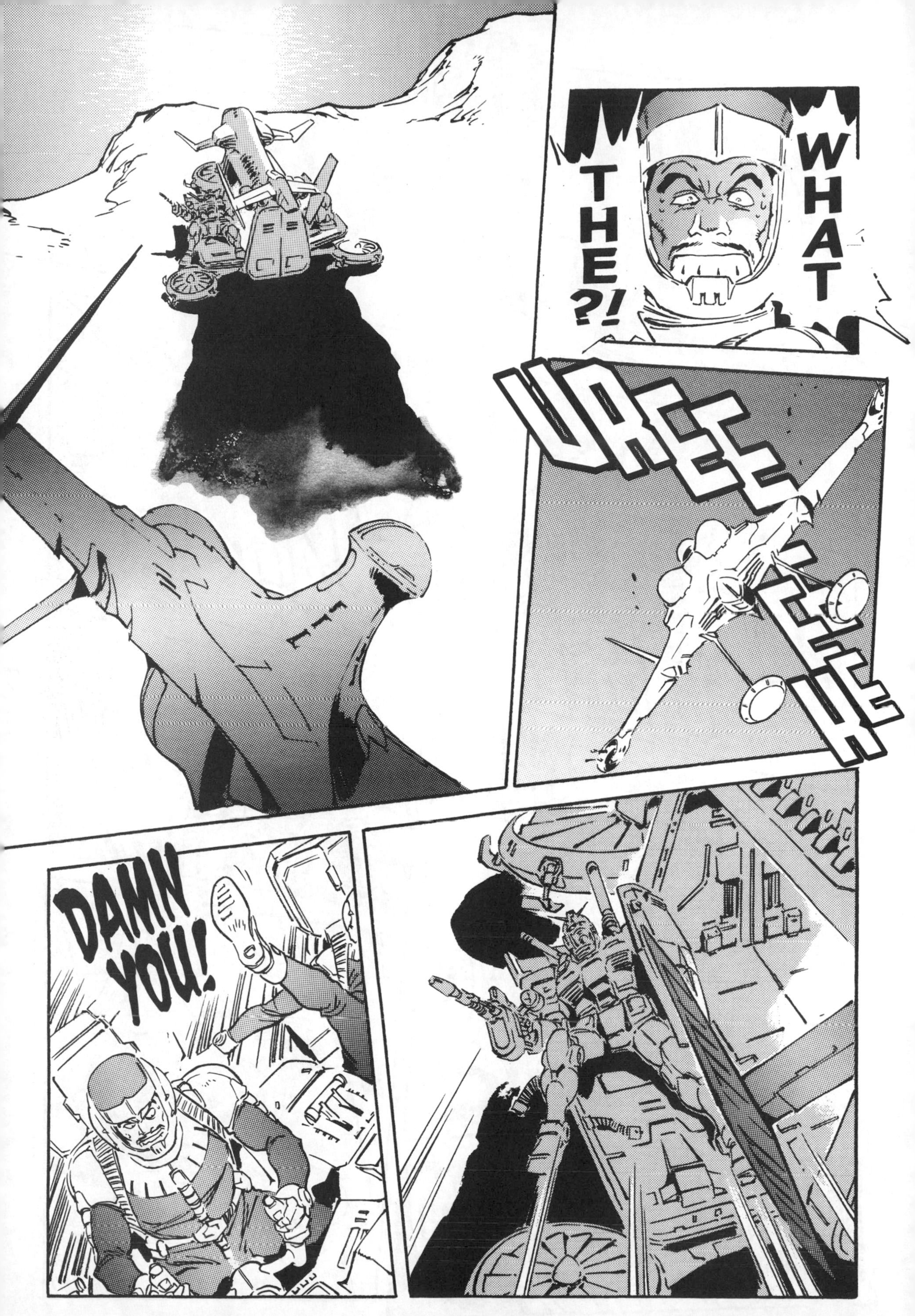
WHAT THE?!
VREEEEEEK
DAMN YOU!

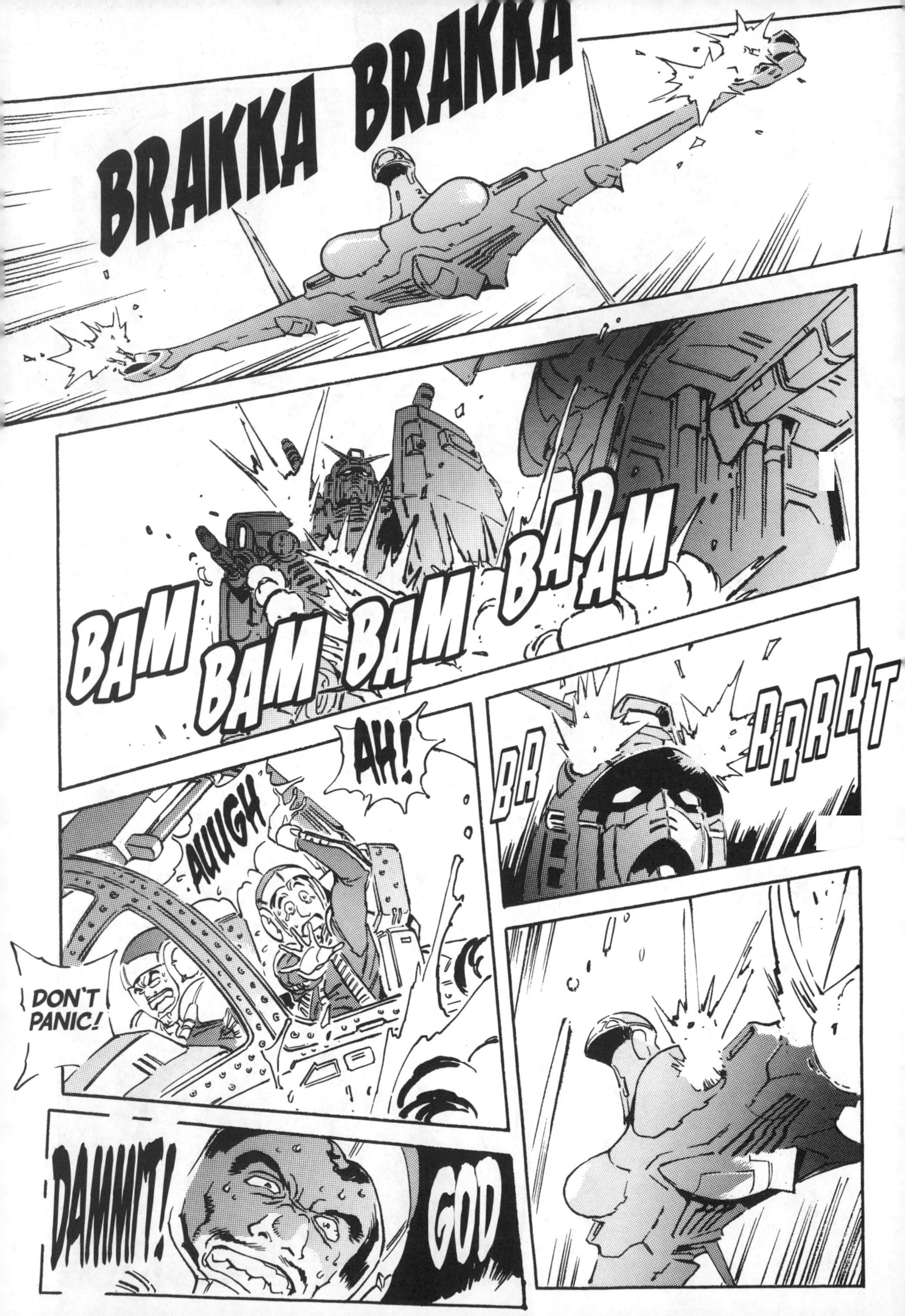
BRAKKA BRAKKA
BAM BAM BAM BADAM
BR RRRRT
AH!
AUUGH
DON'T PANIC!
DAMMIT!
GOD

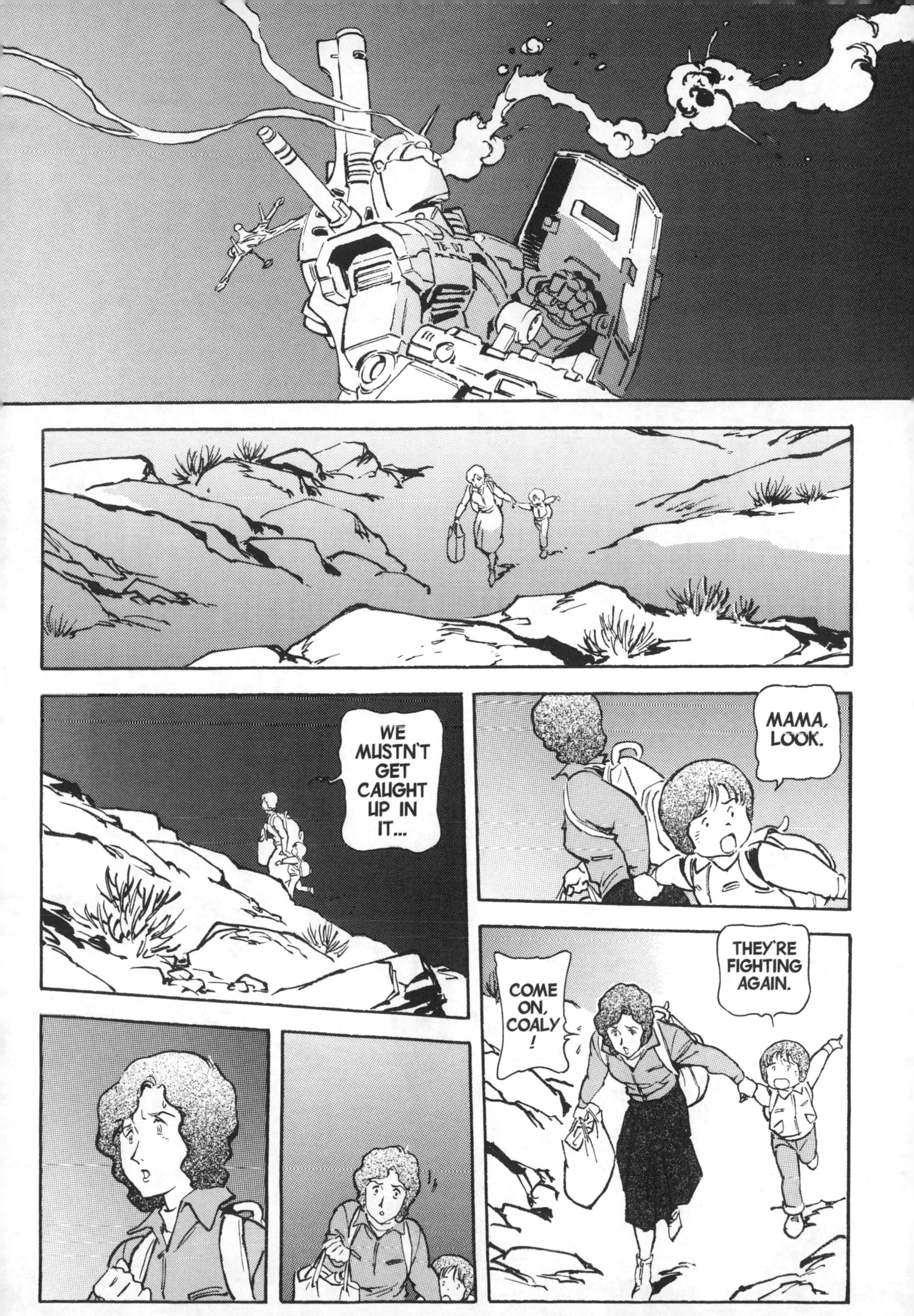
MAMA, LOOK.
THEY'RE FIGHTING AGAIN.
COME ON, COALY!
WE MUSTN'T GET CAUGHT UP IN IT...

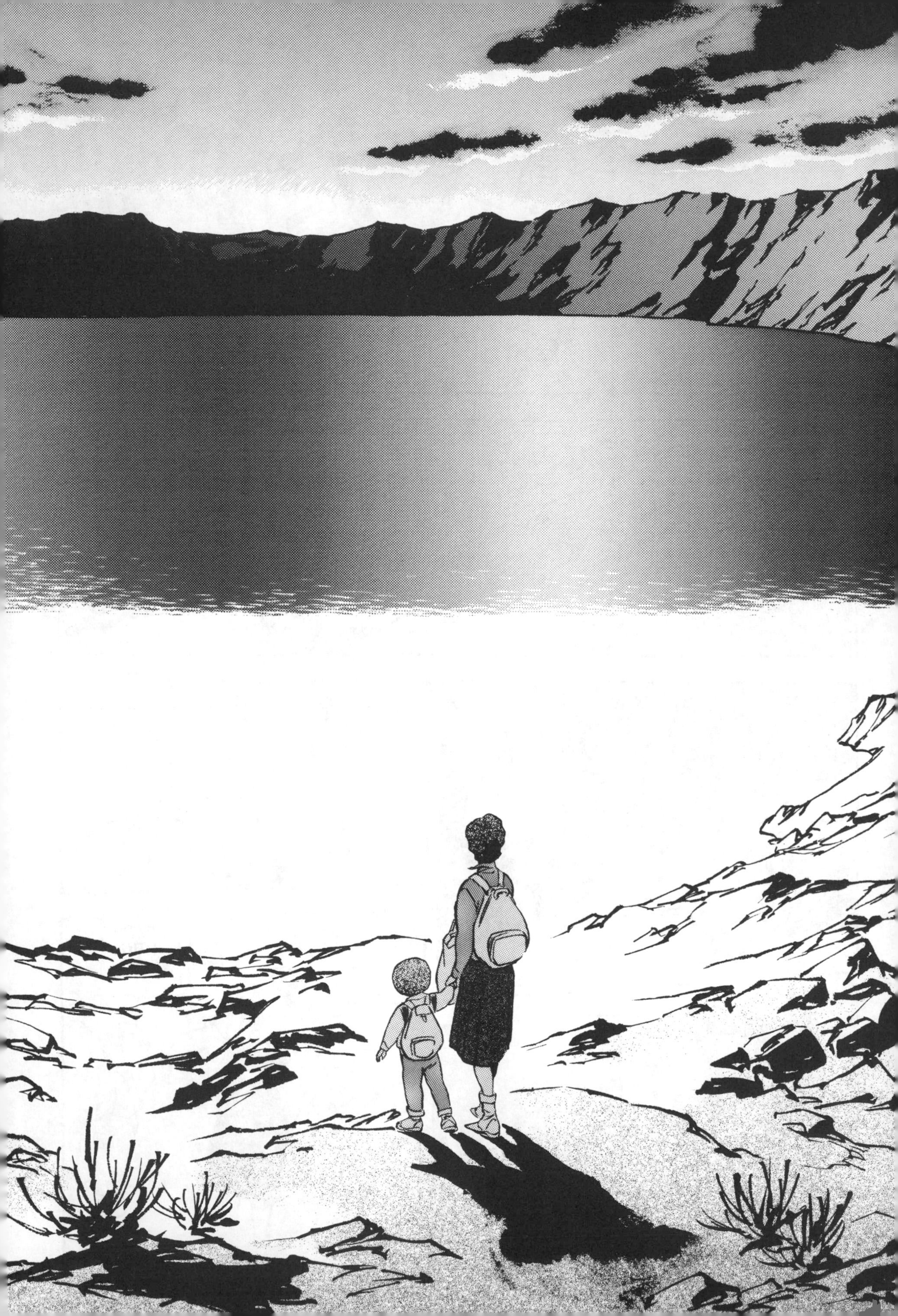

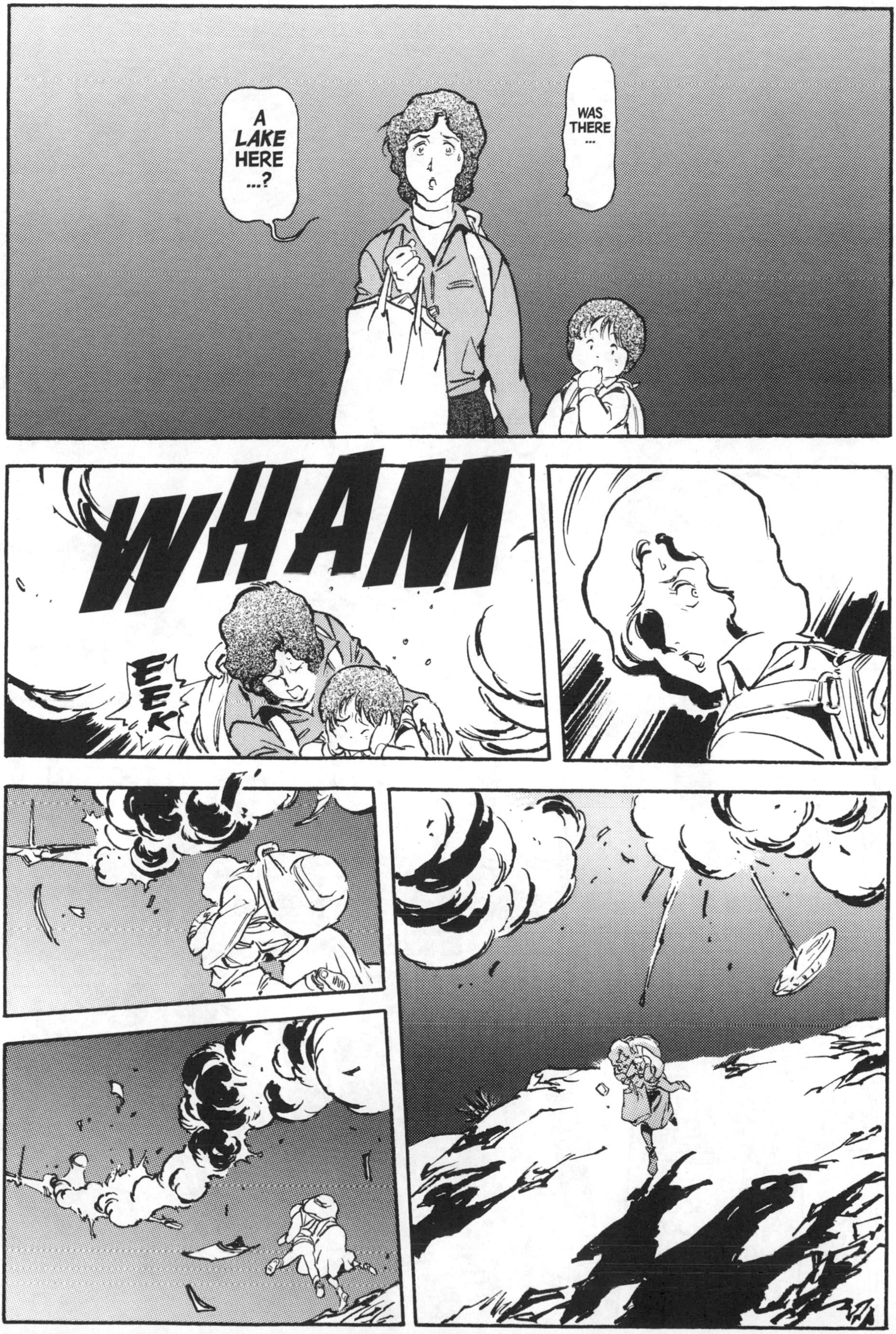
WAS THERE ...
A LAKE HERE ...?
WHAM
EEEK

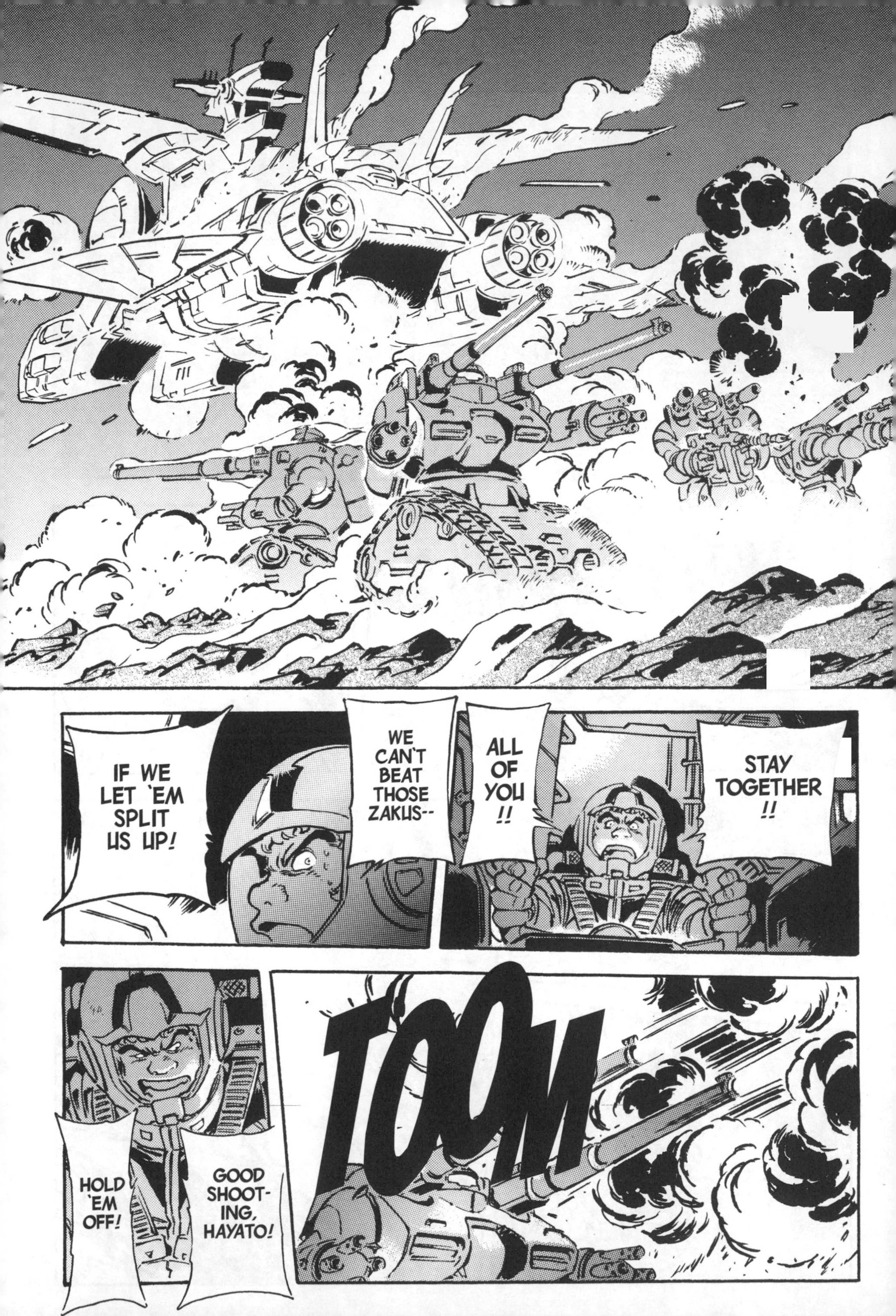
STAY TOGETHER!!
ALL OF YOU!!
WE CAN'T BEAT THOSE ZAKUS--
IF WE LET 'EM SPLIT US UP!
TOOM
GOOD SHOOT-ING, HAYATO!
HOLD 'EM OFF!

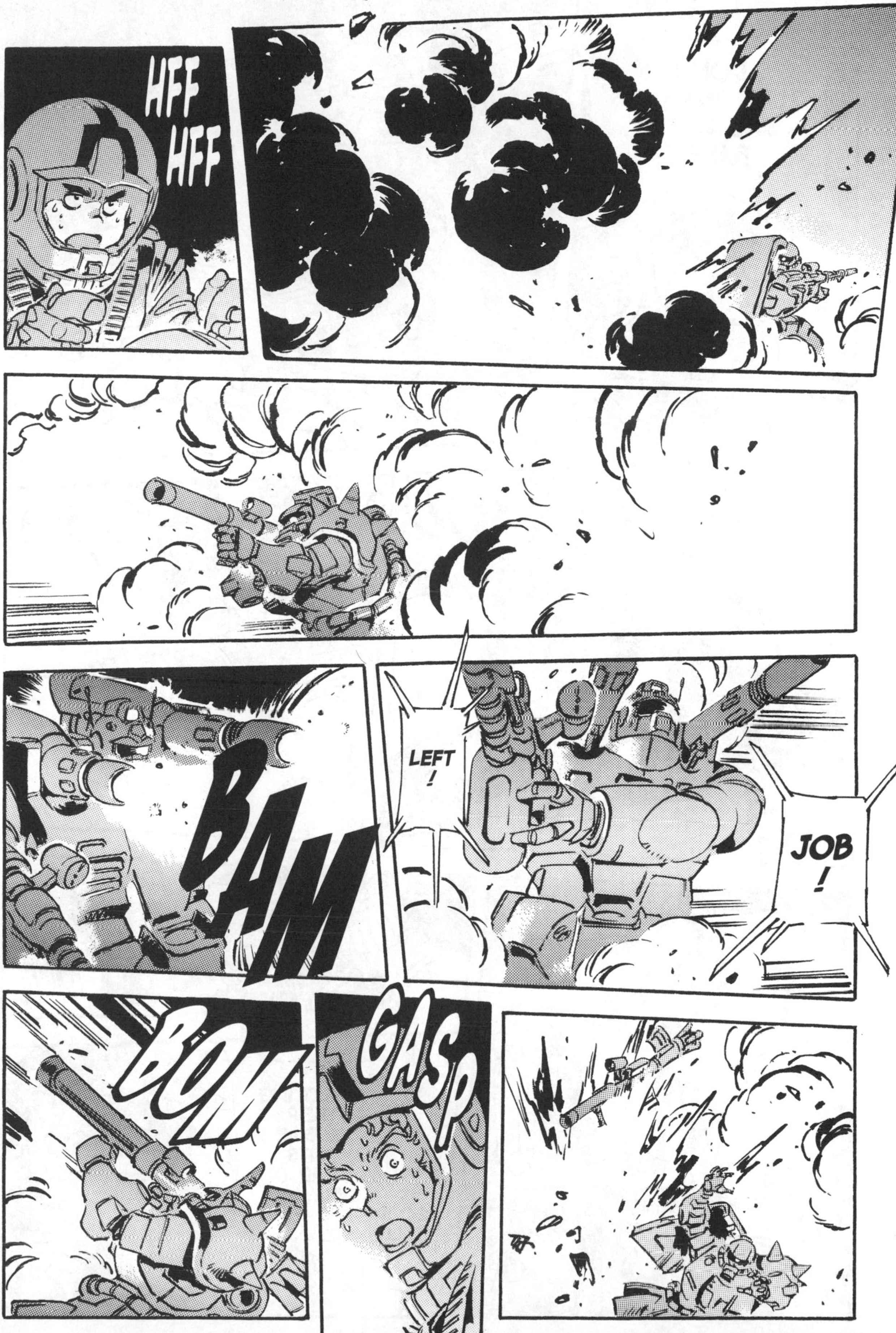
HFF
HFF
JOB!
LEFT!
BAM
GASP
BOM

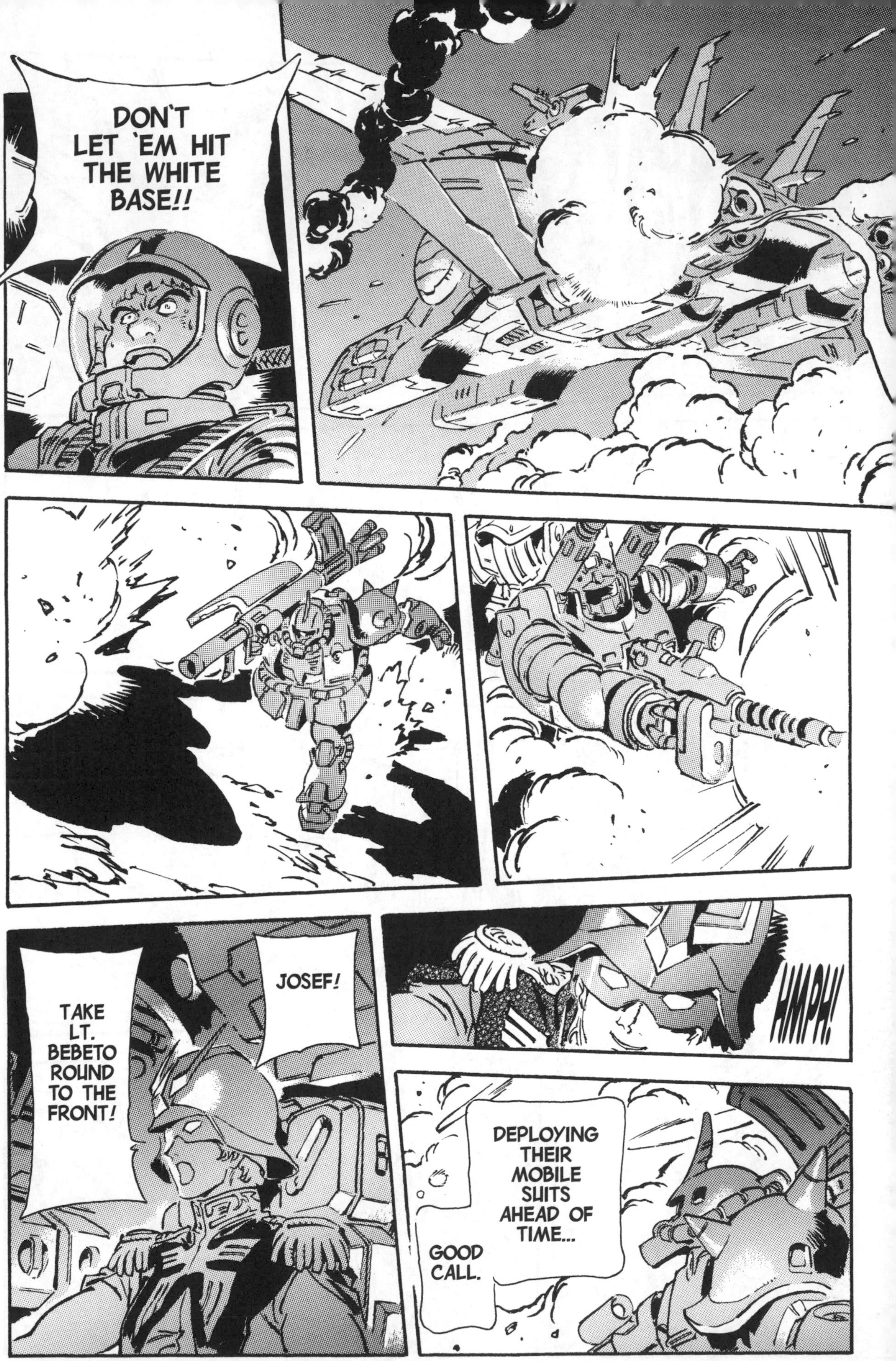
DON'T LET 'EM HIT THE WHITE BASE!!
HMPH!
DEPLOYING THEIR MOBILE SUITS AHEAD OF TIME...
GOOD CALL.
JOSEF!
TAKE LT. BEBETO ROUND TO THE FRONT!

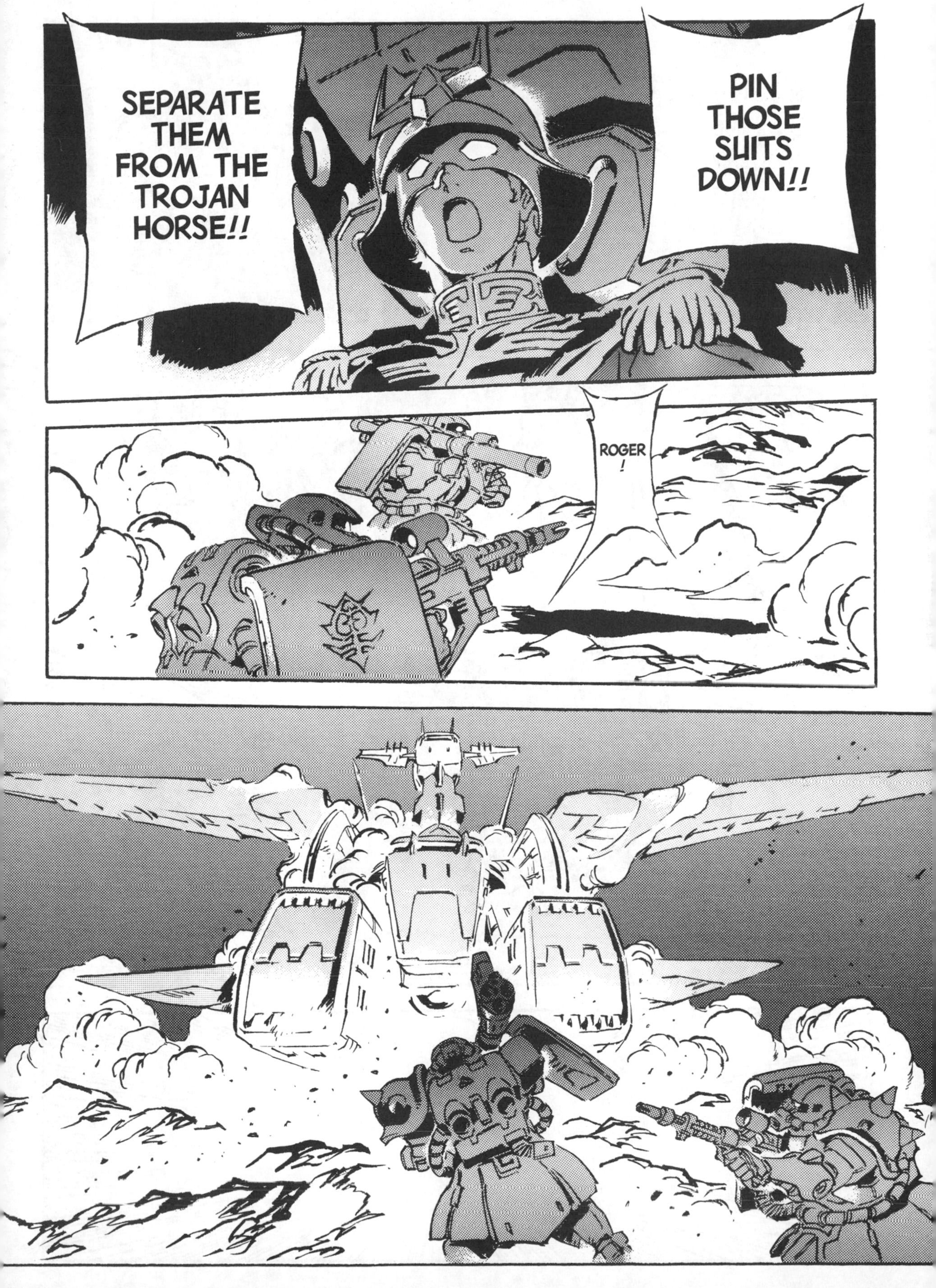
PIN THOSE SUITS DOWN!!
SEPARATE THEM FROM THE TROJAN HORSE!!
ROGER!

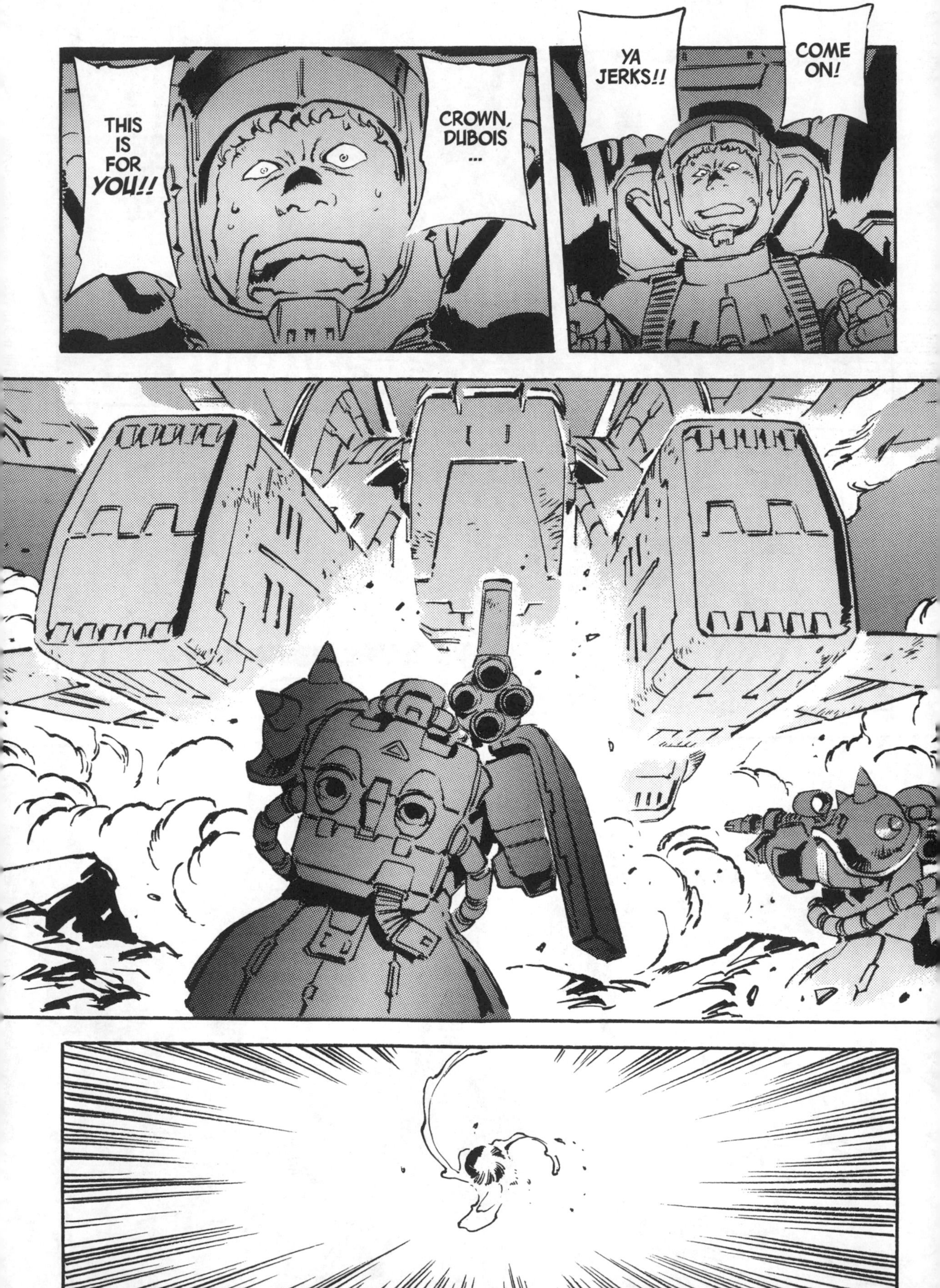
COME ON!
YA JERKS!!
CROWN, DUBOIS ...
THIS IS FOR YOU!!

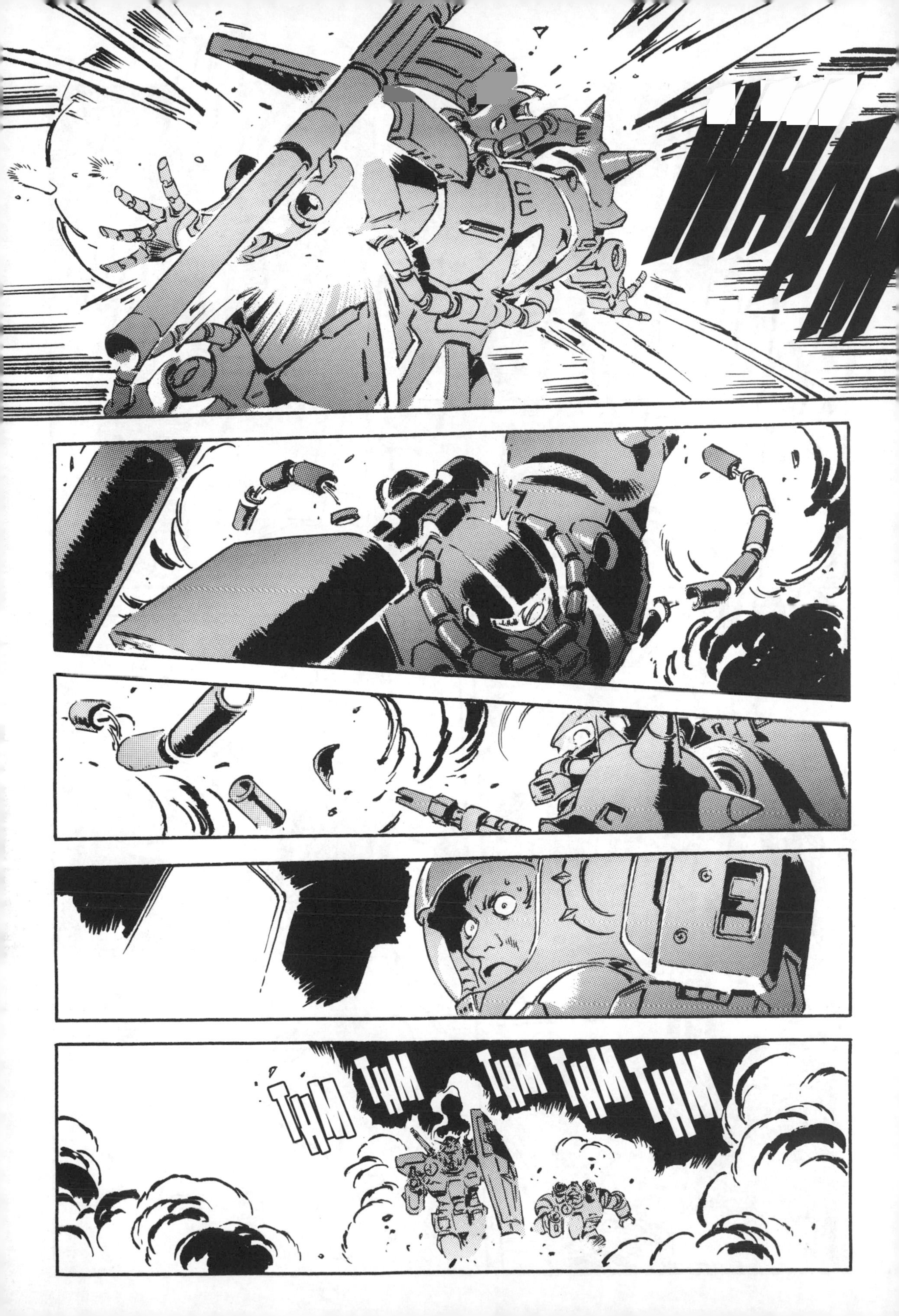
THM THM THM THM THM

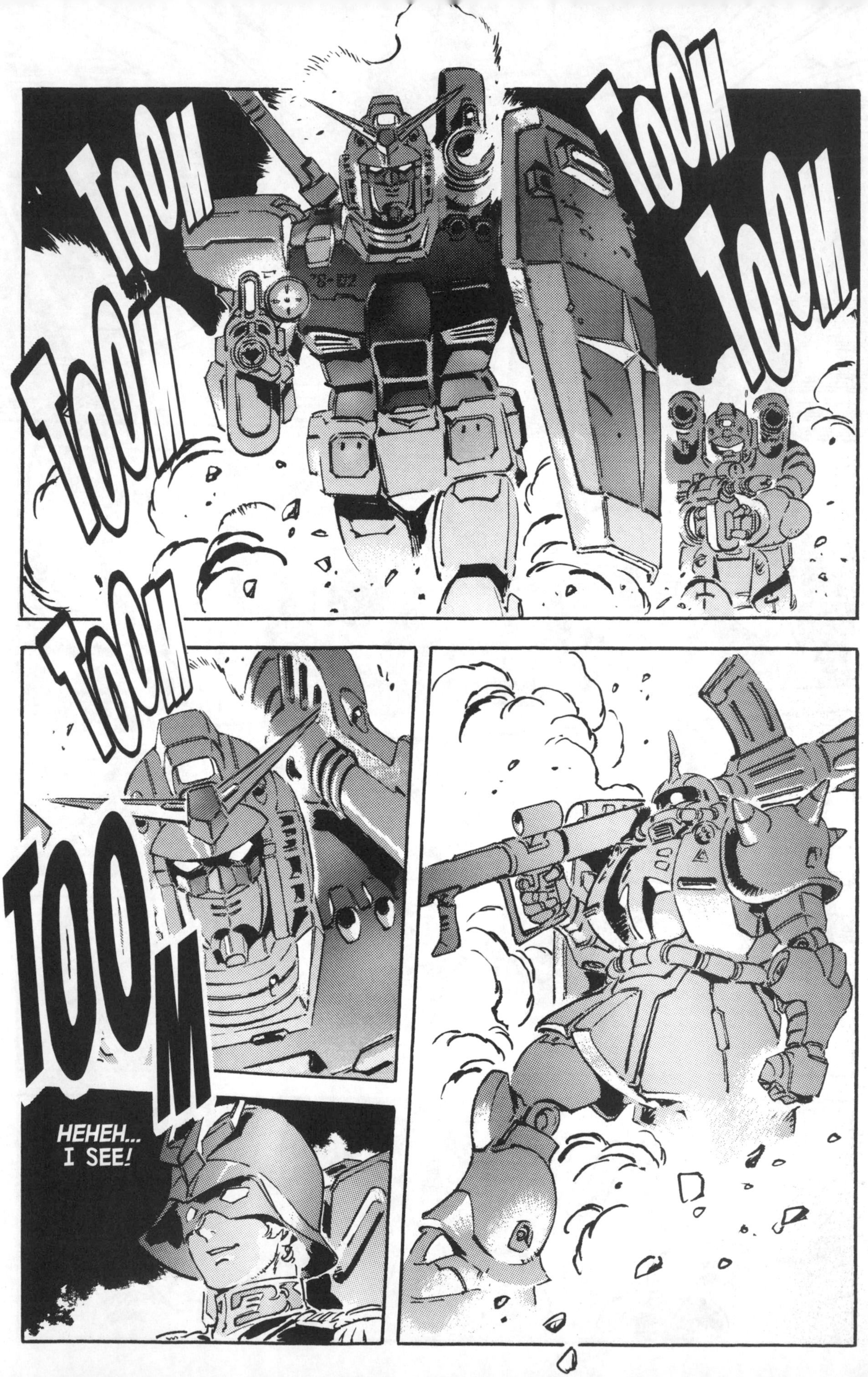
TOOM
TOOM
TOOM
TOOM
TOOM
TOOM
HEHEH... I SEE!

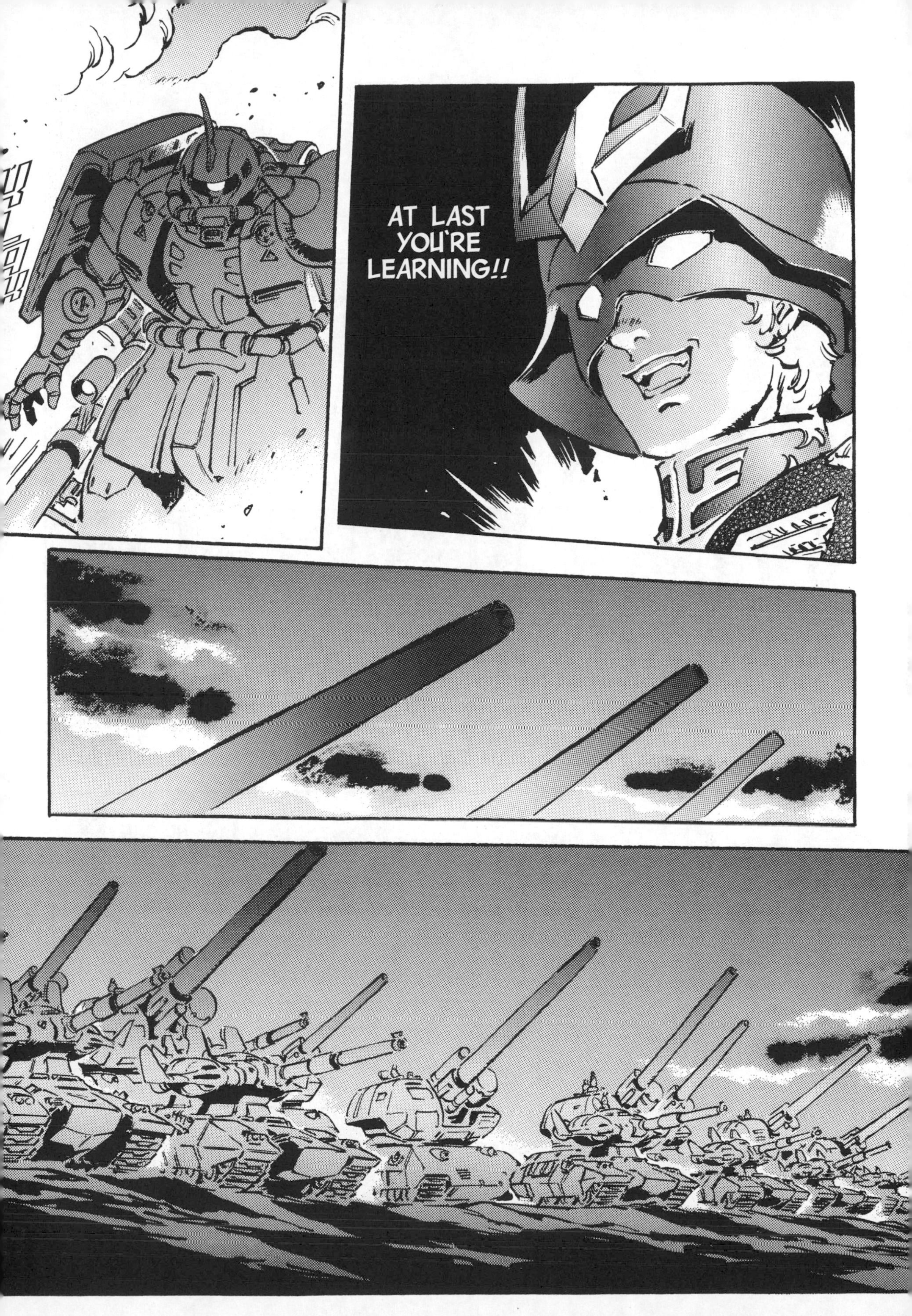
AT LAST YOU'RE LEARNING!!

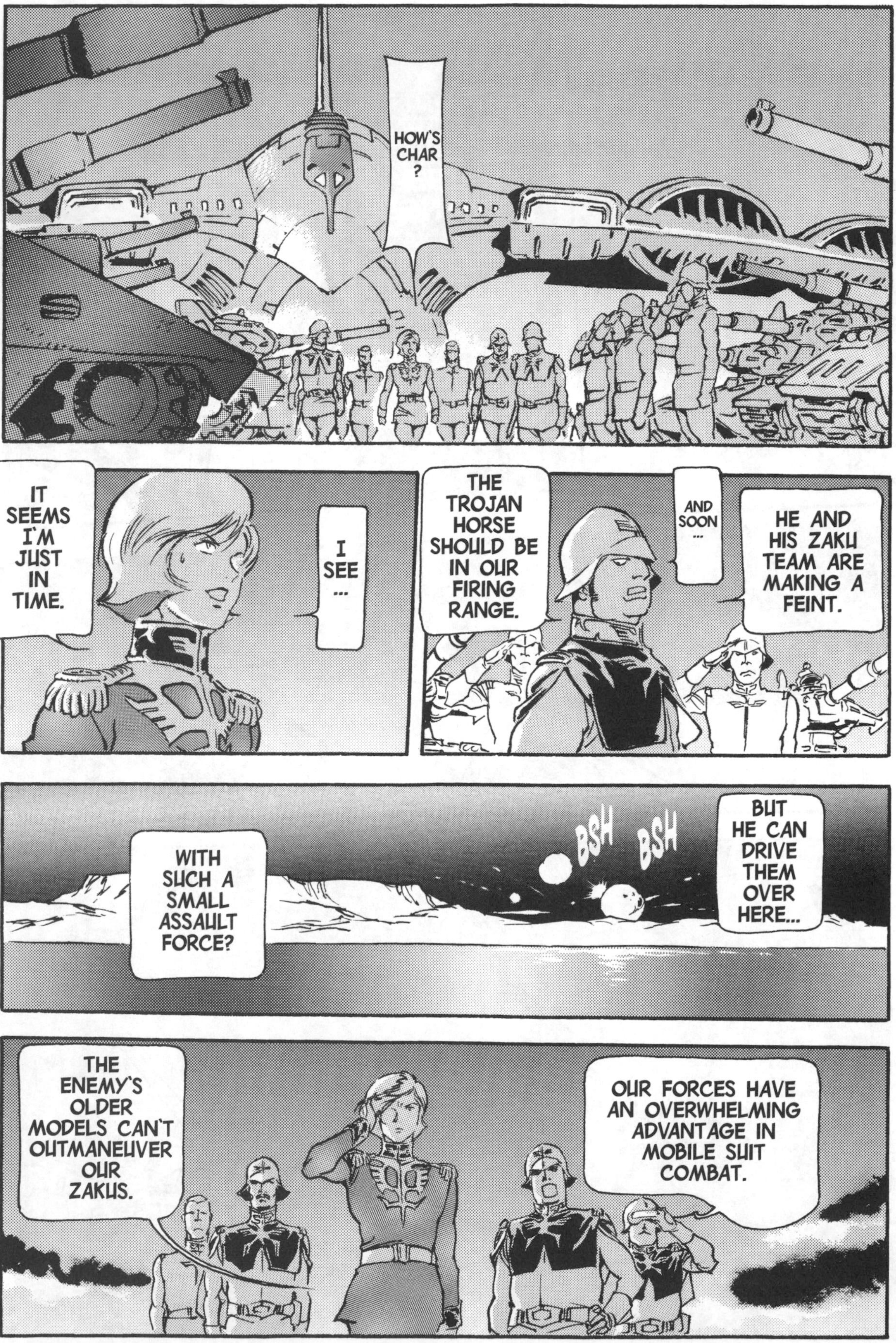
HOW'S CHAR?
HE AND HIS ZAKU TEAM ARE MAKING A FEINT.
AND SOON...
THE TROJAN HORSE SHOULD BE IN OUR FIRING RANGE.
I SEE...
IT SEEMS I'M JUST IN TIME.
BUT HE CAN DRIVE THEM OVER HERE...
BSH
BSH
WITH SUCH A SMALL ASSAULT FORCE?
OUR FORCES HAVE AN OVERWHELMING ADVANTAGE IN MOBILE SUIT COMBAT.
THE ENEMY'S OLDER MODELS CAN'T OUTMANEUVER OUR ZAKUS.

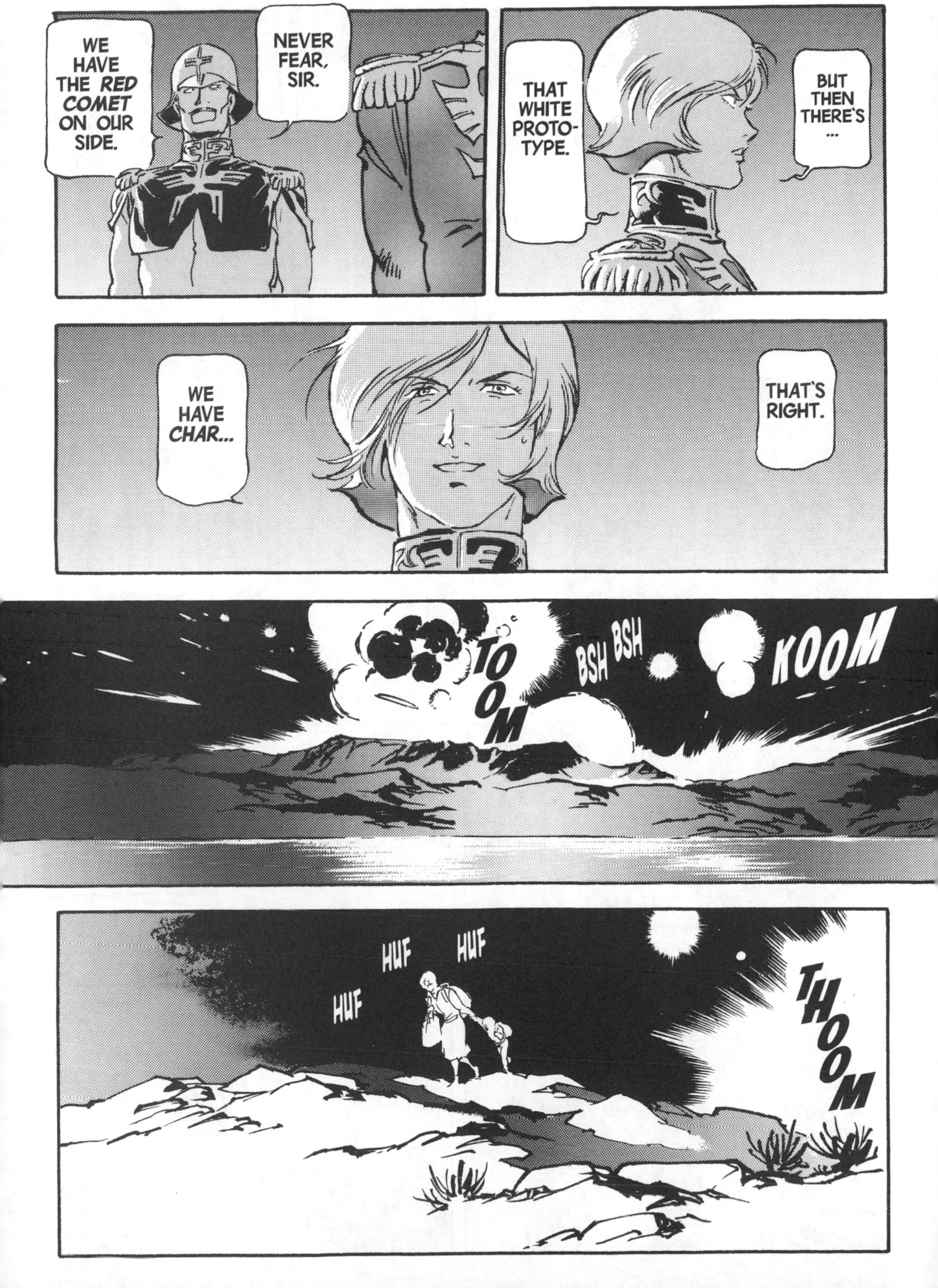
BUT THEN THERE'S ...
THAT WHITE PROTOTYPE.
NEVER FEAR, SIR.
WE HAVE THE RED COMET ON OUR SIDE.
THAT'S RIGHT.
WE HAVE CHAR...
KOOM
BSH BSH
TOOM
THOOM
HUF HUF
HUF

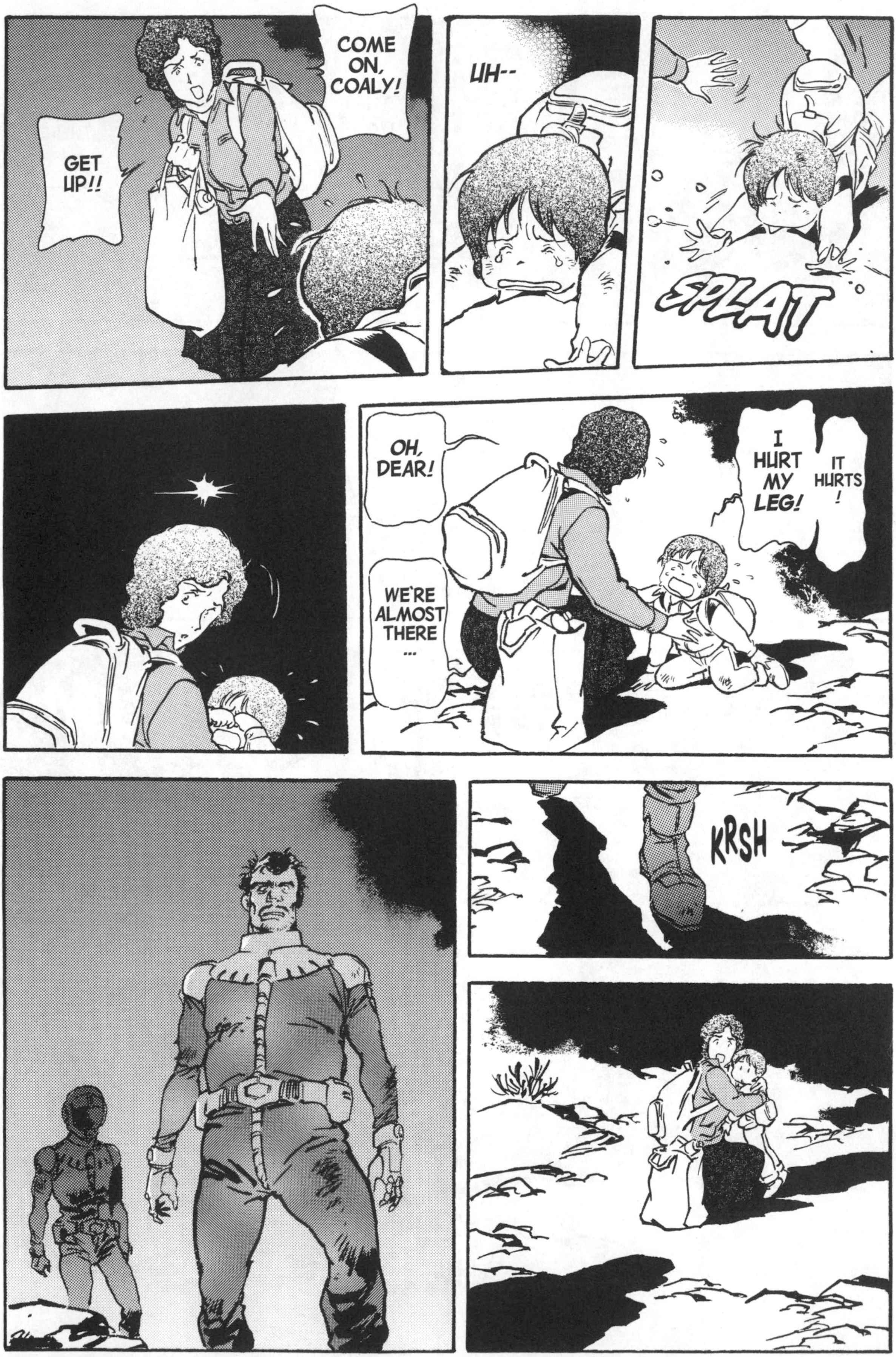
SPLAT
UH--
COME ON, COALY!
GET UP!!
I HURT MY LEG!
IT HURTS!
OH, DEAR!
WE'RE ALMOST THERE ...
KRSH

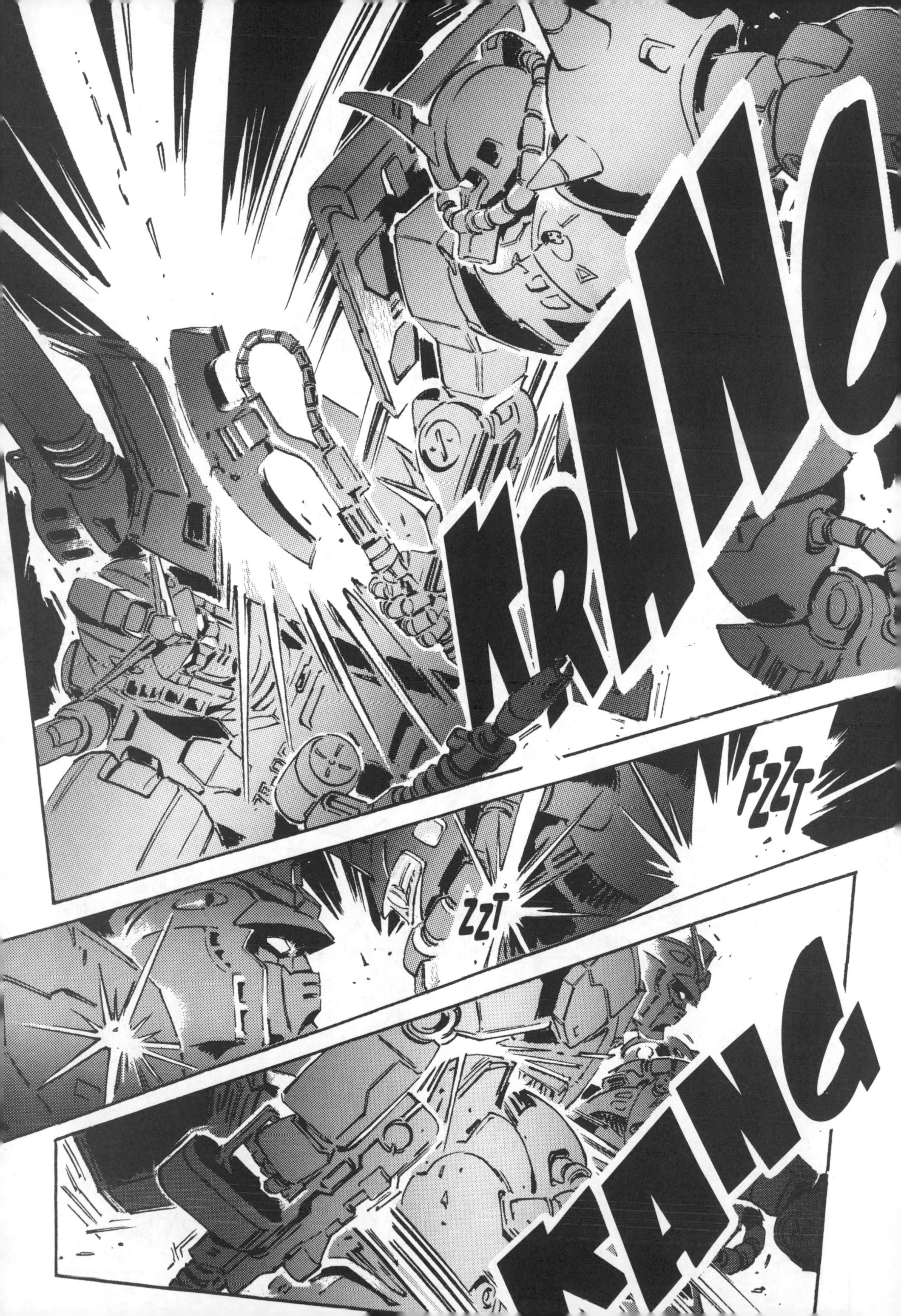
KRANG
FZZT
ZZT
ZANG

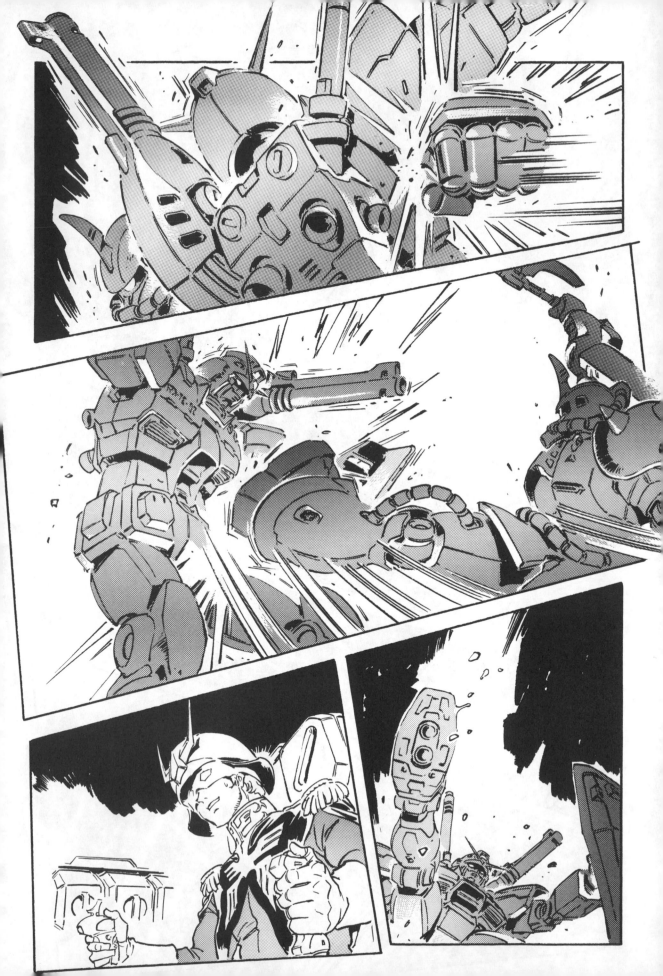

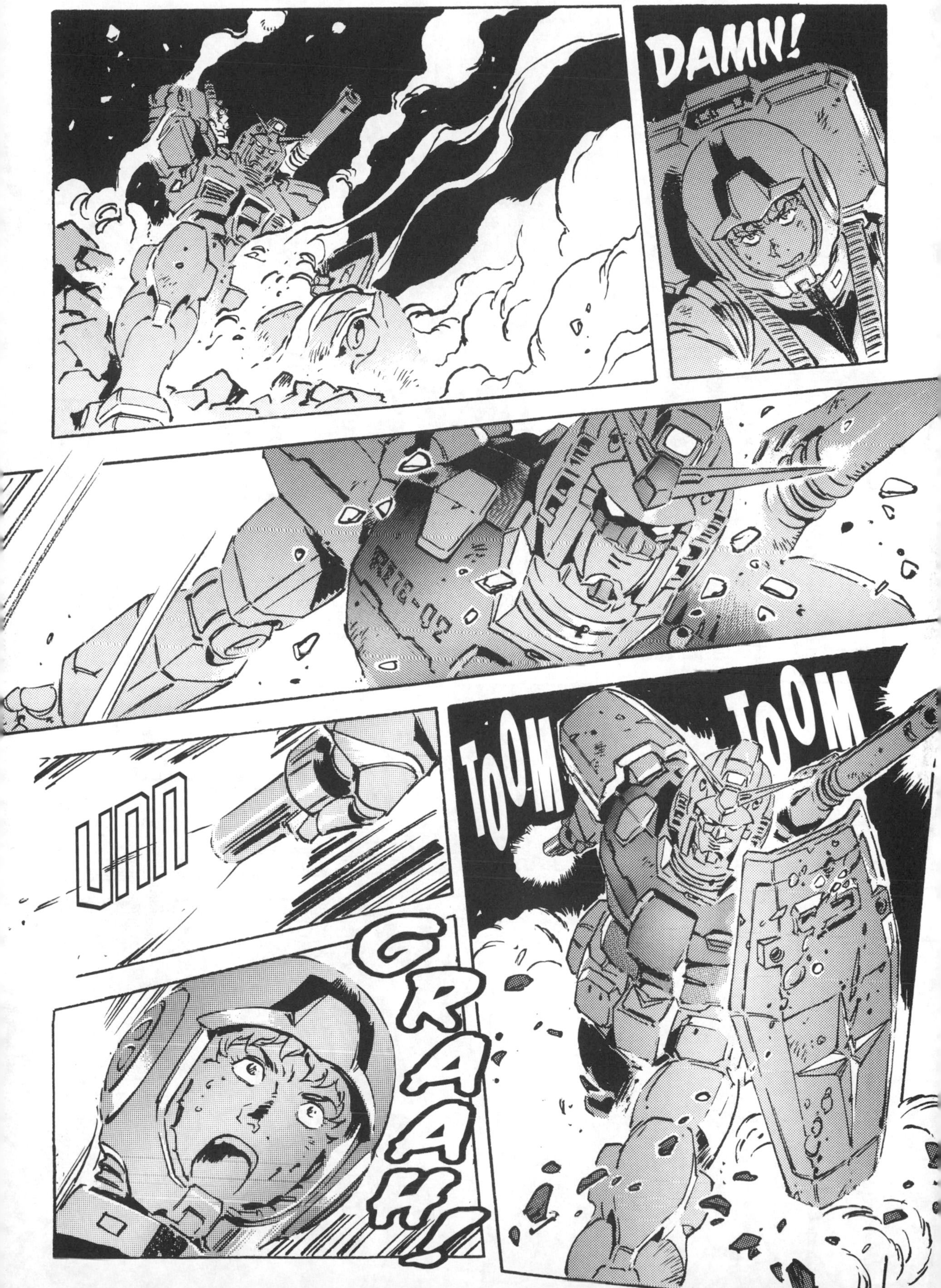
DAMN!
TOOM TOOM
UNN
GRAAH!

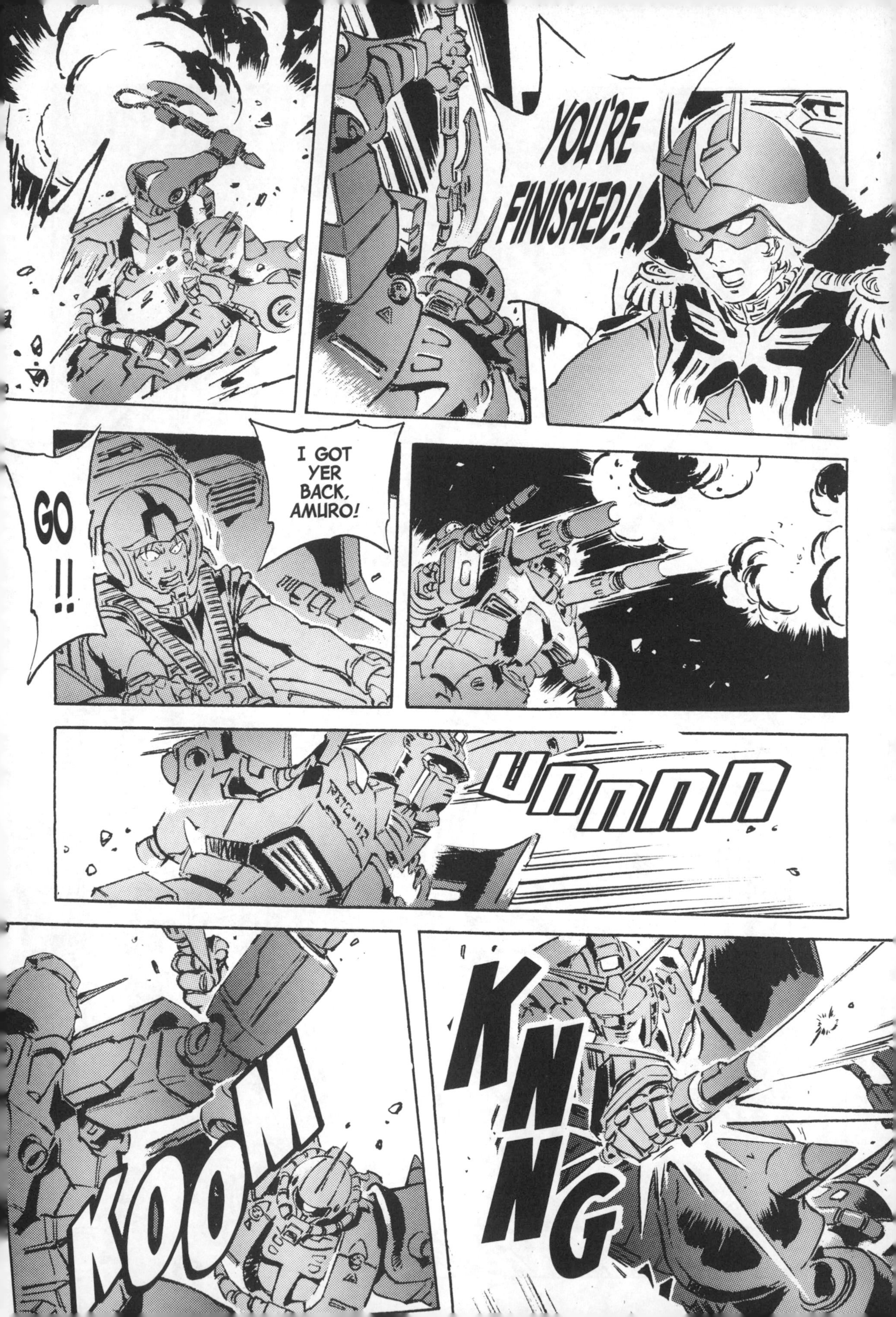
YOU'RE FINISHED!
I GOT YER BACK, AMURO!
GO!!
UNNNN
KNNG
KOOM

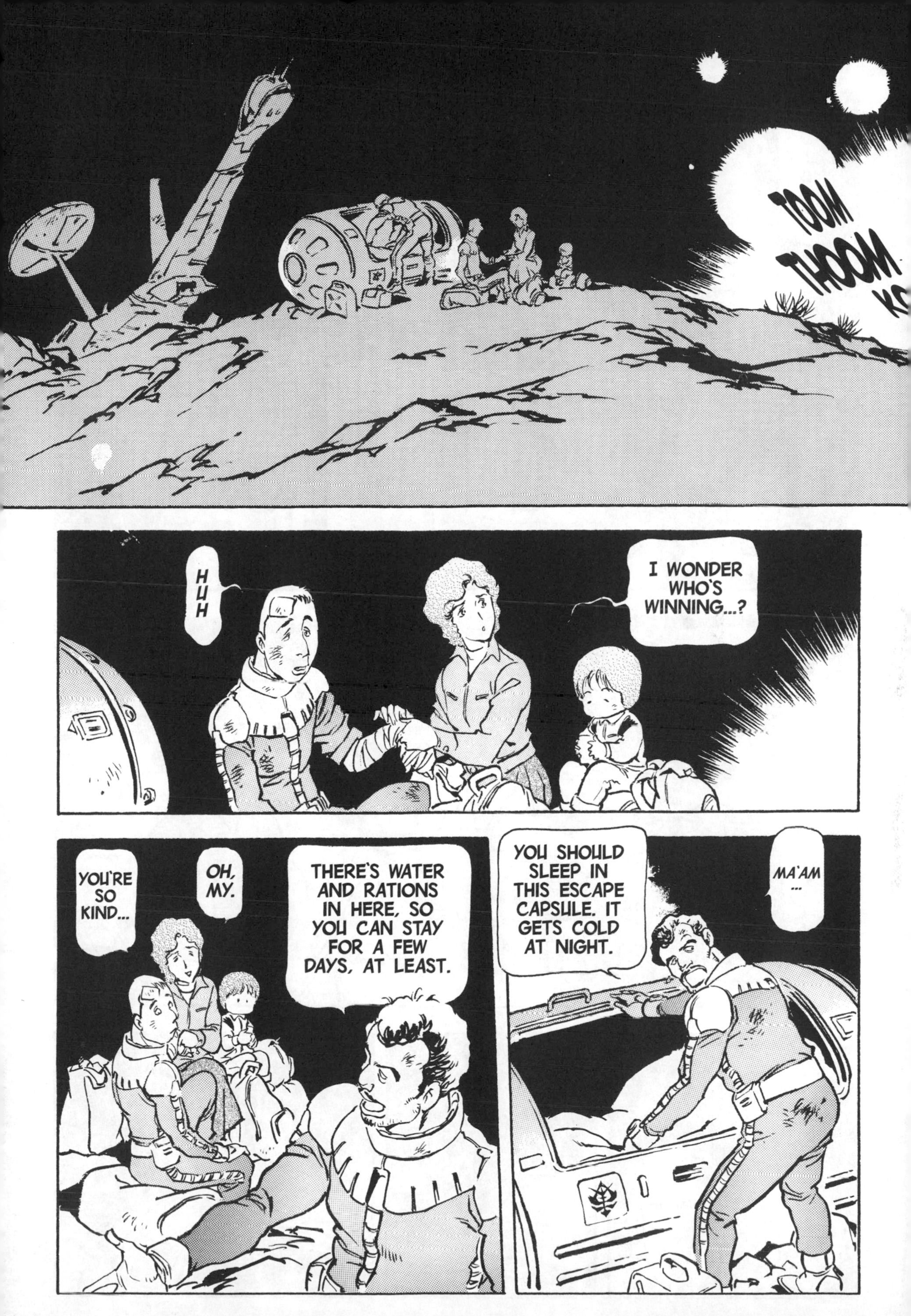
TOOM
THOOM
I WONDER WHO'S WINNING...?
HUH
MA'AM ...
YOU SHOULD SLEEP IN THIS ESCAPE CAPSULE. IT GETS COLD AT NIGHT.
THERE'S WATER AND RATIONS IN HERE, SO YOU CAN STAY FOR A FEW DAYS, AT LEAST.
OH, MY.
YOU'RE SO KIND...

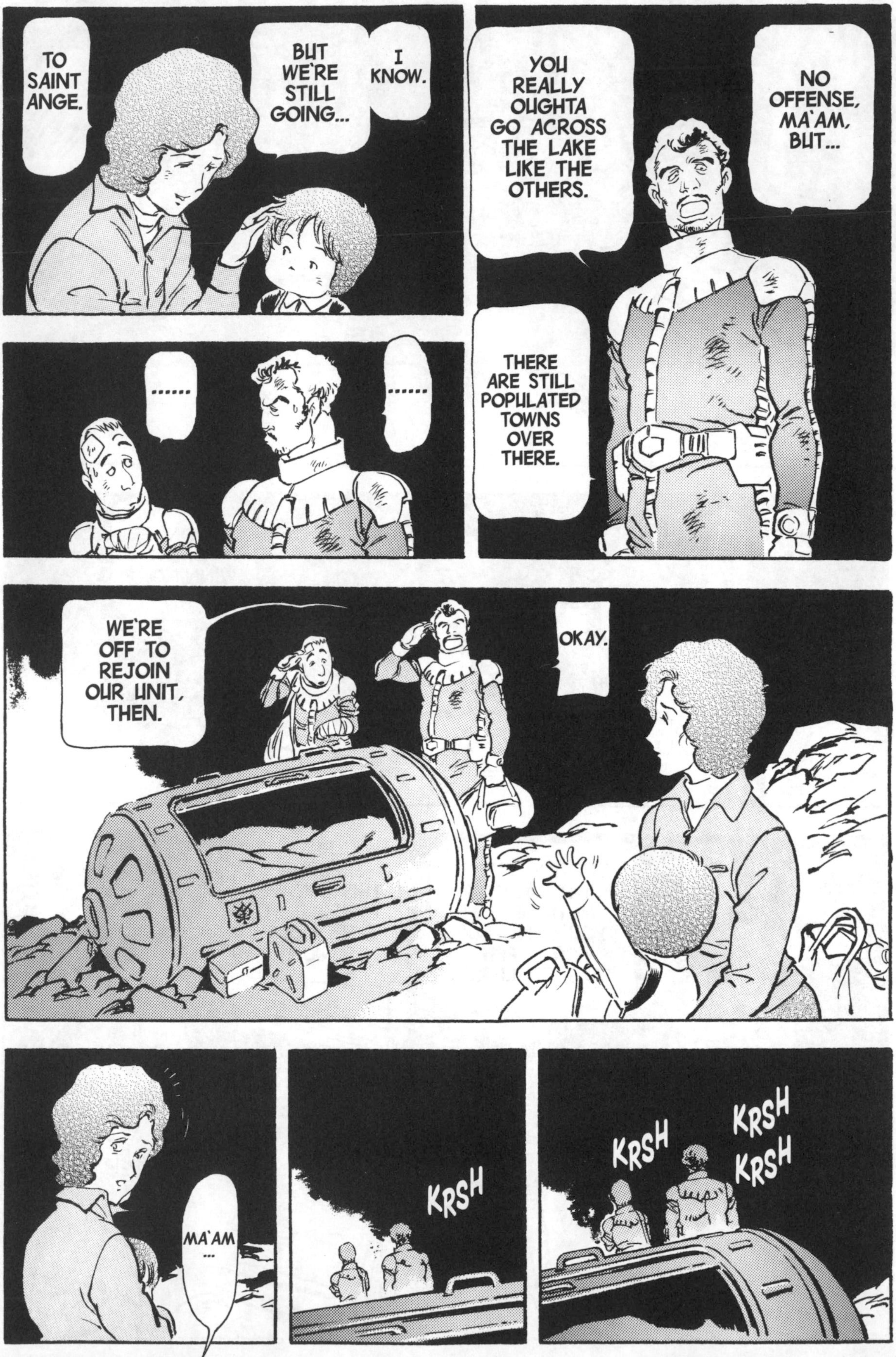
NO OFFENSE, MA'AM, BUT...
YOU REALLY OUGHTA GO ACROSS THE LAKE LIKE THE OTHERS.
THERE ARE STILL POPULATED TOWNS OVER THERE.
I KNOW.
BUT WE'RE STILL GOING...
TO SAINT ANGE.
......
......
OKAY.
WE'RE OFF TO REJOIN OUR UNIT, THEN.
KRSH
KRSH
KRSH
KRSH
MA'AM ...

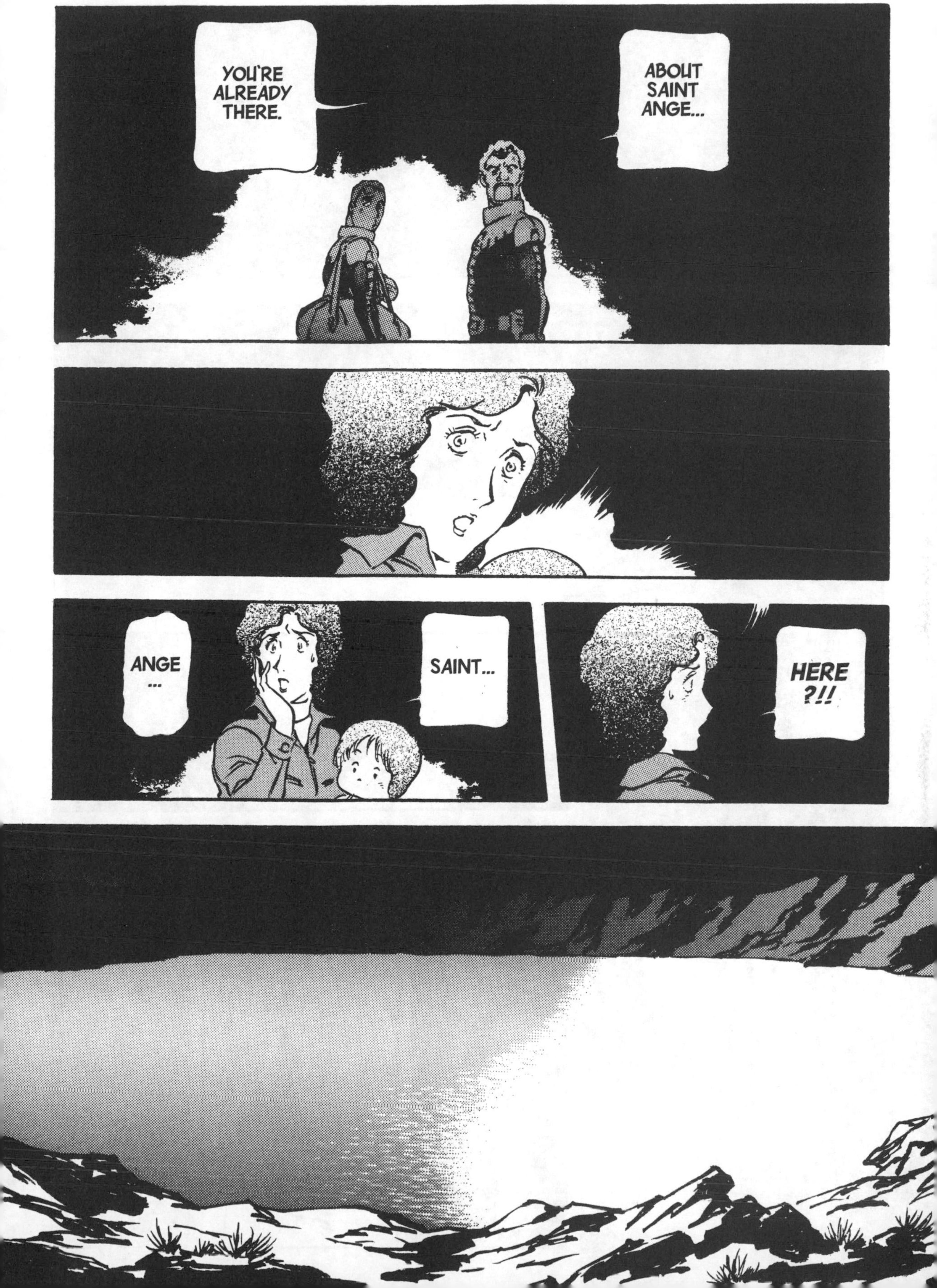
ABOUT SAINT ANGE...
YOU'RE ALREADY THERE.
HERE ?!!
SAINT...
ANGE ...

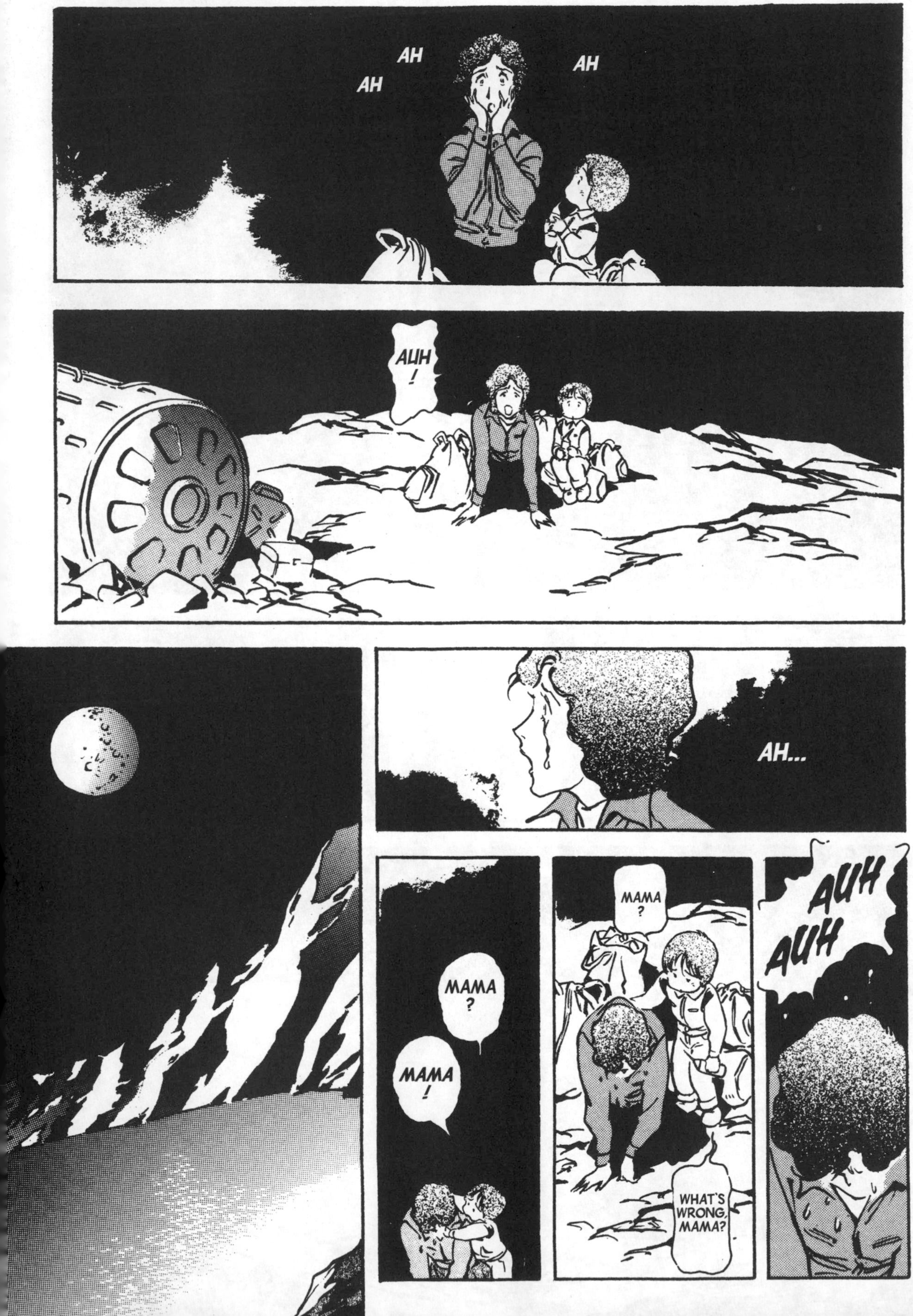
AH
AH
AH
AUH!
AH...
AUH
AUH
MAMA?
WHAT'S WRONG, MAMA?
MAMA?
MAMA!

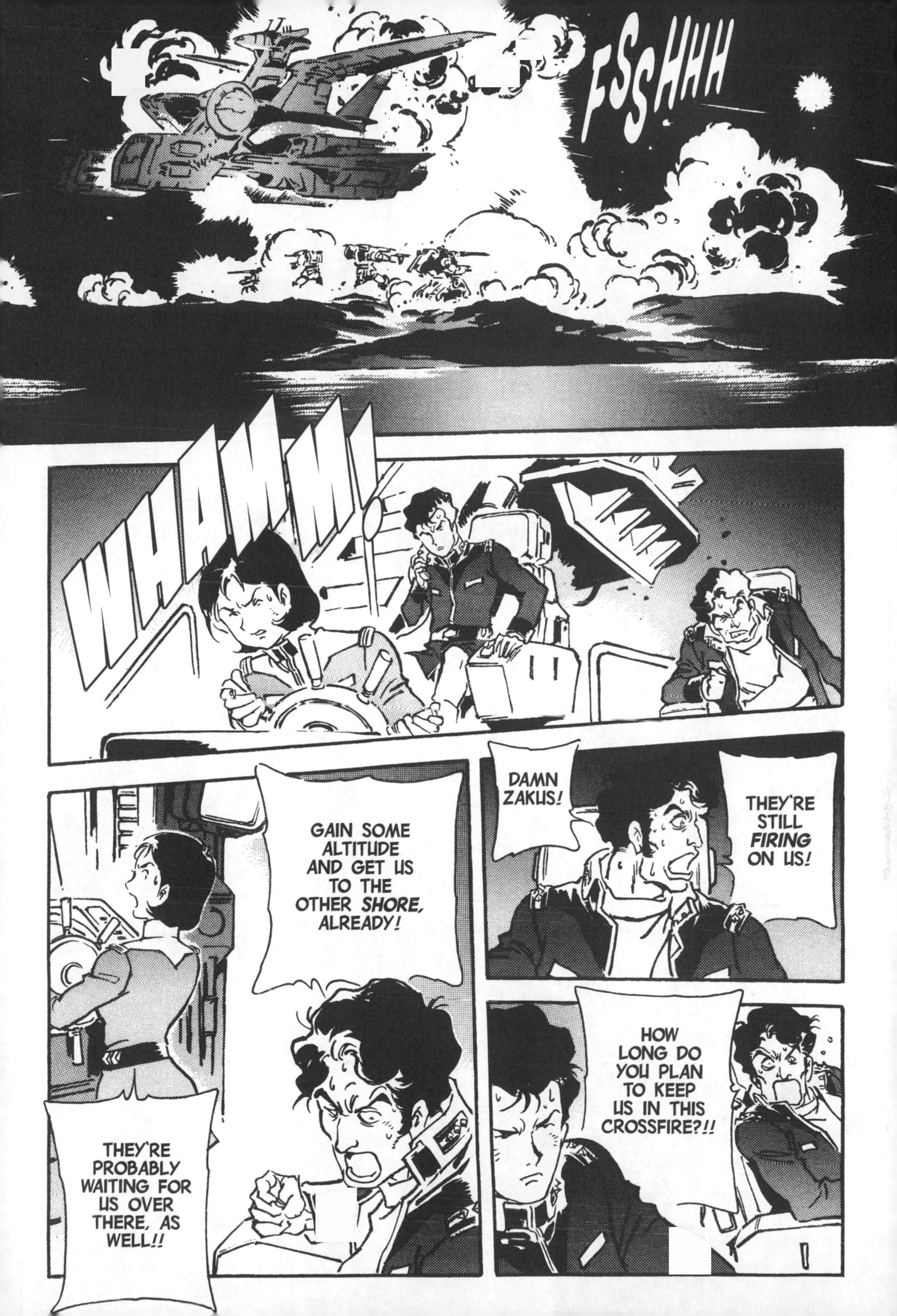
FSSHHH
WHAMM
THEY'RE STILL FIRING ON US!
DAMN ZAKUS!
HOW LONG DO YOU PLAN TO KEEP US IN THIS CROSSFIRE?!!
GAIN SOME ALTITUDE AND GET US TO THE OTHER SHORE, ALREADY!
THEY'RE PROBABLY WAITING FOR US OVER THERE, AS WELL!!

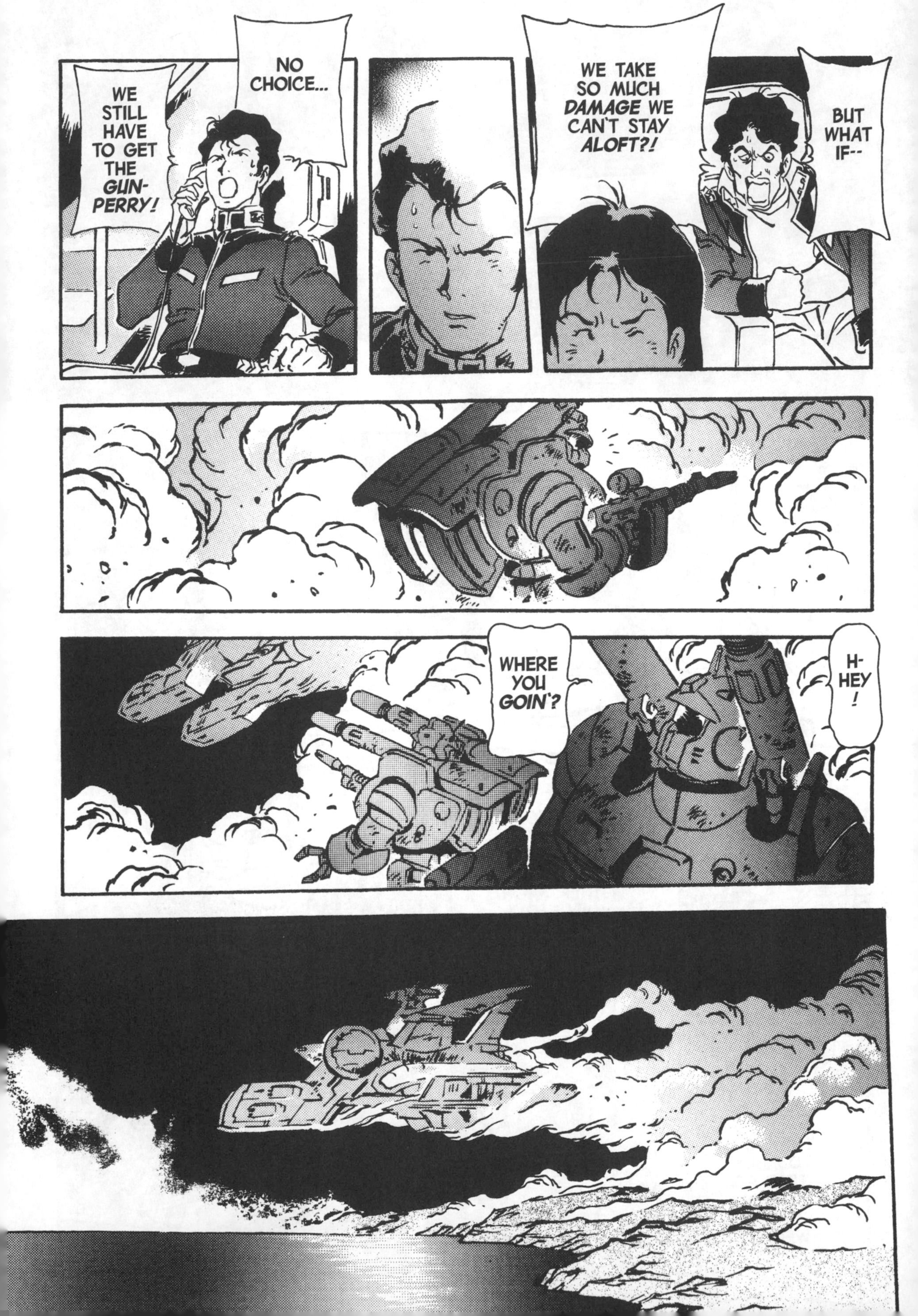
BUT WHAT IF--
WE TAKE SO MUCH DAMAGE WE CAN'T STAY ALOFT?!
NO CHOICE...
WE STILL HAVE TO GET THE GUN-PERRY!
H-HEY!
WHERE YOU GOIN'?

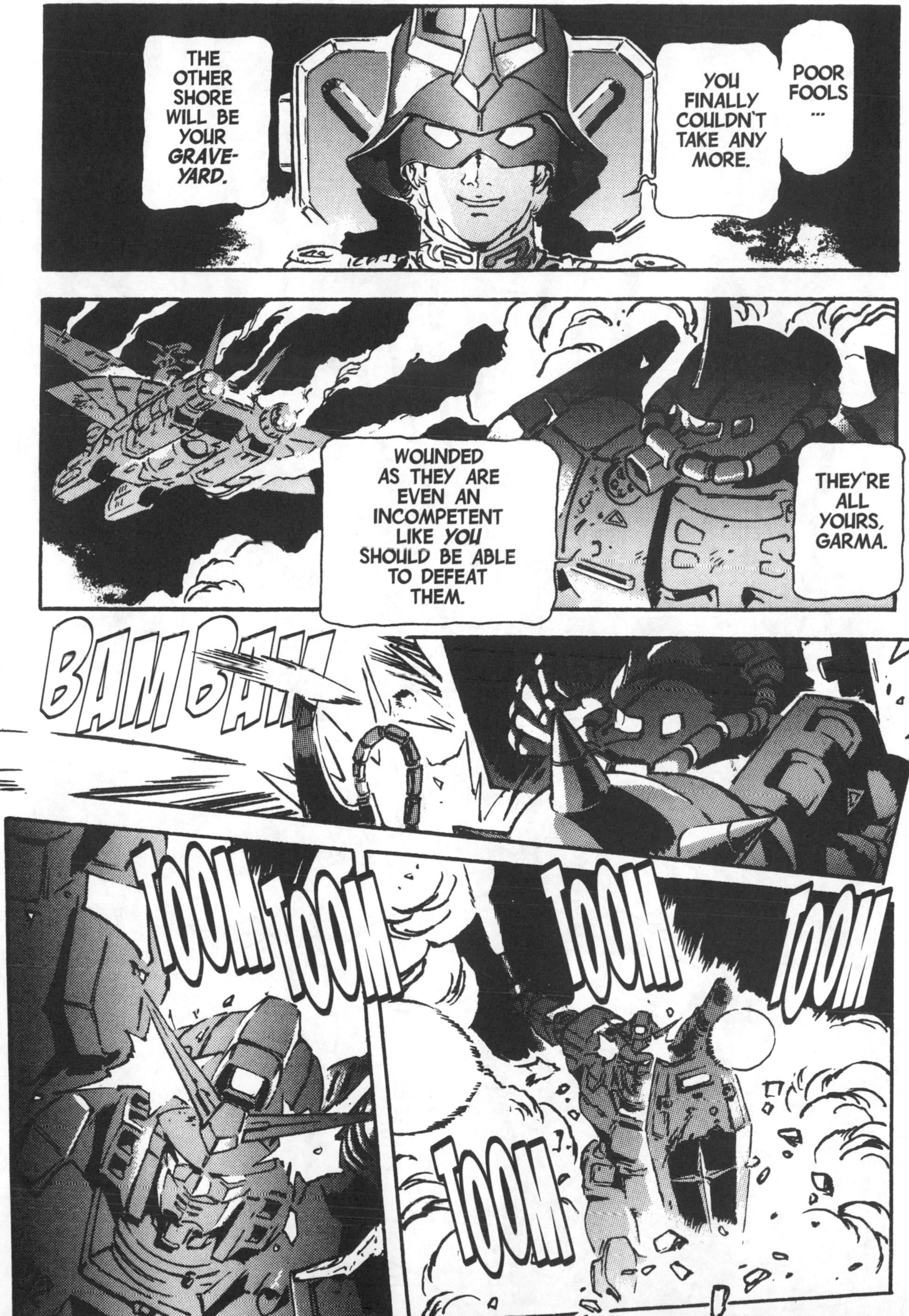
POOR FOOLS ...
YOU FINALLY COULDN'T TAKE ANY MORE.
THE OTHER SHORE WILL BE YOUR GRAVE-YARD.
THEY'RE ALL YOURS, GARMA.
WOUNDED AS THEY ARE EVEN AN INCOMPETENT LIKE *YOU* SHOULD BE ABLE TO DEFEAT THEM.
BAM BAM
TOOM
TOOM
TOOM
TOOM TOOM

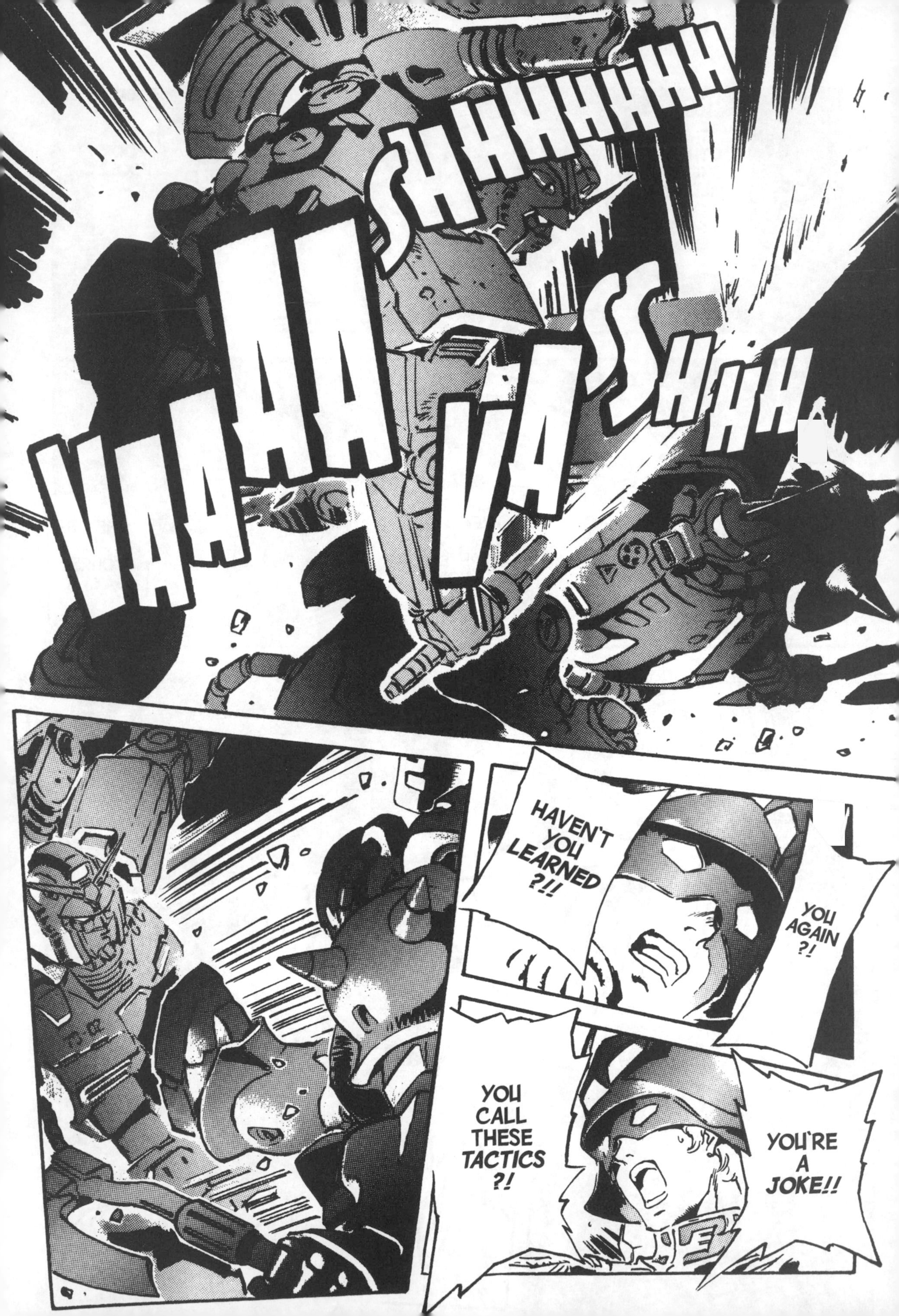
VASHHH
VAAAASHHHHHHHH
YOU AGAIN?!
HAVEN'T YOU LEARNED?!!
YOU'RE A JOKE!!
YOU CALL THESE TACTICS?!

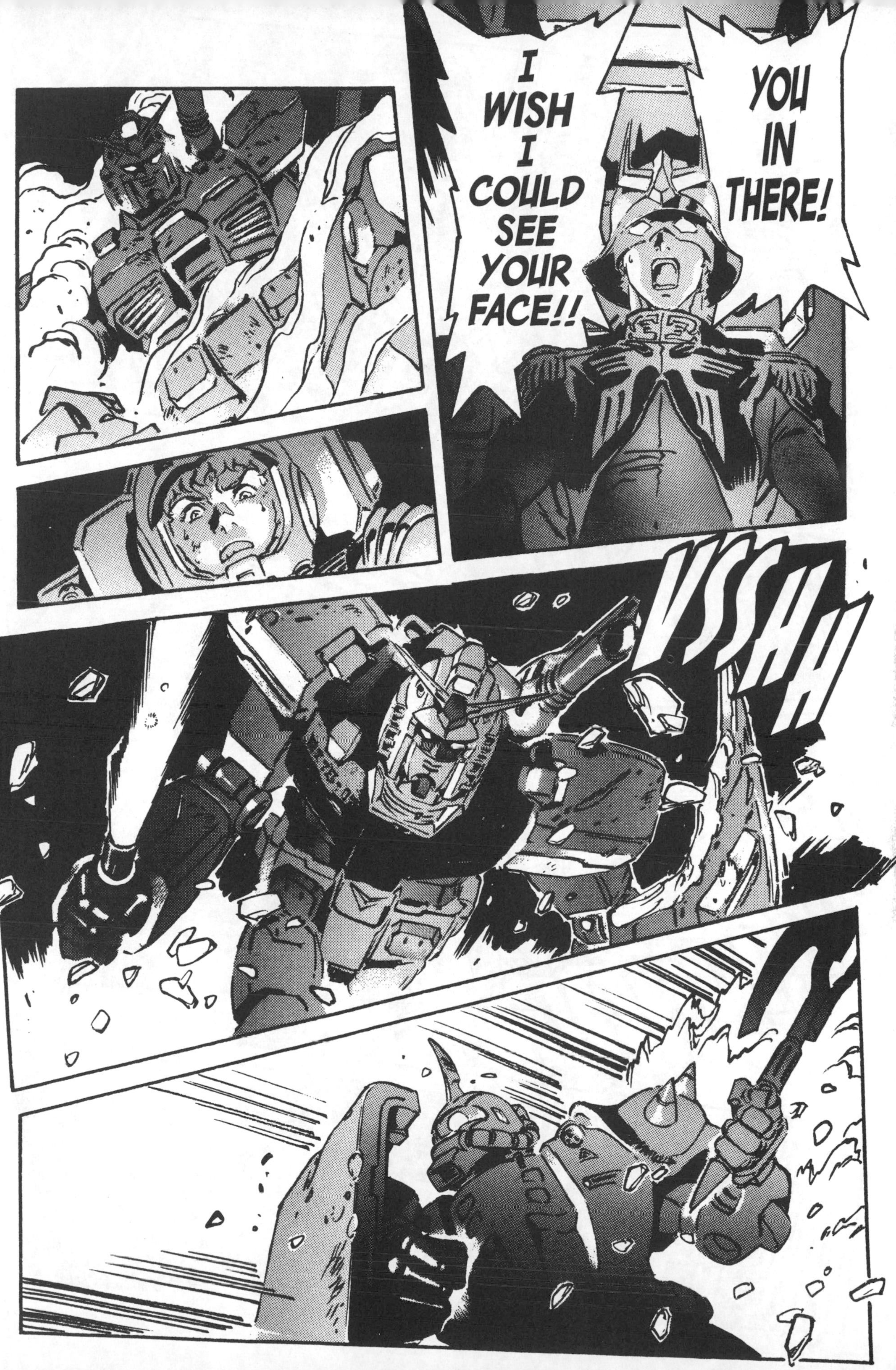
YOU IN THERE!
I WISH I COULD SEE YOUR FACE!!
VSSHH

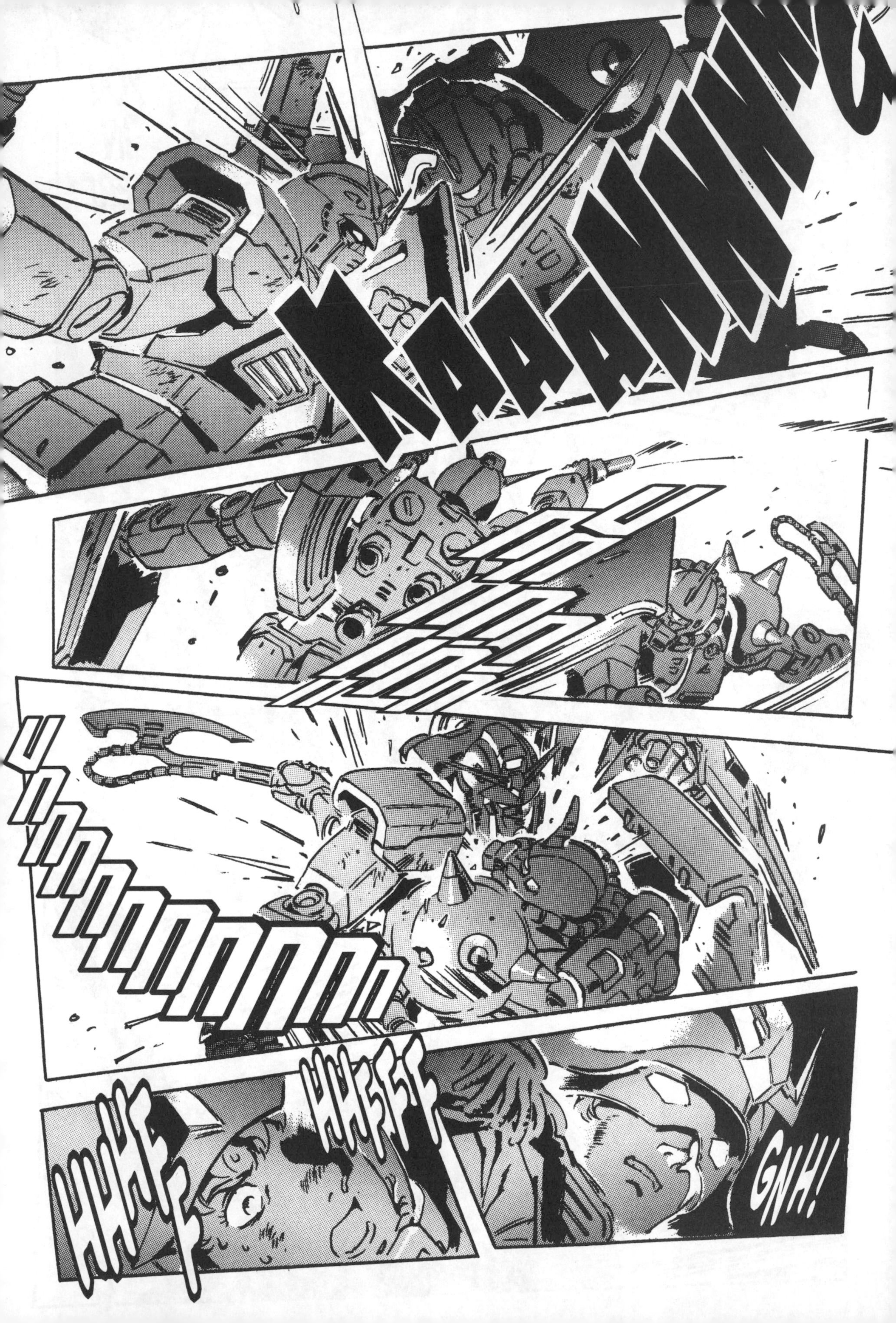
GNH!

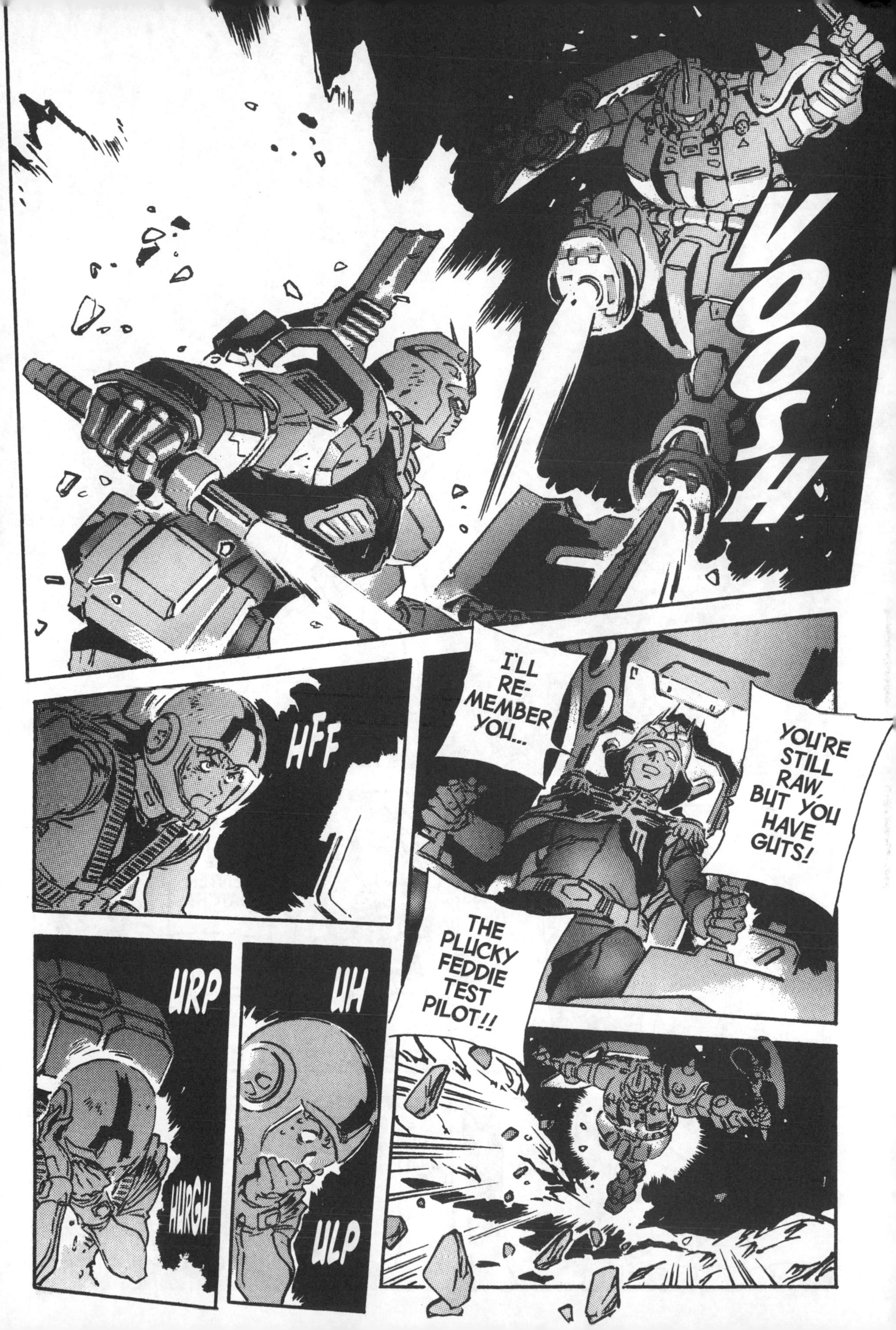
VOOSH
YOU'RE STILL RAW, BUT YOU HAVE GUTS!
I'LL REMEMBER YOU...
THE PLUCKY FEDDIE TEST PILOT!!
HFF
UH
ULP
URP
HURGH

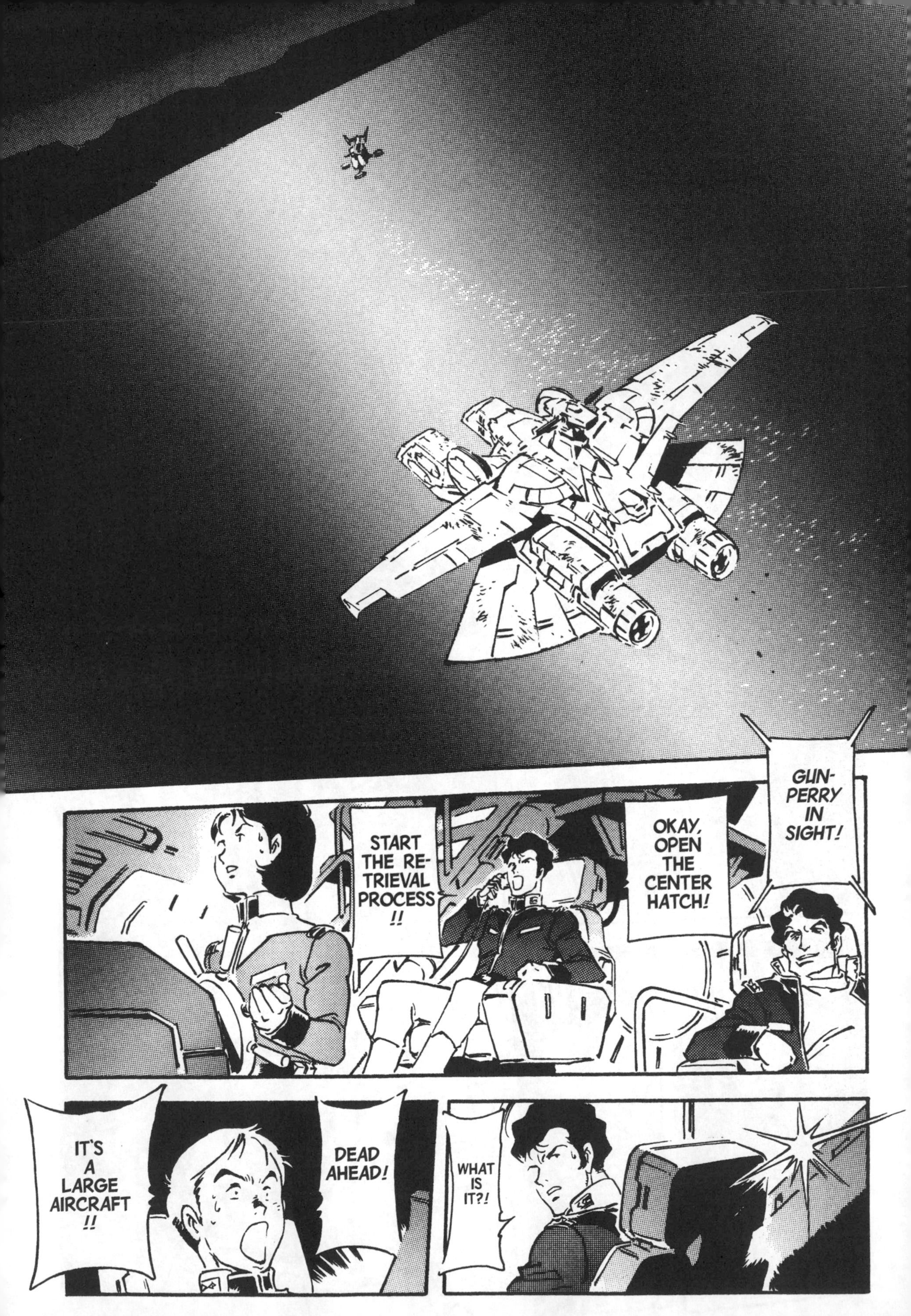
GUN-PERRY IN SIGHT!
OKAY, OPEN THE CENTER HATCH!
START THE RE-TRIEVAL PROCESS !!
WHAT IS IT?!
DEAD AHEAD!
IT'S A LARGE AIRCRAFT !!

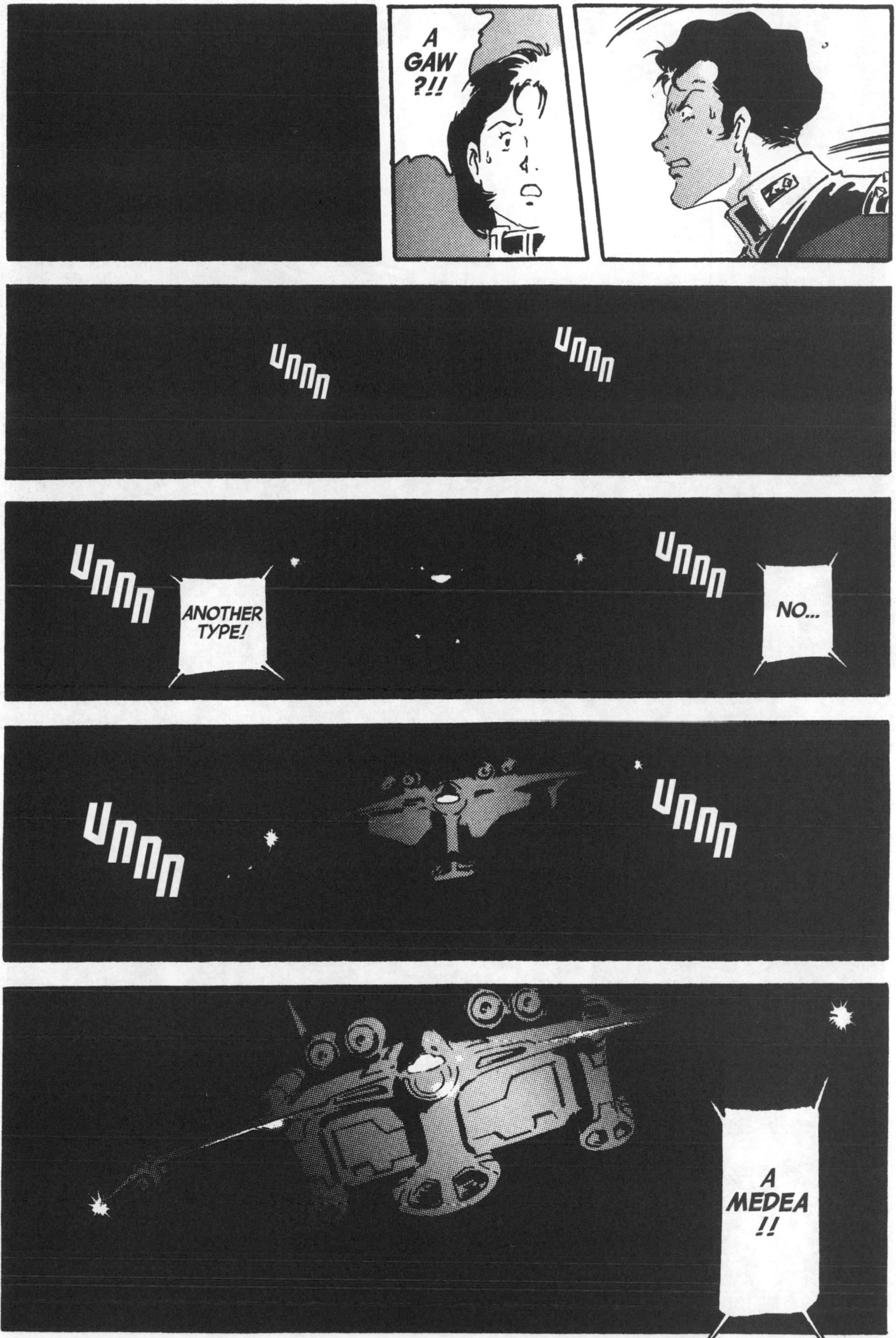
A GAW ?!!
UNNN
UNNN
UNNN
NO...
UNNN
ANOTHER TYPE!
UNNN
UNNN
A MEDEA !!

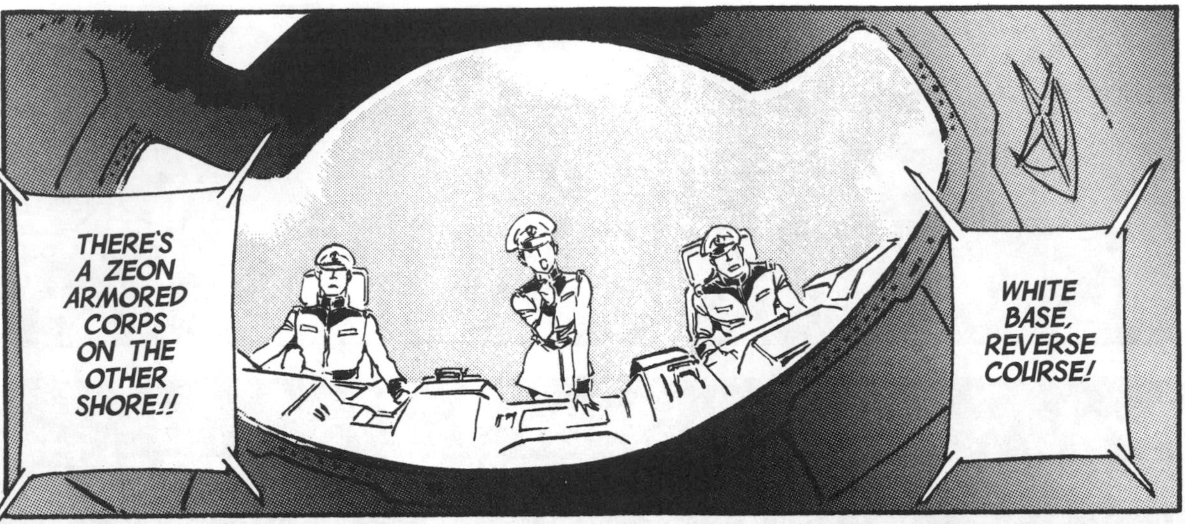
WHITE BASE, REVERSE COURSE!
THERE'S A ZEON ARMORED CORPS ON THE OTHER SHORE!!
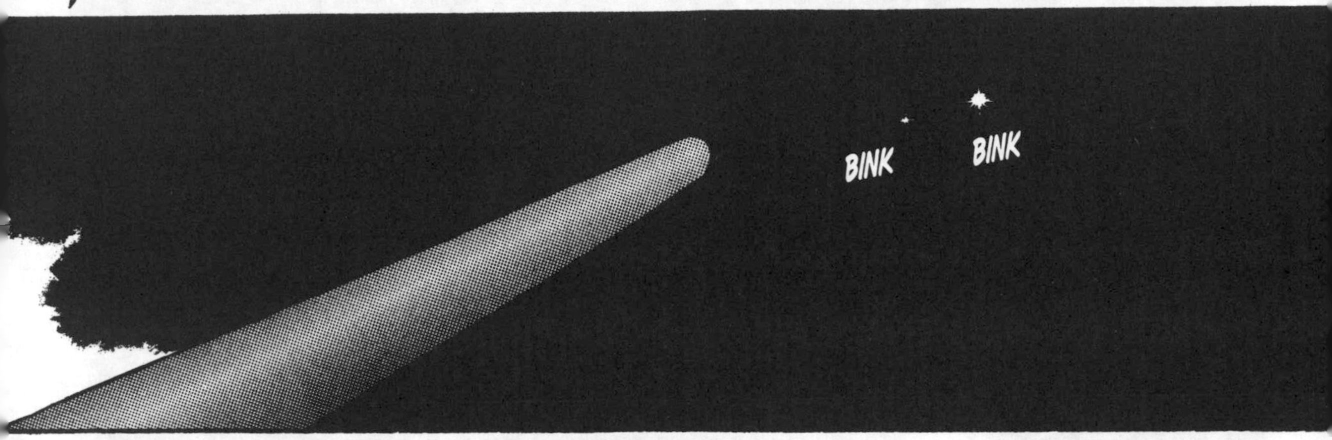
BINK
BINK
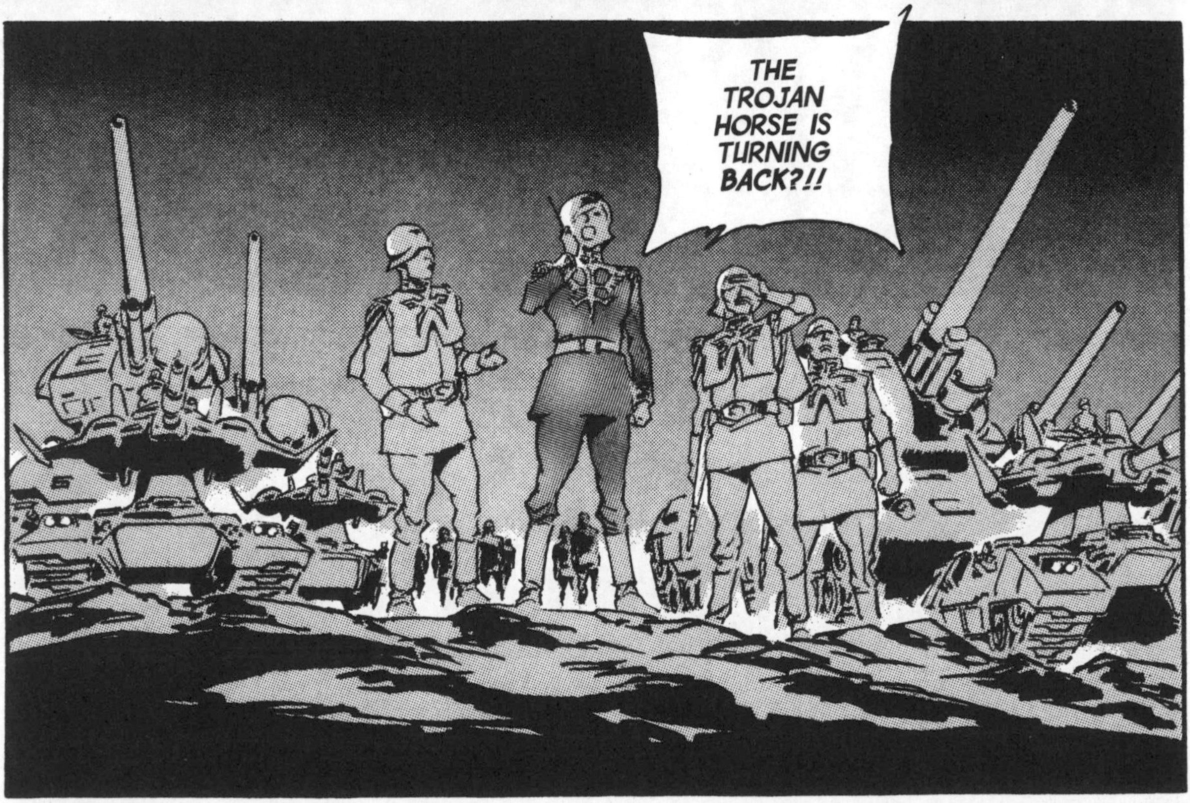
THE TROJAN HORSE IS TURNING BACK?!!

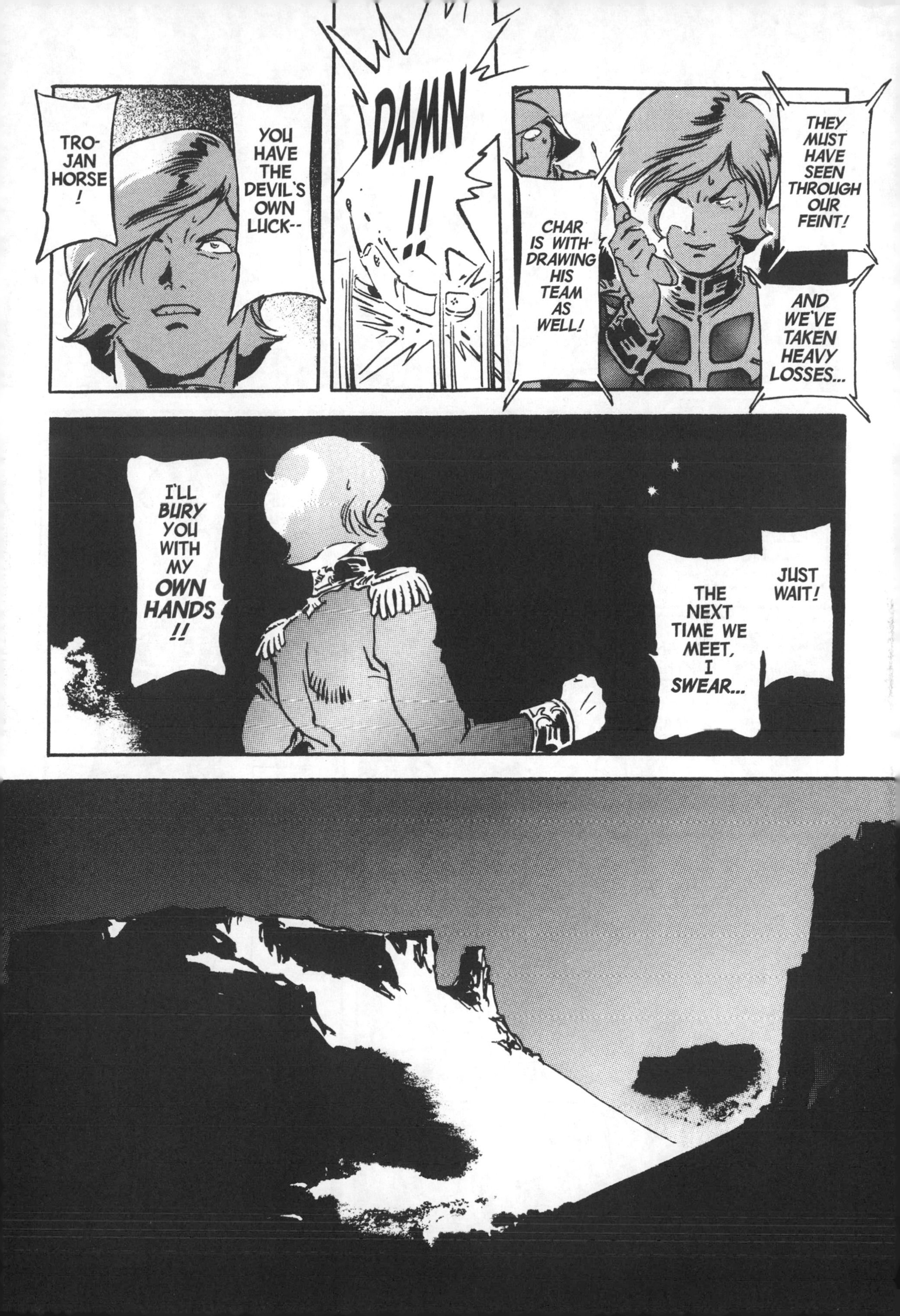
THEY MUST HAVE SEEN THROUGH OUR FEINT!
AND WE'VE TAKEN HEAVY LOSSES...
CHAR IS WITH-DRAWING HIS TEAM AS WELL!
DAMN!!
YOU HAVE THE DEVIL'S OWN LUCK--
TRO-JAN HORSE!
JUST WAIT!
THE NEXT TIME WE MEET, I SWEAR...
I'LL BURY YOU WITH MY OWN HANDS!!

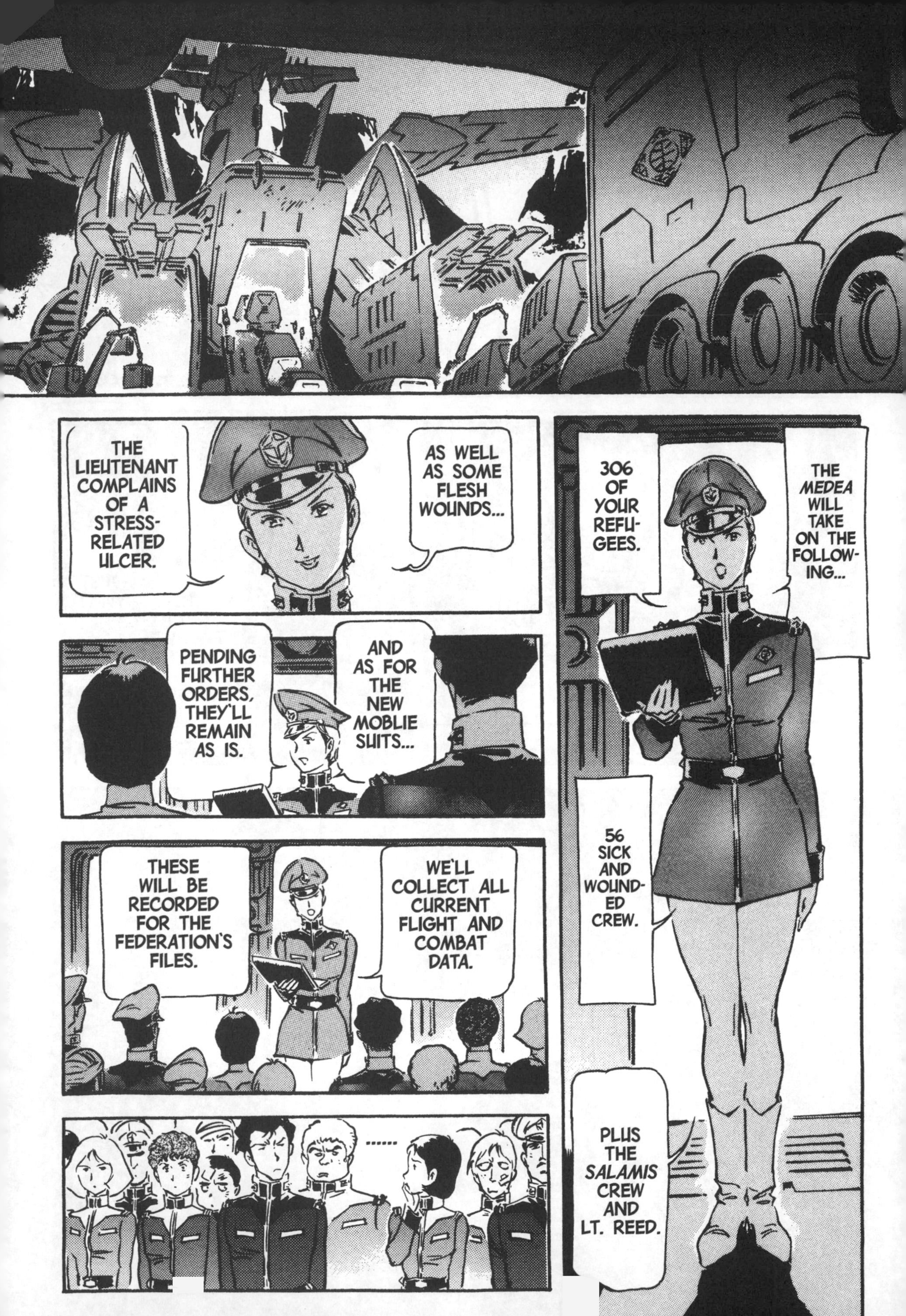
THE *MEDEA* WILL TAKE ON THE FOLLOWING...
306 OF YOUR REFUGEES.
56 SICK AND WOUNDED CREW.
PLUS THE *SALAMIS* CREW AND LT. REED.
AS WELL AS SOME FLESH WOUNDS...
THE LIEUTENANT COMPLAINS OF A STRESS-RELATED ULCER.
AND AS FOR THE NEW MOBLIE SUITS...
PENDING FURTHER ORDERS, THEY'LL REMAIN AS IS.
WE'LL COLLECT ALL CURRENT FLIGHT AND COMBAT DATA.
THESE WILL BE RECORDED FOR THE FEDERATION'S FILES.
......

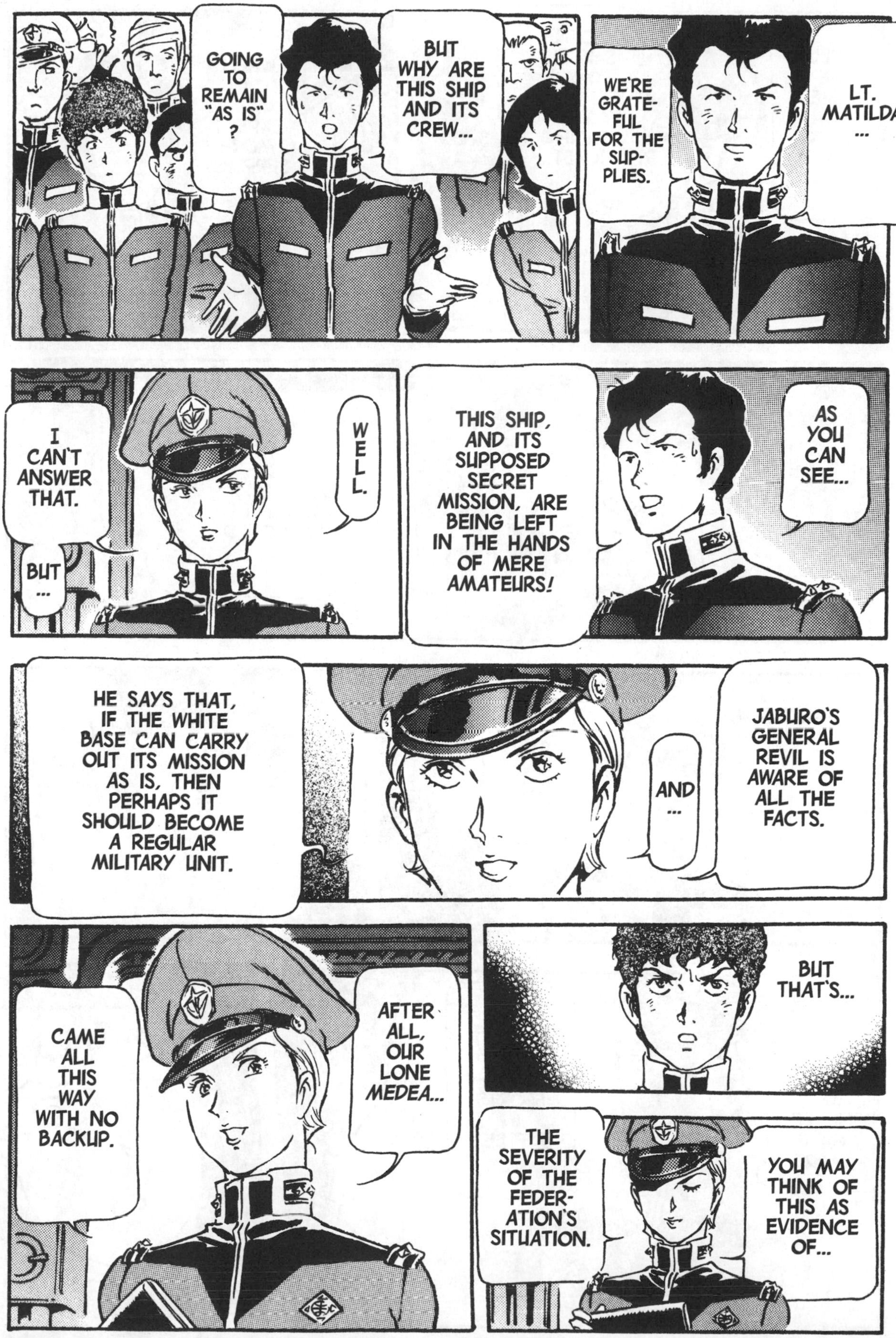
LT. MATILDA ...
WE'RE GRATEFUL FOR THE SUPPLIES.
BUT WHY ARE THIS SHIP AND ITS CREW...
GOING TO REMAIN "AS IS"?
AS YOU CAN SEE...
THIS SHIP, AND ITS SUPPOSED SECRET MISSION, ARE BEING LEFT IN THE HANDS OF MERE AMATEURS!
WELL.
I CAN'T ANSWER THAT.
BUT ...
JABURO'S GENERAL REVIL IS AWARE OF ALL THE FACTS.
AND ...
HE SAYS THAT, IF THE WHITE BASE CAN CARRY OUT ITS MISSION AS IS, THEN PERHAPS IT SHOULD BECOME A REGULAR MILITARY UNIT.
BUT THAT'S...
YOU MAY THINK OF THIS AS EVIDENCE OF...
THE SEVERITY OF THE FEDERATION'S SITUATION.
AFTER ALL, OUR LONE MEDEA...
CAME ALL THIS WAY WITH NO BACKUP.

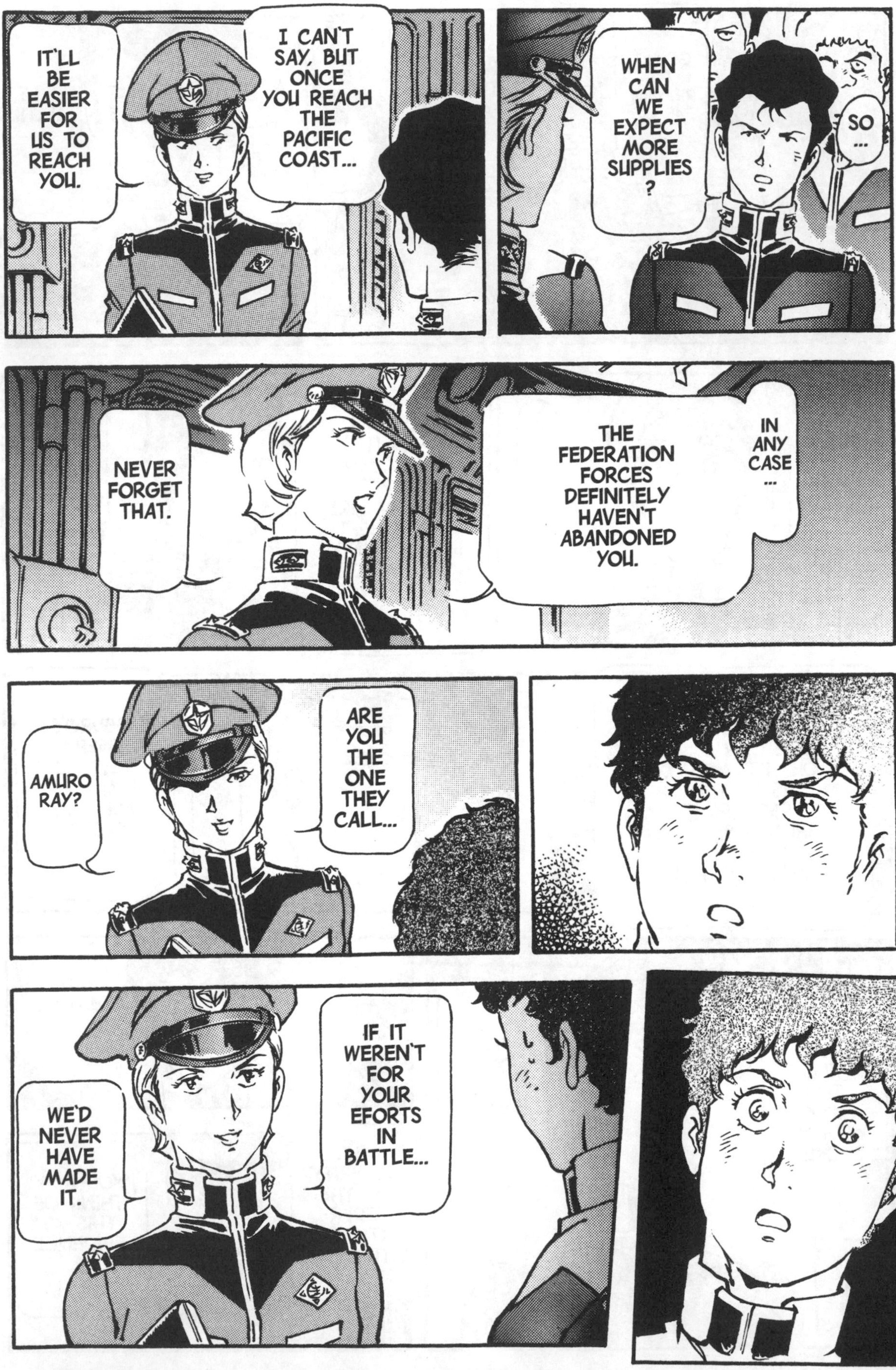
SO ...
WHEN CAN WE EXPECT MORE SUPPLIES ?
I CAN'T SAY, BUT ONCE YOU REACH THE PACIFIC COAST...
IT'LL BE EASIER FOR US TO REACH YOU.
IN ANY CASE ...
THE FEDERATION FORCES DEFINITELY HAVEN'T ABANDONED YOU.
NEVER FORGET THAT.
ARE YOU THE ONE THEY CALL...
AMURO RAY?
IF IT WEREN'T FOR YOUR EFORTS IN BATTLE...
WE'D NEVER HAVE MADE IT.

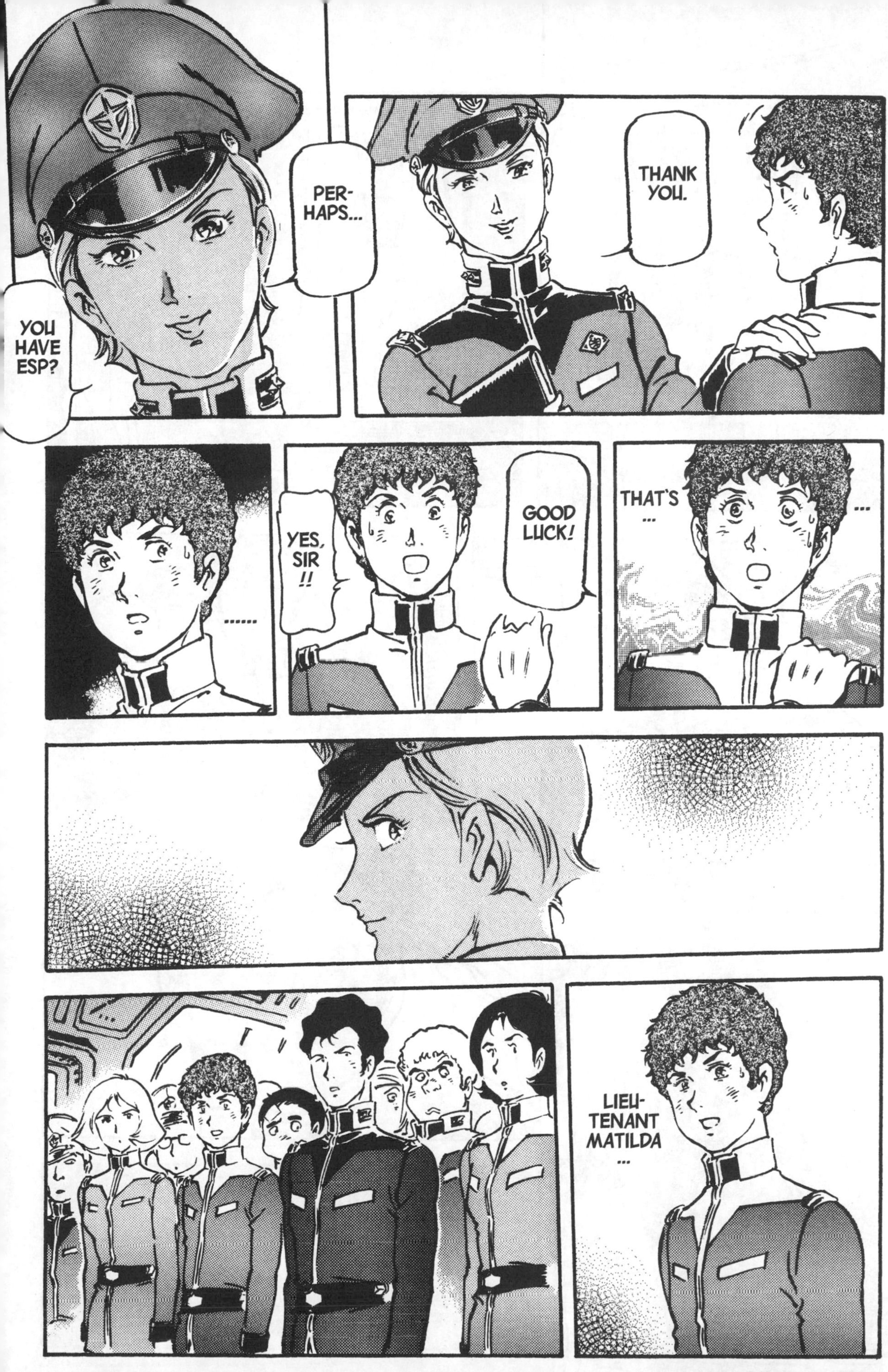
THANK YOU.
PER-HAPS...
YOU HAVE ESP?
THAT'S ...
...
GOOD LUCK!
YES, SIR !!
......
LIEU-TENANT MATILDA ...

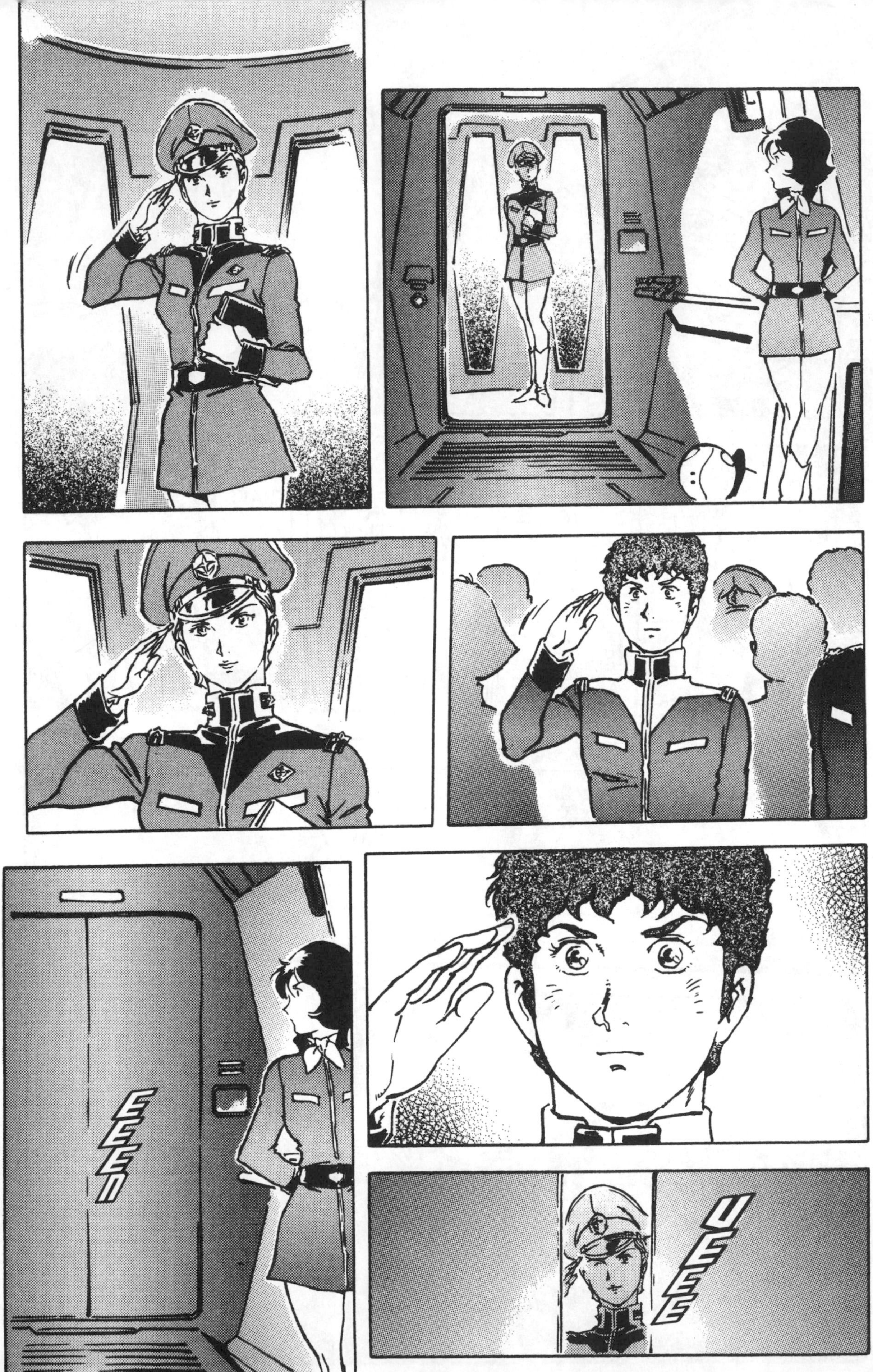
UEEE
EEEN

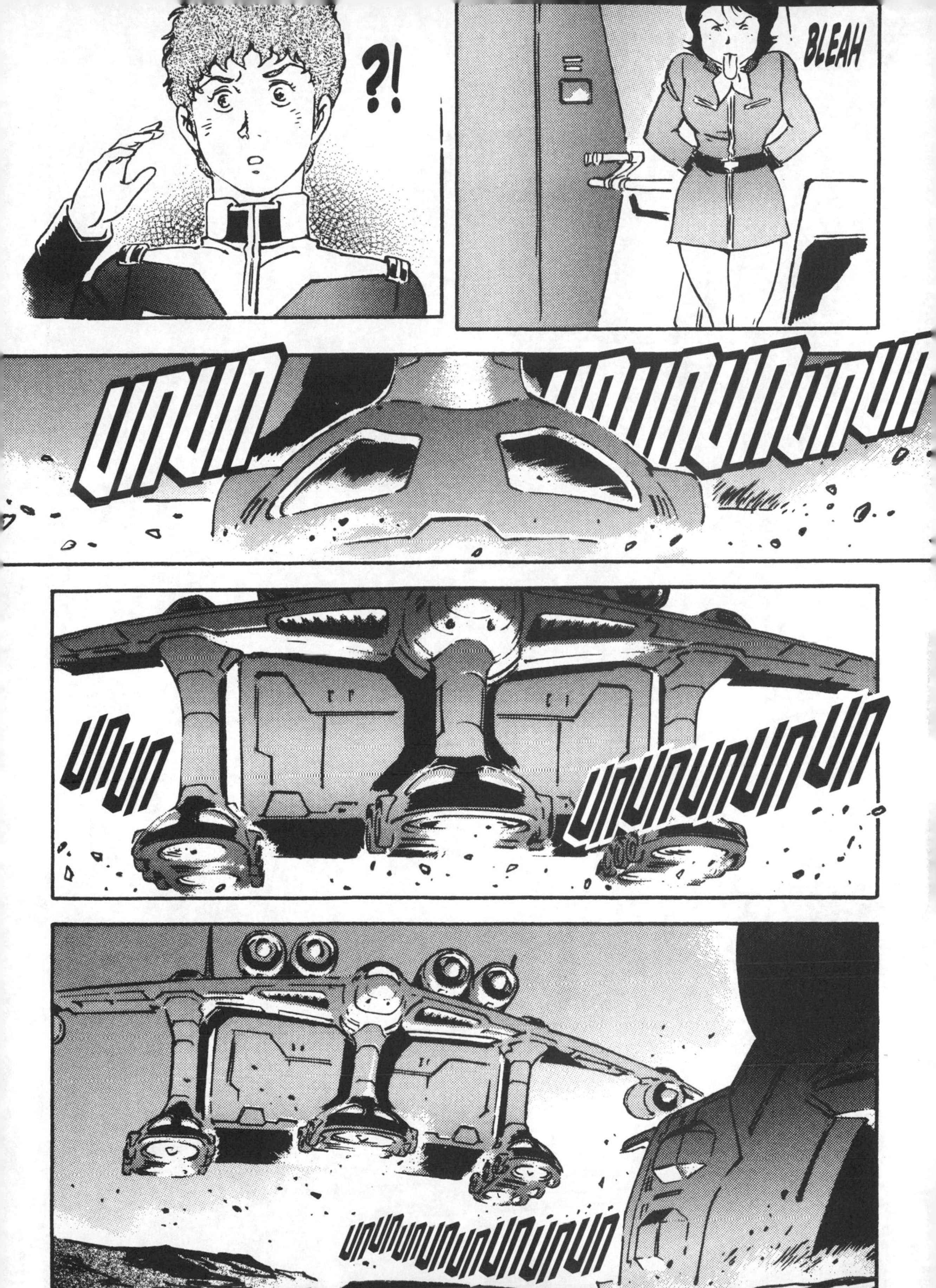
BLEAH
?!
UNUNUNUNUN
UNUN
UNUNUNUNUN
UNUN
UNUNUNUNUNUNUNUN

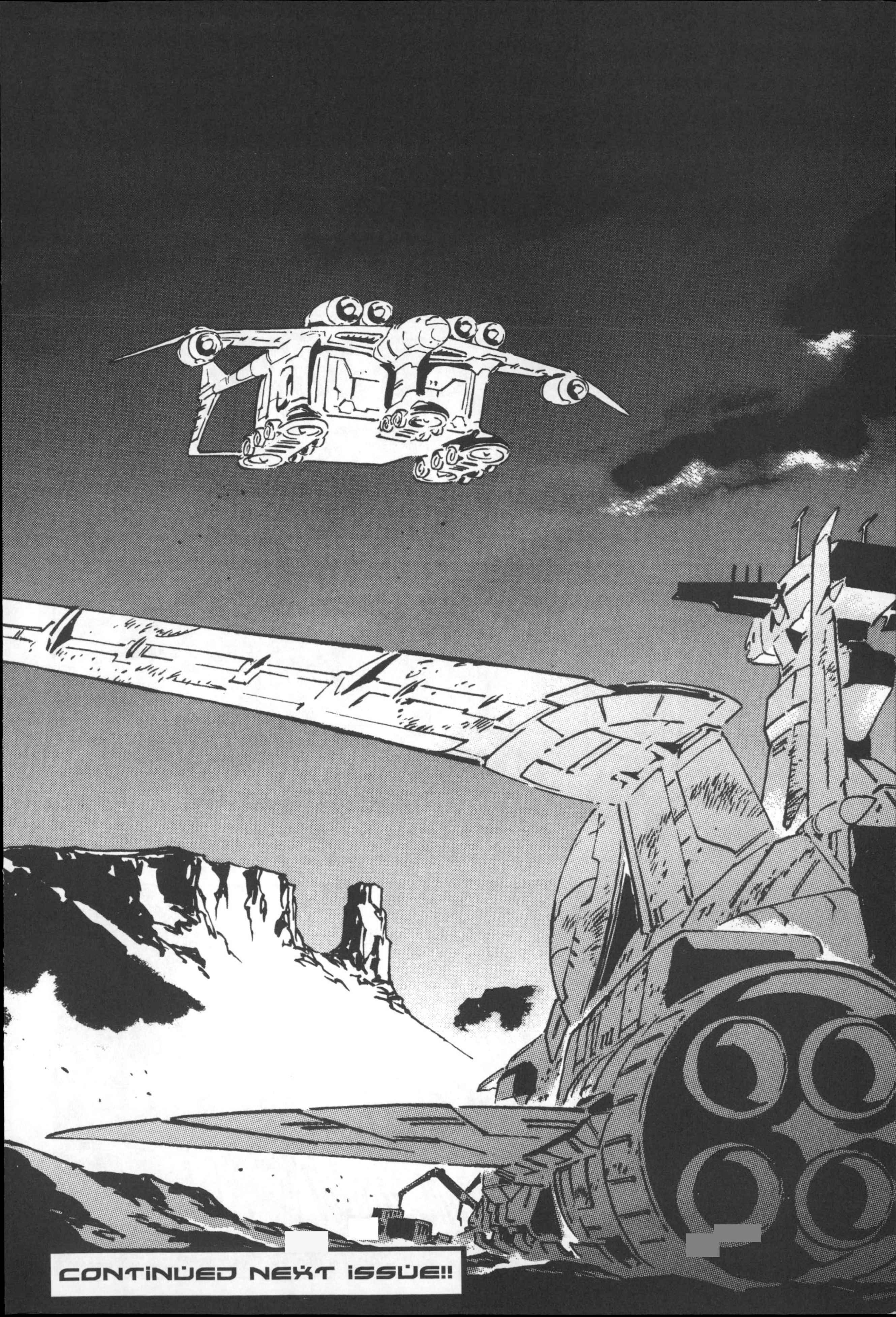
CONTINUED NEXT ISSUE!!

COMPLETE OUR SURVEY AND LET US KNOW WHAT YOU THINK!

☐ Please check here if you DO NOT wish to receive information or future offers from VIZ

Name: _____

Address: _____

City: _____ **State:** _____ **Zip:** _____

E-mail: _____

☐ **Male**   ☐ **Female**   **Date of Birth** (mm/dd/yyyy): ___ / ___ / _____ (Under 13? Parental consent required)

What race/ethnicity do you consider yourself? (please check one)

☐ Asian/Pacific Islander   ☐ Black/African American   ☐ Hispanic/Latino

☐ Native American/Alaskan Native ☐ White/Caucasian   ☐ Other: _____

What VIZ product did you purchase? (check all that apply and indicate title purchased)

☐ DVD/VHS _____

☐ Graphic Novel _____

☐ Magazines _____

☐ Merchandise _____

Reason for purchase: (check all that apply)

☐ Special offer   ☐ Favorite title   ☐ Gift

☐ Recommendation   ☐ Other _____

Where did you make your purchase? (please check one)

☐ Comic store   ☐ Bookstore   ☐ Mass/Grocery Store

☐ Newsstand   ☐ Video/Video Game Store   ☐ Other: _____

☐ Online (site: _____)

What other VIZ properties have you purchased/own? _____

_____

How many anime and/or manga titles have you purchased in the last year? How many were VIZ titles? **(please check one from each column)**

ANIME	MANGA	VIZ
☐ None	☐ None	☐ None
☐ 1-4	☐ 1-4	☐ 1-4
☐ 5-10	☐ 5-10	☐ 5-10
☐ 11+	☐ 11+	☐ 11+

I find the pricing of VIZ products to be: **(please check one)**

☐ Cheap ☐ Reasonable ☐ Expensive

What genre of manga and anime would you like to see from VIZ? **(please check two)**

☐ Adventure ☐ Comic Strip ☐ Detective ☐ Fighting

☐ Horror ☐ Romance ☐ Sci-Fi/Fantasy ☐ Sports

What do you think of VIZ's new look?

☐ Love It ☐ It's OK ☐ Hate It ☐ Didn't Notice ☐ No Opinion

THANK YOU! Please send the completed form to:

NJW Research
42 Catharine St.
Poughkeepsie, NY 12601

All information provided will be used for internal purposes only. We promise not to sell or otherwise divulge your information.